Homer and the Bronze Age

Homer and the Bronze Age

The Reflection of Humanistic Ideals in Diplomatic Practices

PETER KARAVITES

GORGIAS PRESS
2008

First Gorgias Press Edition, 2008

Copyright © 2008 by Gorgias Press LLC

All rights reserved under International and Pan-American Copyright Conventions. No part of this publication may be reproduced, stored in a retrieval system or transmitted in any form or by any means, electronic, mechanical, photocopying, recording, scanning or otherwise without the prior written permission of Gorgias Press LLC.

Published in the United States of America by Gorgias Press LLC, New Jersey

ISBN 978-1-59333-985-2

GORGIAS PRESS
180 Centennial Ave., Suite A, Piscataway, NJ 08854 USA
www.gorgiaspress.com

Library of Congress Cataloging-in-Publication Data
Karavites, Peter.
  Homer and the Bronze age : the reflection of humanistic ideals in diplomatic practices / Peter Karavites.
       p. cm.
  Includes bibliographical references and index.
  1. Middle East--Foreign relations. 2. Bronze age--Middle East. 3. Homer--Knowledge--Diplomacy. I. Title.
  JZ1670.K37 2008
  327.39'4--dc22
                                          2008012787

The paper used in this publication meets the minimum requirements of the American National Standards.

Printed in the United States of America

To my granddaughter Kristina

Table of Contents

Table of Contents v
Preface ix
Abbreviations xiii
1 Introduction 1
   The Focus 4
   Problems with the Sources 7
   Past Developments 11
   The Eastern Archival Material and Homer 15
   The World of the Gods 17
   The Term Messenger 17
2 Diplomacy during the Egyptian Imperium 19
   The Form of Address 22
   Messengers 26
   Treatment, Dangers, Escorts 34
   Marriage Alliances 39
   Gift-Symbolism 45
3 Messengers in Western Asia 53
   Messenger Hospitality 65
   Messenger Credentials and Welcome 68
   The Significance of Gifts 70
   Traveling, Dangers, and Escorts in Mesopotamia and the Littoral ... 72
   Envoys as Informants 77
   Intermediaries of Royal Marriages 81
4 Homeric Messengers 87
   Introductory Remarks 87
   Continuity vs. Discontinuity 92
   Pre-Trojan War Stories 99
   Messengers in the *Iliad* 101
   Personal Honor 105
   The Route to Reconciliation 110
   The Speeches in Achilles' Quarters 114
   Priam's Embassy 117

	Other Messenger Cases	123
	Divine Messengers	127
	Messengers in the Odyssey	133
	Hermes Visits Calypso	140
	Cyclopes, Laestrygonians, Lotus-Eaters, and Aeolus.	140
	Summation	142
5	Homeric and Near Eastern Analogies	145
	Instructions	146
	Libations and Prayers	147
	Envoys' Departure	148
	Hospitality, Identification, Purpose	148
	Credentials	149
	Sacrosanctity, Dangers, Escorts, Provisions	150
	Gifts	154
	Relationships and Gift Exchanges	156
	Bride-price	158
	Salutation and Posture	159
	Verbatim Delivery	161
	Sons of Kings as Envoys	164
	Archives	165
6	Concluding Remarks	169
Afterword		185
The Diachronic Endurance of Messenger Practices		187
	Berridge's View	197
	Continuity of Contact	200
	Qualifications of Diplomatic Personnel	201
	Bureaucratic Directions	202
	Mediation	204
	Methods for Underpinning Agreements	204
	Flexibility	205
	Weak Conditions	206
	Ancient Roots	207
Bibliography		215
	Near Eastern Bibliography	215
	The Amarna Letters	215
	Lexicon of Ancient Cultures	215
	General Bibliography	215
	Homeric and Other Bibliography	222
	Lexica	222

Some Homeric Texts and Commentaries 222
Index..235

PREFACE

This book has been long in the making. Several of the arguments in it had appeared a number of years ago in an article in *RIDA*, vol. 34 (1987) 41–100 but it was not until recently that these arguments have been enlarged and combined with Near Eastern material to form a book-size unit. This unit enjoys the benefits of recent discussions on Near Eastern findings, the new publication of the Amarna Letters by Johns Hopkins University Press and the new archaeological reevaluation of the prehistoric Aegean.

These factors rekindled my interest in messenger activities and diplomatic envoys of the Near East and Homer and led me to the conclusions described in this book. My study of the envoy practices between the Near East and Homer guided me ultimately to the conclusion that the practices described by Homer could not have been the figment of the poet's imagination but must have been in force long before he composed his poetic masterpieces around the eighth century BC. Along with the ideas and practices of his age, Homer used ideas and practices bequeathed to his age *mutatis mutandis* from preceding ages before the time of the Trojan War. After all, it has by now become evident that Greece's past is immensely longer than either the Greeks themselves imagined or modern scholarship previously believed. It reached a peak or two, the Minoan and the Mycenaean Ages, before it "declined" into the recession of the Dark Ages toward the end of the Bronze Age and the beginnings of the Iron Age. It then reemerged reinvigorated in the eighth century BC. Consequently, the period classified earlier by us as Dark Ages does not seem to have been as dark as we formerly thought, and the name we ascribed to this period might have simply been a misnomer.

The Mycenaean Civilization was contemporary with the New Kingdom period in Egypt, the Hittite Civilization in Asia Minor, and the period of the Middle Assyrian Kingdom in Mesopotamia. Unfortunately, unlike its contemporary Near Eastern cultures, the Mycenaean Civilization left no significant written documentation from which its history can be reconstructed, but did, however, leave a lot of archaeological remains. It has also left to us a mass of legends contained in poets like Homer and Hesiod, and some often vague remembrances recorded in the form of information by people like Herodotus, Thucydides, and other historians and poets. Consequently, we are often compelled to resort to the contemporaneous evidence from the Near Eastern states in order to fill in some of our historical gaps regarding the Mycenaean culture. This is the method I use in my effort to investigate the messenger practices in Greece in the pre-Homeric period.

Some modern scholars feel that the safest position to adopt in the analysis of the early Greek civilizations rests upon archaeology. It is their hope that future archaeological discoveries may shed further light on the informational material about the Bronze Age and the Archaic Greek civilization and may even provide us with new material that will enable us to understand the Greek past better. Others have sought to make sense of the Homeric epic material which manifestly contains elements of the past, although there is no agreement whether these elements advert to the Bronze Age time or simply to the period of the Dark and the Homeric Ages.

My position is that the Aegean Bronze Age is a period vital to the cultural cohesion of later Greek history and that some of its practices and customs have been transmitted, albeit metamorphosed, to the succeeding Dark Ages and beyond. To avoid any misunderstandings by my references to the Bronze Civilization of Greece, let me explain at the outset that whether the Mycenaeans were Greeks or proto-Greeks is not the question to be answered here. What is important is that the Mycenaeans were part of a dynamic civilization that flourished on the soil of Greece and became part of the Greek civilization. The people we call Mycenaeans (if they came from outside of Greece c. 2000 BC) were bound to have absorbed customs and practices from the residents they found in Greece, unless these earlier residents were totally destroyed branch and root, something that is rather unlikely to have happened. The same is true of the Minoan culture; the Minoans and their culture were absorbed by the Mycenaeans, who, in their turn, must have absorbed much from the conquered. Out of this amalgam of reciprocal influences arose the people and culture known since the so-called Dark Age as Greek Civilization.

By a limited but systematic comparison of the traditional envoy practices as described by Homer with the abundant messenger practices of the Near East, I intend to prove that the Homeric envoy practices as described in Homer predate the Homeric poems by many centuries. We need not wonder at the similarity of practices between the Near East and Homer. They may not necessarily be a product of borrowing in one direction or another. After all, many things in a given historical and cultural setting are arrived at independently by more than one group, simply because there are only limited options available. That two groups use the same or similar methods does not always mean that one has copied from the other. Even where there is a direct dependence, one must determine its nature and significance.

I have no special quarrel with those who see the historical situation differently from the way I do, either in whole or in specific parts. My hope is that the facts as presented here are useful to those students of the subject whatever the interpretive framework they choose to adopt. The purpose of this essay is to illuminate the historical setting in as many of its ramifications as is feasible so as to understand better the real world in which the pre-Aegean people lived. The better one sees and understands the background of the Aegean Civilization, the more clearly he can see its cutting edge.

In one respect I owe an apology to the reader of this study. Because of the comparative methodological nature used, a certain degree of repetition is unavoidable. The envoy material from the Near East is more plentiful so that a variety of examples of envoy practices can be adduced to exemplify different points. In contrast, the examples in Homer are somewhat limited, and one has often to use the same Homeric event to illustrate a variety of envoy customs.

Another quick explanation relating to the organization of this study might be necessary. In view of the recent flurry of publications regarding the Amarna Letters, I have decided to begin the discussion of the "diplomatic" activities of the Near East not with Mesopotamia, as is often customary, but with Egypt. My decision to do so should not be interpreted as implying an earlier date for the beginnings of the history of Egypt. That is an entirely different issue into which I cannot enter here.

I would like to thank several people for their help in the preparation of this book, most notably those friends and colleagues from whose opinions I benefited. Undoubtedly, their help in the improvement of some sections of this book is appreciated, but the responsibility for the ideas and the mistakes contained in it are mine. Thanks are owed to the Department of Alte Geschichte of the University of Heidelberg, especially to Professor Dr. Angelos Chaniotis, now at Oxford, as well as Professor Dr. Geza Alföldi and Mrs. Alföldi for their kindness and hospitality during my very short stay in Heidelberg. Professor Dr. Emeritus Fritz Gschnitzer, a friend and mentor, read the paper and offered some very valuable suggestions, and for that he has my immense gratitude. I am especially indebted to Professor Carol Thomas of the University of Washington for her willingness to read the initial version of the ms and for her valuable recommendations. Thanks are due equally to Professor Kurt A. Raaflaub for reading and commenting on an earlier version of this paper; to my wife for proof-reading and correcting many errors; to three personal friends, Dr. George Capernaros, Dr. Valerie Warrior, and Dr. Athanasios Douvris of Athens, who made comments and corrections to the manuscript. Finally, I would like to express my gratitude to Ms. Sharon Rice of Bridgewater State College for several stylistic suggestions and to Katie Stott from Gorgias Press for the many valuable editorial suggestions.

Peter (Panayiotis) Karavites
Quincy, MA
October 15, 2007.

ABBREVIATIONS

ABL	Assyrian and Babylonian Letters
AbB	Altbabylonische Briefe
AFO	Archiv für Orientforschung
AHB	Ancient History Bulletin
AJA	American Journal of Archaeology
AJPh	American Journal of Philology
AM	Athenische Mitteilungen des Deutschen Archäologischen Instituts. Athenische Abteilung
ANET	Ancient Near Eastern Texts Relating to the Old Testament
AOS	American Oriental Society
AO	Archiv Orientalni
AR	Archaeological Reports of the Society for Hellenic Studies
ARI	Assyrian Royal Inscriptions
ARM	Archives Royales de Mari
AS	Anatolian Studies
BASOR	Bulletin of the American Schools of Oriental Research
BCH	Bulletin de Correspondence Hellénique
BICS	Bulletin of the Institute of Classical Studies of the Univ. of London
BIN	Babylonian Inscriptions in the Collection of J. B. Nies
Bi Or	Bibliotheca Orientalis
BSA	Annals of the British School of Archaeology at Athens
CAD	Chicago Assyrian Dictionary
CAH	Cambridge Ancient History
CAJ	Cambridge Archaeological Journal
CPh	Classical Philology
CQ	Classical Quarterly
CTH	Catalogue des Textes Hittite, L. Laroche, Paris 1966-71 and Supplements
CW	The Classical World
DHGE	Dictionnaire d'Histoire et de Geographie Ecclesiastique

EA	El-Amarna (Tablets)
ELA	Enmerkar and the Lord of Aratta
GdGR	Geschichte der Griechischen Religion
GRBS	Greek Roman and Byzantine Studies
HSCP	Harvard Studies in Classical Philology
IG	Inscriptiones Graecae
IEJ	Israel Exploration Journal
ISQ	International Studies Quarterly
JAOS	Journal of the American Oriental Society
JBL	Journal of Biblical Literature
JCS	Journal of Cuneiform Studies
JEA	Journal of Egyptian Archaeology
JESHO	Journal of the Economic and Social History of the Orient
JHS	Journal of Hellenic Studies
JMA	Journal of Mediterranean Archaeology
JNES	Journal of Near Eastern Studies
JRGZM	Jahrbuch des Römisch-Germanischen Zentralmuseums, Mainz
JSOR	Journal of the Society of Oriental Research
JSSEA	Journal of the Society for the Study of Egyptian Antiquities
KBo	Keilschriftexte aus Bogazköi
KUB	Keilschrifturkunden aus Bogazköi
LAS	Letters from Assyrian Scholars to the Kings of Esarhaddon and Assurbanipal
MDOG	Mitteilungen der Deutschen Orient-Gesellschaft
MVAG	Mitteilungen der Vorderasiatisch-Ägyptischen Gesellschaft
NB	Neubabylonische Briefe
OJA	Oxford Journal of Archaeology
OLZ	Orientalistische Literaturzeitung
OpAth	Opuscula Atheniensia
PCPS	Proceedings of the Cambridge Philological Society

PEQ	*Palestine Exploration Quarterly*
PDK	*Politische Dokumente aus Kleinasien, Bogazköy Studien,*
PN	Personal Name
RA	*Revue d'Assyriologie et d'Archéologie Orientale*
RCAE	*Royal Correspondence of the Assyrian Empire*
RIDA	*Revue Internationale de Droits de l'Antiquité*
SAA	*State Archives of Assyria. The Correspondence of Sargon II*
SIMA	Studies in Mediterranean Archaeology
SLA	*State Letters of Assyria*, by R. Pfeifer, AOS 6. New Haven: American Oriental Society, 1935.
TAPA	*Transactions of the American Philological Association*
TAPS	*Transactions of the American Philosophical Society*
Theth	*Texte der Hethiter (Heidelberg)*
TCL	*Textes Cunéiformes, Musées du Louvre*
VAB	*Vorderasiatische Bibliotheque*
VT	*Vetus Testamenum*
WO	*Die Welt des Orients*
YOS	Yale Oriental Society
ZAW	*Zeitschrift für Alttestamentliche Wissenschaft*

1 Introduction

It is customary to date the history of diplomacy from classical Antiquity, or, at the utmost, from the historical peoples of the Ancient Near East. Yet international law is seldom spoken of before the appearance of the Renaissance Dutch jurists, with Hugo Grotius the most prominent of them. Others, like Archbishop Germonius in his *De Legatis*, trace the origins of diplomacy to God Himself, who created the angels to be his legates. If, however, we do not wish to lose ourselves in the labyrinth of religion, we must be content with the fact that the roots of diplomacy have hardly been traced farther back in time than the ancient peoples around the Mediterranean and the Orient. Of course, it is by no means impossible to prove that diplomacy—the solution of intertribal or interethnic problems—can be traced back to primitive surroundings. Rudimentary forms of diplomacy evolved as a result of communities living side by side. It has been necessary for them to maintain some sort of mutual relations, through the occasional dispatch of messengers and other suchlike representatives.

In this early stage of diplomacy, there is no evidence of written rules to regulate interethnic solutions but of traditional customs which are suggestive of international law. Some scholars of jurisprudence may be unwilling to categorize these customs as laws. But we must remember that most laws originate as customs and that customs often prove stronger that law. The rise of certain forms of international law is not conditioned by the existence of societies with written law, but of societies which enter into diplomatic relations or peaceful relations with each other, no matter whether these relations had religious, commercial, or political motives. I must stress that when I speak of primitive tribes, groups, or societies, I am not thinking in terms of evolutionary anthropology or history but of peoples in a primitive stage of civilization without a written history. Since I am primarily concerned here with the diplomatic activities of the historical peoples of the Near East—which may help extract evidence about the diplomatic activities of the Mycenaean world—I will limit whatever references I make to the primitive societies to the footnotes.

In a book published a few years ago, I sought to underline the continuity of Greek civilization from Mycenaean to early Greek times and beyond by working backwards and by showing the similarities in the evidence between Homeric culture and Near Eastern culture.[1] The topic is not new, of course. Trade and other kinds of relations between the Aegean and Eastern Mediterranean in the Bronze Age have long fascinated scholars and general readers alike. During the past twenty years, these topics have once again become hotly debated issues, as new archaeological evidence has been unearthed or older material reevaluated. Also, theories such as that of Martin Bernal's *Black Athena* triggered a lively controversy which was followed by a flood of new and spirited literature. Proceeding from the work of earlier scholars such as Astour, Gordon, Bass and others, Bernal has argued that the Aegean region was heavily influenced by the hegemony of Egypt and the Near Eastern states during the Late Bronze Age, though there is no definitive evidence to support the theory that the Hyksos, whom he mainly credits for this process, exercised substantial influence in the area of the Aegean The outpouring of animated discussions as a result of the "furor" Bernal's theory produced is, one may add, the most positive aspect of the entire controversy. The evidence about them—archaeological, pictorial, and literary—does not substantiate the claim that the Egyptians ever exercised hegemony over the Aegean region. Nonetheless, Bernal's theories have triggered heated arguments, causing the scrutiny of old arguments from new angles and generating a flood of new literature.

In *A New Companion to Homer*, Sarah Morris, one of its contributors, discusses the Near Eastern influences that figure in Homer's epics.[2] Morris maintains that although the Homeric epics and epic cycles, as well as Hesiod, belong to the Eastern Mediterranean in their history and literary setting, they share narrative elements with neighboring cultures going back to the Bronze Age and show specific nexuses to Near Eastern mythology and history. In actuality, theories of such connections have been discussed since the nineteenth century, with the increasing discovery and decipherment of Near Eastern texts and the unearthing of new archaeological evidence. Poignant similarities in themes such as human and animal sacrifices, poetic similes, religious and poetic formulas, and oaths and imprecations demonstrate the affinity of the early Greek epics with the Near East. Sumerian and Akkadian epics, the Bible, Hittite and Levantine documents show close connections between Homer and Mesopotamia, the Levant, and Ugarit,

---

[1] P. Karavites, *Promise-Giving and Treaty-Making, Homer and the Near East* (Brill, 1992).

[2] Sarah Morris, "Homer and the Near East," in Ian Morris and Barry Powell, eds., *A New Companion to Homer* (Brill, 1997) 599–623.

while Greek art and myth have drawn diverse and repeated inspiration from Near Eastern subjects. Archaeological discoveries in the Delta and the Levant support the existence of close contacts in the second millennium BC and, along with them, diverse opportunities for mutual influence in the art and culture among the Near Eastern States and the Aegean.[3]

Sarah Morris singles out many of the areas of contact between the Near East and Early Greece but notes that her brief investigation could not cover the entire gamut of similarities between the two. In the following pages, I will focus on one of the areas she understandably fails to mention and on which a plethora of recent studies sheds ample light to help us better understand the nature of these similarities in the Near East and Early Greek customs. This area deals with the beginnings of diplomacy and the dispatch of envoys or messengers. The main thrust of the present chapter concerns the relations between the messenger-envoys of the Near East and those of the Homeric world and aims to underline the extent of institutional similarities between the two worlds in the hope that such a comparison may reveal the origins of the Homeric messenger practices. This study is an attempt to trace the network of relationships, which might have once connected the lands of the Aegean with the lands of the Aegean littoral and somewhat farther East, as far back at least as the second millennium BC. During this time, these regions were host to several small states and mighty empires: the Minoans on Crete and the Mycenaeans on the mainland of Greece, the Egyptians of Upper and Lower Egypt, and later, in the period of New Kingdom from the fourth Cataract to the Euphrates, the Hyksos in Egypt during the Second Intermediate period, the Hittites and the Trojans in Anatolia, the Ugaritans in the coastal area of Syria-Lebanon, the Mitanni and Hurrians of the area of upper Euphrates, the Canaanites of Syro-Palestine, and a bit farther East the Babylonians and Assyrians of Mesopotamia. Thus, the second millennium BC represents a period of continuous political, commercial, and cultural fermentation for all of the above areas. The network of colonies and trade no doubt resulted in the transfer of ideas and innovations in all directions. These innovations might have even led to local changes, which would not be easily identifiable, since we lack adequate documentation. Of greater interest to us here are the intriguing institutional messenger similarities in these cultures which can be discerned and fairly easily documented.

---

[3] Ora Negbi, "The Libyan Landscape from Thera: A Review of Aegean Enterprises in the Minoan IA Period," *JMA* 7 (1994) 73–112.

The Focus

Compared to the Homeric chieftain states as they emerge from the Homeric corpus, the ancient Near Eastern states seem better structured, seeming to have possessed a better organized ambassadorial system than that of the Homeric world. Records of the diplomatic exchanges of the Eastern states demonstrate this organization. In contrast, the gathering of all the Achaean leaders near Troy for the purpose of conducting a war does not always provide us the best natural setting for "normal interstate" exchanges. The proximity of the Achaean armies in the constricted space of a military camp deprives us of the vaster space of a state and the full measures usually undertaken by those responsible for the dispatch of envoys to out-of-state, distant places. These shortcomings notwithstanding, the picture that emerges from the diplomatic exchanges of the Achaean Kings in Troy seems to reflect not only the diplomatic practices of the Dark Ages but also those of the Late Greek Bronze Age. There is no gainsaying the fact that the analysis of these diplomatic activities may entail some minor conjecture owing to the paucity of hard evidence available. However, it does not mean that whatever minor conjectures are made will be logically circular, although that sort of objection is sometimes lodged against studies of this sort. Whereas the paucity of data is a discomfiting problem, one can only say with Chadwick, that it would be "defeatist" to refuse to pursue such an undertaking.[4] More specifically: studies that are long on speculation and short on so-called hard evidence are often unfairly dismissed on the grounds that they can only be circular, with meager data gathered and arranged as evidence using certain criteria that are then "proven." In the present case, the circularity objection may be something like this: certain relatively formal practices of the Ancient Near East have been taken as the model of practices in the Homeric epics selected and then reconstructed. Then the "hypothesis" is made that because the reconstructed Homeric envoy practices are significantly similar to the earlier Near Eastern envoy practices, they are probably copied from those practices either directly or via the interaction between pre-Homeric Greeks and their Near Eastern contemporaries. But then, supposedly, this hypothesis is really a pseudo-hypothesis. Nor is there any question of "probability," an empirical concept, since the point of the circularity objection is that it is not probable but instead only vacuously true that Homeric envoy practices reconstructed in terms of some other culture's conventions will resemble the practices of that culture. Furthermore,

---

[4] John Chadwick, *The Mycenaean World* (Cambridge, University Press, 1976) x.

since this "resemblance" would be obtained, regardless of the times to which the original format belonged, one could hardly go on to assert a causal relationship, for even the most indirect sort of influencing that takes place along temporal lines. Yet, though the Mycenaean and Dark Greek Ages may not have developed the sophisticated structure that existed among the great Near Eastern states, some of the institutional nuclei of the diplomatic practices were definitely in place and can be detected in the practices of the pre-Trojan War times, the Dark Age, and the period that followed it.

Unlike early Egypt and Mesopotamia, which are blessed with ample historical evidence, the Bronze Age period of Greece depends on archaeological material and the Mycenaean documents of Linear B, which, however, do not provide us with firm information about this period. We are therefore compelled to use the only early evidence we possess for the Dark Age and possibly the pre-Homeric times dealing with messengers, namely *The Iliad* and *The Odyssey*. True, Homer may not be a historical chronicler, but it is equally true that "linkages" between the Near Eastern and the Mycenaean Civilization are there if one looks carefully for them. This study is consequently leaning on the background assumption that, in the absence of historical records, poetry can provide substantial historical information. Poetry, especially great poetry, derives its themes from reality, from which it forms a new synthesis. It is frequently inspired by great events and takes its cue from them. But even when it does not, its settings and characterizations contain hard historical kernels. Both epics, though likely chronicled centuries after their inception, draw their account of life around the beginning of the Dark Ages and, as I will show, afford us glimpses into the Mycenaean world. Prior to and contemporaneous with the pre-Homeric age of Greece were the promise-making practices of other Mediterranean and Oriental cultures, many of which practices may very well have flowed over into the Greek world. In this as well as other respects *The Iliad* and *The Odyssey* are dividing lines of cultural streams, that include not only those influences which might have come down from them remotely and indirectly but also those that flowed down from the Mycenaean times. Accordingly this study focuses on the messenger practices depicted in the Homeric epics in the belief that by doing so we can also learn something about times and places adjacent to and preceding Homer's times. For hundreds of years, scholars have laboriously explored and analyzed the contents of these epics as well as related issues from every conceivable angle. The present study revisits the Homeric corpus once again, in hopes that what the poems suggest about the way messengers operated can help us understand better not only the internal structure of the poems themselves, but also the social and international practices that obtained before, during, and even after the times these poems were written We know there were: (A) Near Eastern cultures, some of whose diplomatic customs reached back into the third millennium BC and still earlier; (B) During the second millennium some of these peoples lived alongside and must have interacted with the sophisticated and aggressive Mycenaean people whose civilization endured for several centuries, with its zenith apparently being some time in the thirteenth century; (C) Highlights of the latter period are reflected in the poetic retrievals of those early greater times in *The Iliad* and *The Odyssey*, around roughly 750–700 BC. It would be naturally fallacious to infer anything about the nature of B solely from what we know of A, since temporal and geographic proximity does not of itself imply similarity. It would be likewise fallacious to read straight to B from C, since the Homeric epics were neither meant to be taken as history nor produced in a time or social milieu already known on independent grounds as being close to the Mycenaean age. However, we can infer tentatively, but not fallaciously, to the nature of B if we move to it from A (the Near Eastern practices) and C (the Homeric epics) simultaneously.

The above claim can be stated more carefully, though somewhat ponderously, as follows: if (1) when the A–B relationship is reconstructed by the usual tools of historical scholarship, including the tool of common sense, certain patterns emerge, giving rise to hypotheses about Mycenaean conventions, and if (2) these hypotheses agree with those formed from patterns emerging when the C–B relationship is reconstructed by literary analysis buttressed by historical scholarship, then (3) we have a relatively strong and fairly reliable reason for accepting these hypotheses. The last point is all the more compelling once we recognize that, in the present state of historical evidence for B, to accept these hypotheses is the equivalent of preferring them to the alternative of no hypothesis at all. Although in the eyes of many historians there is nothing inglorious in the passing of a *non liquet* topic, in the presence of relevant and adequate evidence from neighboring and other remote areas, it would be irresponsible not to venture the effort. Relevant evidence exists indeed from many other advanced and primitive cultures aplenty thanks to the efforts of modern anthropologists and sociologists who will be only footnoted, since I have opted to limit the primary evidence to the Near Eastern cultures for the sake of brevity. Acceptance of the hypotheses described above provides us with a fascinating, if at times blurred, image of a distant heroic age, its flavor, customs, beliefs, and institutions. Because this image is at times indistinct, the historian has to sail cautiously through the shifty currents of the existing evidence. At the end, he can be rewarded with a picture that is not bereft of historical significance. Indeed, the final picture may be of more historical value than our initial timidity is ready to accept.

PROBLEMS WITH THE SOURCES

Though our knowledge of the Bronze and Dark Ages is greatly due to the efforts of archaeologists, the nature of this knowledge remains such that it becomes necessary to tackle it with extreme care. Furthermore, in spite of this expansion, historians have to approach this knowledge with unsentimental accuracy. Along with archaeological findings, Homeric texts must be ransacked for whatever pertinent evidence can be ferreted out about diplomatic exchanges in the late Bronze and the Dark Age.

Fortunately for our pursuit of the subject, there are tidbits of information that can reinforce the relevance of our use of the Homeric information. Authors such as Thucydides, Herodotus, Apollodorus, Pausanias, and others corroborate references in Homer about the prevailing conditions in the Late Bronze and Dark Age periods. For example, Thucydides' first book refers to the same troubles that Homer describes. Elsewhere, literary tradition tells us of strife between Perseids and Pelopeids, Heracles and Nestor, Eurystheus and the Heraclidae, the war of the Seven against Thebes, the conflicts of the Epigonoi, the attempt of Hyllus against the Peloponnese, and many other acts of war. It was a tumultuous period begetting violence in pursuit of better land and living conditions (Thuc. 1.12).

Thucydides describes this period as a time without the vine and the olive, indispensable products of the later Greek era. It is hard to know to which time this reference refers, but certainly no later than two thousand BC, because we have evidence that proves the existence of the olive and vine at about this period.[5] Thucydides knew, of course, that vine and olive were common staples in the Homeric and post-Homeric times, and his references to their non-existence express his view of the general trend of Greek History. Aside from a lengthy period of political turbulence and group movements from north to south (1.12.3–4), he knows nothing comparable to our idea of a Dark Age. His description of earlier times when political turmoil was rampant seems to apply to the pre-Trojan war period,

---

[5] Yannis Tzedakis and Holley Martlew, Gen. eds., *Archaeology Meets Science, Minoans and Mycenaeans, Flavors of their Time* (Ministry of Culture, 2001) 36, 41, 93, and passim.

but it also may be a general tale of very ancient times, as Thomas and Conant have suggested.[6] Nothing in Thucydides' general account of the very early times serves as evidence for the widespread destruction and decline in population normally associated with the Dark Ages, and Hesiod appears to be in agreement with this view. Generally speaking, later Greeks found themselves embarrassed by their total historical ignorance of these years. However, we accept the argument of a complete break between the Bronze and Dark Age, and we would do well to examine the implications linked to that break.

The view of a break implies that elements of the Bronze Age civilization were virtually effaced or that the culture of the Mycenaean Age was wiped out, an event which consequently enabled or even forced a fresh start. As a result, the culture of the second millennium could have had no major influence on the culture succeeding it. *The Iliad* may ostensibly be retelling a tale set in the Bronze Age but in reality it describes the world of the Dark Ages. This view of the massive occupation by invaders and the total destruction of the preceding civilization has been slowly revised in the last twenty years. What caused the events of the LH IIIB/C (1340–1190 BC) period is a question that may never receive a clear answer. These proposed theories can be summarized into one of three categories: foreign attacks, internal strife, and natural disasters. Those who favor natural causes think mainly in terms of earthquakes rather than climate change. Kilian attributes all the LH IIIB (1340–1300) destructions at Tiryns to earthquakes, which affected, beyond the Argolid, the entire Peloponnese.[7] Even if earthquakes are accepted as the immediate cause of the destruction of many sites, much remains unexplained. Above all, this is not the disaster for which the Mycenaeans had been preparing with their reinforced constructions of defensive ramparts and storage rooms. This construction makes the threat they ostensibly perceived more mysterious.

The theory that Mycenaean Greece succumbed to raids or invasion from the outside has its adherents. Some scholars interpret the construction of protective walls as evidence of preparations against outsiders, while others attempt to discern signs of an imminent attack in the Linear B tablets

---

[6] Carol Thomas and Craig Conant, *Citadel to City-State The Transformation of Greece, 1200–700 B.C.E.*, (Indiana University Press, 1999) xix; Cynthia Shelmerdine, "Review of Aegean Prehistory VI: The Palatial Bronze Age of the Southern and Central Greek Mainland," *AJA* 101 (1997) 556, 582–83.

[7] Klaus Kilian's reports of the 1976–83 seasons are summarized by S. Iakobides, "Das Werk Klaus Killians," *AM* 108 (1993) 9–27.

from Pylos. The argument that an immediate crisis can be inferred from the Linear B tablets fails to convince those who work with the tablets more closely. Consequently, this theory does not answer the mystery of the collapse. The culprits responsible for these attacks are purported to have been two: first, the Sea Peoples, who caused great damage to Egypt and the Levant in the late thirteenth and early twelfth century BC. There is, however, no archaeological evidence that these pirates assailed the Greek mainland, nor do the Aegean islands seem to have suffered destruction at this time. The second explanation is the coming of invaders from the north or northwestern Greece. The prevalent theory regarding such attacks equates the invaders with the Dorians, people of Greek origin. This theory more recently has given way to a limited scenario of raids, followed by a gradual infiltration over the course of a century or more by West Greek speakers. This theory has also been punctured and some of its weaknesses exposed.

The third view ascribes the decline to internal factors. The Linear B tablets document the highly centralized control of industries and resources and their preoccupation with detail reflect a response to economic decline rather than any immediate threat. Another version of this view ascribes attacks on palatial centers to local uprising or internal warfare rather than foreign incursions. In the latter explanation, new populations figure far less prominently, while evidence of artifacts, cult practices, and thesmic customs attest to continuity.[8] Additionally, new ideas and directions in the field of archaeology are proving beneficial to the study of this period in Greek antiquity.[9] The truth that emerges is that many Mycenaean locations escaped destruction, keeping at the same time their institutions and technical know-how. The population decline and the resulting loss of skillful know-how were not complete. Many people survived to carve out an existence, although often in grim conditions. While survivors sought to remain and pick up their lives others were forced by invaders to depart for distant lands. There is increasing evidence for at least two waves of new Mycenaean settlers on Cyprus in the late thirteenth century to which, very likely, contributed the area of Arcadia and Argolid.[10] Other refugee centers included

---

[8] Shelmerdine, "Review of Aegean Prehistory VI," 580–81: Oliver Dickinson, *The Aegean Bronze Age* (Cambridge University Press, 2001) his introduction; Thomas and Conant, *Citadel*, xix-xxii.

[9] O. T. P. K. Dickinson, "Drought and the Decline of Mycenae, Some Comments," *Antiquity* 48 (1974) 228–30.

[10] Dickinson, *Aegean Bronze Age*, 308–309; Thomas and Conant, *Citadel*, 19–20; A. M. Snodgrass, "An Historical Homeric society," *JHS* (1974) 114–25.

Achaea, the Ionian Islands, sections of Attica, Euboea, and the coast of Ionia. At Mycenae itself, rebuilding efforts on the site of the House of Columns and construction of a viaduct spanning the Chavos ravine attest to a restoration of order and renewed vitality. Perhaps then we should not be speaking so much of a total catastrophe of the old system as much as of a partial, interspersed destruction.[11]

Be that as it may, Thucydides' references to Thessaly, Boeotia, and the Peloponnese pertain to pre-Dorian times. In his praise of Athens, he mentions those groups which escaped to Attica as a safe haven, free of disturbances (Thuc. 1.2.5). In the case of Dark Age Nichoria, there are indications both of continuity with the old population and the addition of new elements. Several sites managed to weather calamity, suffering only slight social and economic dislocations or even profiting from the straightened circumstances. Similarly, the settlement area on Xeropolis in Euboea yielded evidence of continuous occupation from the second half of the third millennium to the end of the twelfth century. The earlier periods of the settlement indicate stability, longevity, even a modicum of prosperity. While many sites in various areas went out of use, habitation continued in many places like the citadels of Mycenae, Tiryns, Midea, and sites like Argos, Korakou, Chalandritsa and Derveni in Achaea. The significant change from LH IIIB to LH IIIC is the demise of palatial administration.[12] Though life went on in Mycenae and Tiryns, the megaron units went out of use. At Midea, the megaron itself was converted to other uses, while Pylos was abandoned, at least for a while. Writing B seems also to have been aban-

---

[11] Thomas and Conant, *Citadel*, 85–91; For a bibliography connected with the modern trends Nancy Demand, "Models in Greek History and the Question of the Origin of the Polis," *AHB* 18 (2004) 61–86; K. W. Catling, "Cyrpus in the 11th Century B.C.—an End or Beginning?" in Vassos Karageorghis, ed., *Cyprus in the 11th century B. C.* (Nicosia, 1994) 133–41; Sigrid Deger-Jalkotzy, "The Post-Palatial Period of Greece: An Aegean Prelude to the 11th Century B. C. in Cyprus," in Vassos Karageorghis, ed., *Proceedings of the International Symposium of the Archaeological Research Unit of the University of Cyprus and the Anastasios G. Leventis Foundation (30–31 October 1993: Cyprus in the 11th Century B. C.* Nicosia 11–30.

[12] R. Hope Simpson and O. T. P. K. Dickinson, *A Gazetteer of the Aegean Civilization in the Bronze Age*, vol. 1: *The Mainland and the Islands* (Sima 52, Göteborg Åstrom, 1979); Kilian, "Zum Ende der Mykenischen Epoche in der Argolis," *JRGZM* 27 (1980) 166–95; for Chalandritsa *Archaeologikon Deltion* 40 (1985) Chron. 136–38; *AR* 192–93, 23 Dervenin and Achaea; T. J. Papadopoulos, *Mycenaean Achaea* (Sima 55, Göteborg, 1979).

doned. Whether this abandonment is related to the collapse of the Mycenaean central authority and bureaucracy or the appearance of the new, easier writing is hard to say. Numerous myths, legends, and genealogies hark back to the Bronze Age and along with them many social, political, and institutional practices may be traced to Mycenaean times. In short, many ideas and customs might have been bequeathed to the Dark and Classical periods by the Mycenaean times. Similarly, hostile activities and feuds cited also in Homer occasionally led to attempts at negotiated solutions. Unfortunately, Thucydides and other writers do not supply us with any clues about attempts at reconciling hostilities or finding solutions to feuds. We have to rely on Homer for the precious little he provides in this regard.[13]

That Thucydides nonetheless sketches what probably several of his contemporaries considered to be the prevailing conditions considerably earlier than the Trojan times becomes evident from his reference to Minos, who, according to legend, became the first to liberate the Aegean from piracy (Thuc. 1.2.5). Excavations in Greece have confirmed this turbulent state since the last phase of Mycenaean IIIB is marked by scattered examples of destruction in the Peloponnese, at Epano Eglianos, Tiryns, Mycenae, Zygouries, Crisa near Delphi, and Gla in Boeotia.[14] In corroboration of his argument, Thucydides cites the instability that prevailed during the times he describes as well as the tendency of many groups to flee from the parts of Greece which suffered from civil strife, seditions, external invasions, and piracy. He further mentions that, in these disturbed times, Attica constituted a safe haven for many groups which escaped there. Similar events cited in Homer occasionally led to attempts at negotiated solutions.

Past Developments

Fortunately or not, there have been many later examples of population movements into the Greek peninsula in the long history of Greece. Some of them are more contemporary, hence much more tangible than the ancient (obscured by the mist of time), which clearly demonstrate the course of historical evolution of these newcomers. One of them is the Slavic invasion that began in the early sixth century AD. Today few Greeks realize that the Slavs penetrated, often in depth, the southernmost lands of the Pelo-

---

[13] Thuc. 1.8; 1.4.1–5; 12.5–6; Hdt. 1.171.1; 3.122.2; Paus. 7.2.1.; Strabo 14.2.1; on the authority of Pherekydes.

[14] G. E. Mylonas, "Priam's Troy and the Date of Its Fall," *Hesperia* 33 (1964) 363–7.

ponnese. This ignorance stems from the simple fact that eventually the Byzantine Hellenic culture absorbed most of the Slavs, especially those south of Mount Olympus. Byzantine norms rooted themselves even among those few Slavs north of Mount Olympus, who kept a Slav ethno-linguistic identity grafted onto a Byzantine cultural, institutional, and religious identity. In the Morea, one or two of these tribes remained unabsorbed linguistically until the coming of the Turks in the fifteenth century AD. These wild mountain tribes resisted Byzantine authority but not Orthodoxy and Byzantine civilization. When the Crusaders burst forth onto the Peloponnesian scene in the thirteenth century AD, the *Melingoi* and *Eziretai* tribesmen resisted the western intrusion with an equal zeal as that of the Byzantines. Following the capture of Constantinople in the beginning of the thirteenth century, many of the old Crusaders slowly melted into the local population and were absorbed by it.[15]

The alien Franks and their Frankish politico-military regime in the thirteenth century AD in the Peloponnese proved to be an enterprise doomed to eventual demise. Destruction and dislocation constituted the main impact of their half-century rule. The universal rejection by the Byzantines, both noble and serf, of Frankish culture and Catholic religion, and the discontinuance of inward migration from the West presaged the end of the Frankish experiment. Lacking adequate numbers of women, many of them turned to the local population who eventually conquered them, sealing their doom. As Kazantzakis artfully, romantically, and somewhat superciliously relates in his *Journey to the Morea*, the landscape and the native wheat-brown, black-haired, and wide-eyed women melted Frankish resistance, and the Franks gradually disintegrated. They mingled with the locals and forgot their homeland. Their children emulated the customs of their mothers and spoke their mothers' tongue, becoming part of the Greek population. Over generations, the infants' Frankish blood became so diluted as to be nonexistent. Their Catholic fervor thawed into Orthodoxy, and another foreign "conquest" came to an end. Something similar must have transpired with the Late Bronze Age groups which presumably settled in parts of the Greek mainland and the islands. Something similar happened in the modern times to the numerous bands of Albanians who settled in the Peloponnese and the stretch of land from Menidi (Acharnae) to Thebes. In contrast, the di-

---

[15] Socrates Kougeas, "Peri tôn Melinkôn tou Taÿgetou," in *Pragmatiae Akademias Athênôn* 15.3 (1950) 1–34; A. Bon, *Le Péloponnèse Byzantine jusqu'en 1204* (Paris 1951) 63; R. Janin, *Dictionnaire d'Histoire et de Geographie Ecclesiastique* 16 (1967) 292.

vide between Turks and Greeks was too wide to be bridged, even by the four hundred plus years occupation of Greece by the Turks. The causes that kept them apart belong to another chapter of history.

Like its epic poetry, Greek religion emerged in the Dark Ages as a complex amalgam of ancient, perhaps even pre-Hellenic, and contemporary native and foreign elements. The process of borrowing and discarding practices and beliefs, gods, and goddesses, was an ancient and consistent feature of Greek religion, and there is no reason to believe that Mycenaean civilization was any more static than Classical civilization. Nor are the Mycenaeans to be censured for things they might have absorbed and appropriated from others through their daily contact with outside groups. Most dynamic ethnic groups have done so throughout history. Irrespective of what they might have absorbed, however, there seems to be a significant continuity between the above two periods, the Mycenaean Age and the age that followed it, as pointed out by examination of the Linear B tablets and the attestation of names of several Greek gods such as Zeus, Athena, Hera, Poseidon, Dionysus, and Ares. Aside from these deities, other practices, as we shall see in the discussion that follows, seem to have their roots in the Mycenaean times, perhaps even earlier.

The Mycenaeans flourished at a time when the Pharaohs were reaching the pinnacle of power in the Near East, and the Hittites were creating an extensive empire reaching out from Anatolia. The cultures of the Greek mainland and neighboring islands had become increasingly complex during the third and second millennia, reaching a high point of power, wealth, and culture during the second millennium between 1600 and 1200 BC Named for its most famous location, this first civilization of Greece has been dubbed the Mycenaean Age. The synchronous flourishing of the Mycenaean civilization, the Egyptian New Kingdom, and the Hittite Empire may or may not be attributable to the same reasons that caused the zenith of these other civilizations. In other words, the commonality of Mycenaean diplomatic and social practices with those of the Near Eastern peoples cannot be interpreted as absorption from the other civilizations.

Homeric poetry may share features with the Near Eastern cultures, and the Old Testament poetry may share features with Egyptian poetry. In fact, Homeric poetry and the books of the Old Testament were taking shape at about the same time. In the view of some scholars, the parallels between the Near Eastern and Greek cultures point to the direction of Near Eastern antecedents for the Greek epics. Cyrus Gordon persistently argued more than fifty years ago that the roots of both the Greek epics and the Hebrew biblical compositions were to be located in the literature of

Mesopotamia, Egypt, and the Levant. Thus, Odysseus has adventures in common with the Egyptian sailor Sinuhe, or he wanders widely after the fashion of the Mesopotamian hero Gilgamesh. Were such stories, however, the exclusive property of the above cultures, or did they posses common elements that belonged to the whole Near Eastern world, including the Aegean? That is something, of course, we will never know inasmuch as the Aegean world had bequeathed us no written sources. But as Jeffrey M. Hurwit said, Greece was "not a dry sponge," and the same could also be true of the Mycenaeans as well.[16] Historians may be justifiably concerned with who borrowed what morsels, but the important thing on such occasions is what people do with the material they have, instead of focusing on which parts may have been borrowed.

Some scholars maintain that Near Eastern diplomacy displays certain special characteristic forms. The participating states, for example, in what has been called the Amarna club, "volunteered" to use a common diplomatic language and script, which necessitated the hiring of specialist translators and scribes. The exchange of communications took place on a frequent basis and was facilitated by an extensive network of semi-secure travel routes. But the same is also true about the chieftains of the Homeric epics. Despite the differences in their local dialects, their language and script seem to have been common. If they had to communicate with outsiders, they too must have used interpreters. Were the Trojans Greek, and did they speak the Greek language? Or did the Greeks speak the Trojan language? In either case, they seemed to have had no problem in communicating directly, and the same must have been true on the occasions that the Greeks had to communicate with people who spoke different languages. If exchange of communications took place on a frequent basis, it was facilitated by an extensive network of more or less secure travel routes, but then the same seems to be true among the Mycenaeans and the later Greeks. The Homeric aristocratic society, it has been said, was largely egalitarian and formed a single social fabric. In contrast, the Amarna peers—in some respects the Egyptian kings did not consider the other kings to be their equals, despite their professions of equality—were not tied by an organic unity but headed separate states, each with its own distinct culture. They had made the conscious and deliberate choice to communicate on the basis of equality, and that is perhaps the real hallmark of their diplomatic culture. Something

---

[16] Jeffrey M. Hurwit, *Art and Culture of Early Greece, 1100–800 B.C.* (Cornell University Press, 1985) 19.

similar occurred with the inhabitants of Greece. The various kings who gathered at Troy seem to have been peers who had made the conscious and deliberate choice to elect Agamemnon as their leader and to treat one another more or less as equals. What about the Mycenaeans? How do we know that the kings of Pylos, Thebes, or other places did not consider themselves the equal to those of Mycenae?

THE EASTERN ARCHIVAL MATERIAL AND HOMER

In the Homeric epics, the picture of envoys and messengers is somewhat atypical compared to that of the Near East; yet one has to work with the material he has and hopefully be compensated at the end. There is already plenty of information from the Near East which touches upon treaties and related diplomatic issues which has been collected and published. In addition to this older material, the Amarna documents, in the new English translation, have recently triggered an outpouring of research on the diplomatic activities of the Near East, most of it extremely enlightening.[17] Written on clay tablets and in the Akkadian language, these documents span the reigns of the Egyptian Eighteenth Dynasty rulers from Amenophis III to Akhenaten, and possibly another king Smenkhare or Tutankhamun, and they represent the culmination of a tradition, developed over centuries. Forces at work in the middle of the second millennium BC were conducive, it appears, to the emergence of a regular and clearly recognizable system of continuous international contacts and relationships based on permanent institutions and defined structures.

In its stark simplicity, the Amarna archive reveals much about the assumptions and conventions necessary for the working of diplomatic institutions. It identifies essential features about the conduct of diplomacy, its tools, and its objectives. The Amarna Letters thus preserve a body of material that permits us to observe in detail a comprehensive phase in the development of a central feature of Western civilization. The diplomatic forms and practices that appear here, having evolved over centuries, are precursors, to some extent, of the structures of the modern world.

---

[17] William L. Moran, ed. and trans., *The Amarna Letters* (The Johns Hopkins University Press, 1992) and the excellent analysis of it in the *Amarna Diplomacy, The Beginnings of International Relations*, Raymond Cohen and Raymond Westbrook, eds. (John Hopkins University Press, 2000). Also Mario Liverani, *International Relations in the Ancient Near East, 1600–1100 BC* (Palgrave, 2001); Guy Kestemont, *Diplomatique et Droit International en Asie Occidentale (1600–1200av.J.C.)* (Louvain-la-Neuve, 1974).

Not only does the Amarna correspondence reflect key mechanisms that we have come to take for granted in diplomatic exchanges, such as negotiations on good faith, written and oral communications, protocol, diplomatic reporting, treaties, protests, claims for compensation, resident missions, and several other features, it also mirrors working principles that underpin present-day diplomacy, such as the need for truth, accuracy, credibility, the sanctity of agreements, diplomatic inviolability and immunity, and unhindered communication and reciprocity. In the correspondence, the parties haggle over a variety of items, including dowries and gifts. If envoys are lucky, a single diplomatic mission takes three months; if unlucky, it takes several months or, on rare occasions, years. They may be robbed en route, delayed by pestilence, or forced into service.

The exact chronology of the archive is uncertain, but it does cover roughly the period referred to by Near Eastern archaeologists as the Late Bronze Age, between 1600–1200 BC. This period coincides with the political and cultural apogee of Egypt and its domination of the eastern Mediterranean littoral, while the Amarna correspondence illustrates this dominance and Egyptian international contacts between the other great powers of Western Asia and Egypt in a brilliantly illuminating fashion. There are earlier references to contacts between the XVIII Dynasty king of Egypt and the Kassite rulers which come from the annals of Tuthmoses III (1480–48).[18] The climax of Tuthmoses' military conquests was achieved by his crossing of the Euphrates and penetrating the Mitanni kingdom. His defeat of the Mitanni established Egypt's claim to control the southern parts of the Levant. Egypt became a power with which the great states needed to establish formal links and work out new political relations. It was not surprising that one of the results was the arrival of embassies bearing congratulatory gifts from Hattussas and Babylonia. The visits of these embassies set the stage for the flood of correspondence which comprised the Amarna Documents.

A smaller number of ill-preserved letters were found at Boğazköy and date to the first half of the thirteenth century, showing that diplomatic correspondence was a normal and continuous part of Near Eastern political life. Although individual legal systems varied greatly, there was a common legal tradition throughout the ancient eastern Mediterranean world that continued into the first millennium BC. As a result, it is possible to draw

---

[18] The dates of the Eighteenth Dynasty rulers are somewhat "shifty." There are upper and lower dates but the differences are not great.

examples of customs and practices from different periods and countries. In addition, the Mari archives belonging to the first half of the eighteenth century, combined with some other contemporary texts from the area, prove that many of the rules and principles recognized in the fourteenth century as governing the relations of civilized states were already established centuries earlier.

THE WORLD OF THE GODS

An additional common element during this time is that the Near Eastern peoples believed strongly in the existence of gods who were part of Man's world: they had created it, supervised it, and constantly intervened in it. The divine legal system affected human behavior no less than natural activities. Natural calamities, violations of oaths taken in the name of the gods, and defeat in war were almost always attributed to divine justice and not infrequently steps were taken to make legal reparations in light of them. For example, in his plague prayers, the Hittite King Mursilis identified the cause of a plague afflicting Hatti as the punishment for a breach of an Egyptian treaty by his father Suppiluliumas, and he seeks to assuage the gods by making reparations to Egypt.[19] David takes a similar action regarding a breach of a treaty by his predecessor Saul (2 Sam. 21.1–11). Though the Greeks in the Homeric epics commonly appear much more skeptical regarding their gods, Agamemnon takes the same action when the plague strikes the Achaean troops in Troy (*Il.* 1.43, 94–95).

THE TERM MESSENGER

Before the conclusion of these preliminary remarks, additional explanatory notes are in order. First, the term "messenger" used in this paper is the most commonly used term recently to cover a gamut of functions. Each of these functions may need a special analysis in its own right. "Messenger" could be a "personal agent," a "state agent," a "religious agent," an "envoy," a "representative," or an "ambassador," depending on the situation.[20] The present work is intended as a partial analysis of those messengers who fulfilled one aspect of this diversity: namely, the role of a mediator. As a

---

[19] "Plague Prayers of Mursilis," Pritchard, ed., *ANET*, vol. 1, 3rd ed., (Princeton University Press, 1969) 394–397; P. H. J. Houwink ten Cate, "Hittite Royal Prayers," *Numen*, 16 (1969) 81–98.

[20] *EA* 149.83; J. M. Mann-Rankin, "Diplomacy in Modern Asia in the Early Second Millennium BC," *Iraq* 18 (1956) 99; *EA* 24.111.22–23, 156–62.

result, the term envoy is occasionally employed in the place of the messenger.

The "messenger" is a prime key to understanding the diplomacy of the Ancient Near East. Messengers controlled the diplomatic and sometimes the economic intercourse between important powers. They served as bearers, readers, interpreters, and defenders of their lords' messages. Because of their numerous functions, they were usually people of importance, generally associated with the palace, although exceptions are often noted. They were commissioned to build diplomatic bridges among nearby or more distant lands, large or small; they were the agents on whose prudence and ability the success or failure of a state's foreign relations depended. In our story, they are also the instruments whose activities illuminate further the informational qualities of the Homeric epics and suggest a different interpretation of the historical path of early Greece, an interpretation that sees the Dark Age not as a divide between the preceding Mycenaean civilization from the Classical times but as the bridge that joined the Mycenaean with the Classical world.

Secondly, the theory that the diplomatic rules seen in Homer are the product of the Dark Ages and the period that followed it and are in essence products of the process of borrowing from or an influence of the Near East on the Greeks is not considered as a valid historical explanation. While it is true that people who live in proximity to each other often borrow ideas from one another, there is no hard corroborative evidence that the diplomatic practices explored in this book were borrowed by the residents of Greece from the Near East or that the Homeric diplomatic practices did not exist in the Greek Bronze Age. To be sure, there is no hard historical evidence to prove the existence or type of diplomatic practices among the residents of Greece of the Bronze Age. Nonetheless there is sufficient "peripheral," evidence for the view that diplomatic practices existed in Bronze Age Greece and that they could not have been much different from those we find in Homer.

2 Diplomacy during the Egyptian Imperium

The Amarna Letters provide remarkable insight into the ancient Near East civilization in general and diplomacy in particular. The letters are an archive of nearly 500 cuneiform tablets containing the correspondence of the Egyptian court with neighboring rulers in the fourteenth century BC.[1] Discovered accidentally by a peasant woman at El-Amarna in Middle Egypt in 1887, the cuneiform tablets were soon dispersed in museums and private collections throughout Europe and the United States. Most of the letters are in Akkadian, the diplomatic language of the day, the rest being in Hittite or Hurrian. Most of the letters are by the Mesopotamian and Western Asian kings addressed to the Egyptian King and the great majority of them are written by the Egyptian vassals in the area of Palestine and Syria. Of these letters, very few are by the Egyptian King, addressed to correspondents.

As we shall see, most of the correspondence ostensibly deals with minor political matters or such fascinating items as the betrothal of royal princesses; the exchange of precious gifts such as gold, lapis lazuli, ivory and precious stones; travel arrangements; and the treatment of messengers. Under the surface of such issues, one perceives the real, and remarkably contemporary, matters at stake: spheres of influence, prestige, alliance formation, trade, rebellious activities, matters of protocol, safety of traveling officials and merchants, among others. The Amarna Letters corpus places unedited diplomatic exchanges at our disposal, offering us a panoramic view far removed from abstract philosophical categories.[2]

---

[1] The practice of the Near Eastern peoples to keep records in special archival places continued in the Greek and Roman times, and of course, the modern times, see P. Karavites, *Promise-Giving and Treaty-Making* (Brill, 1992) 187–93.

[2] Raymond Cohen, "On Diplomacy in the Ancient Near East: The Amarna Letters," in *Diplomacy and Statecraft* 7 (1996) 246.

From the standpoint of Near Eastern history, these exchanges are not very old since we have in our possession diplomatic material dating back as far as the mid-third millennium BC. However, in their unique scope and comprehensiveness of detail they illuminate a critical period in the diplomatic history of Egyptian foreign relations and the diplomatic exchanges of the ancient Near East almost indispensable for our knowledge of the area. Although the torch of diplomatic initiatives had passed to Egypt, the cuneiform language remained dominant in diplomatic relations.

The decipherment of the Amarna tablets reveals a complex world composed of organized polities in the form of states which engaged in the frequent exchange of messengers, negotiations, formation and breaking of alliances, and making of treaties. The states mentioned in the tablets perceived themselves as separate, having different interests, often striving for expansion and hegemony, thereby following on the tracks of preceding states and hegemonial powers. Egypt became the major superpower in the Near East in the second half of the sixteenth century BC During its hegemony the horizons of Egyptian diplomacy expanded vastly reaching the border of the fourth cataract south of Egypt to the borders of Iran north and east of Egypt. When the New Kingdom finally collapses, eventually Egyptian hegemony is succeeded by other states but most of the diplomatic practices of the Amarna Age survived and remained as international principles, guiding relations among states that emerged from the ashes of the old world.

Whether similar evolutionary formation developed in the contemporaneous Mycenaean states cannot be dismissed. There is no definite answer to this central question because no contemporaneous "hard" evidence survived the Mycenaean collapse that would help support such a theory. The earliest information we possess is in the form of the meager evidence in the Writing B tablets, whatever archaeological evidence remains, and the myths and sagas which may have originated in Mycenaean times, but which were written down in all probability in the eighth century BC To be sure there were plenty of contacts between the Mycenaeans and the Levant. These contacts have been richly documented in Near Eastern literature as well as by recent archaeological findings in Greece.[3] Large numbers of Canaanite jars used for carrying wine or olive oil have been located in Egypt and Mycenaean Greece. Pottery from Cyprus and Mycenae was imported in

---

[3] Oliver Dickinson, *The Aegean Bronze Age* (Cambridge University Press, 2001) chap. 1.

large quantities into Palestine, evidence of trade traffic in the opposite direction. Imports from Mycenae increased sharply in the fifteenth century. Their presence is also valuable for establishing the Amarna years. A recent discovery of Mycenaean pottery in a fourteenth-century temple at the Amman airport points to trading activities from the Aegean to the territory east of the Jordan River, either directly or through intermediaries. These findings testify to the existence of far-flung commercial relations of the Aegean with the Near Eastern world, whatever implications these contacts may denote.[4] Contact between the Aegean and eastern Mediterranean world through cosmopolitan centers such as Ugarit and Cyprus is already well-known.[5] Beyond this type of archaeological material, which is always subject to controversial interpretation, the Amarna Letters preserve a body of written material enabling us to observe in more concrete form comprehensive practices in diplomacy which may provide an inkling to contemporaneous Mycenaean diplomatic practices.

Is it possible that the Mycenaeans followed many of the same diplomatic practices in their interstate relations? To be sure, we have no definitive way of knowing. However, information from events and diplomatic practices referred to in Homer and evidence from the Homeric epics themselves lead us to the inference that the Mycenaean world was made up of states enjoying political independence and following diplomatic practices similar to those in the area of the Levant. In their extensive commercial contacts with the Levantine states it is possible that Mycenaean diplomatic contacts took the form of messenger-exchanges, hospitality for messengers, intermarriages among prominent families, gift-exchanges, and so on, and implemented diplomatic rules not so radically different from their Eastern neighbors. A possible answer to this question will be facilitated by the recent publication in the English language of the Amarna Letters, which draws on almost a century of international scholarship that has provided a fresh stimulus to the research of Near Eastern and Egyptian diplomacy. This research resulted in a number of refreshingly interesting and fruitful

---

[4] Kathleen M. Kenyon, "Palestine in the Time of the Eighteenth Dynasty," *CAH*, 3rd ed., vol.2, pt. 1, 575–81; Mario Liverani, " The Great Powers' Club" in R. Cohen and R. Westbrook, *Amarna Diplomacy, The Beginnings of International Relations* (Johns Hopkins University Press, 1999) 18, hereafter simply *Amarna Diplomacy*.

[5] Michael W. Several, "Reconsidering the Egyptian Empire in Palestine During the Amarna Period," *PEQ* 104 (1972) 123–33; M. Weinfield, "Covenant Terminology in the Ancient Near East and Its Influence on the West," *JAOS* 93 (1973) 190–99.

studies, and the same publication serves as the spring board for the discussion in this chapter and the following chapters as well. Since the old kings of the Amarna Letters used a salutation at the opening part of their correspondence, I will begin the discussion with a few brief comments on the form of address.[6]

THE FORM OF ADDRESS

The form of the Amarna Letters is fairly uniform throughout, although it occasionally differs, depending on the circumstances or the addressee. In the usual form, the address is of the type, "Say to PN2, thus says PN1."[7] It is addressed to the messenger who carries the communication in either oral or written form, or most probably both. This form of address is of Babylonian origins and does not carry any implications of the relative social status of the correspondents. Another type of address, "thus PN: Say to PN," appears in two letters from Egypt (*EA* 5 and 31) and in one form from Boğazköy (*EA* 41). In this form, the sender, superior or equal names himself first, whereas in the first form of address, the addressee ("Say to PN…") is employed only by an inferior addressing a superior. Throughout these case studies of individual forms of address, we are frequently reminded that status, age, gender, power, and prestige—i.e. social or political hierarchy in just about any form—are as much at issue in the choice of a vocative as they are in society in general.[8]

---

[6] E. Westermarck, *The Origin and Development of the Moral Ideas*, vol. 2 (London, 1906–08) 196 has shown that the custom of primitive peoples is not merely the habit of a certain circle of men, but at the same time involves a moral rule, and that laws which are based on customs naturally express moral ideas prevalent at the time when they are established. Also that in India, especially in the South, custom has always been greatly superior to written laws, vol. 1. p.163. Similarly, W. H. R. Rivers argues that custom in primitive societies is of immense importance as an unwritten and intuitive method of regulating the social organization, *Kinship and Social Organization* (London, 1914) 169–70.

[7] PN=personal name. See W. L. Moran, *Amarna Letters*, hereafter AL, xxii; W. F. Albright, "A Case of Lèse-Majesté in Pre-Israelite Lachish, with Some Remarks on the Israelite Conquest," *BASOR* 87 (1942) 33, n.7.

[8] Moran AL, xxiii; Jean Nougayrol, *Le Palais Royal d'Ugarit, IV, Textes Accadiens des Archives Sud, Archives Internationales* (Paris, 1956) 66. Eleanor Dickey, *Latin Forms of Address. From Plautus to Apuleius* (Oxford University Press, 2002); Dickey, *Greek Forms of Address. From Herodotus to Lucian* (Oxford University Press, 1996). Forms of address may not be everybody's cup of tea but are significant as part of utterance or

Another form of address that seems to have developed in the Mesopotamian area in the Old Babylonian Period consists of two parts. The first is a report of well-being: "For me all goes well." This part is often omitted in the Assyrian letters (*EA* 15–16); consequently, it may have been optional or, rather, cultural. The second part, never omitted and therefore not optional, is an expression of good wishes for the addressee, commonly beginning with "May all go well with you," the wishes elaborated and extended to the household, to wives and children, courtiers and troops, even horses and chariots.⁹

Some of the subjects addressed in these letters concern the relationships between rulers as allies or vassals, acknowledgements of gifts received, praise of the quality of gifts, or a frank expression of disappointment over the gifts received. Other subjects involve the expression of motivation behind the exchange of gifts, demands of counter-gifts in response to gifts being dispatched, dispatch of messengers, treatment and safety of messengers, and many other concerns. The number of topics with which these letters deal is so great that it would be unwise to array here all of the existing evidence in the Amarna Letters or the cuneiform tablets. A representative sampling of these letters will hopefully suffice to demonstrate the forms of address the correspondents used. For example, a letter from a Pharaoh complains to the Babylonian King about certain matters:

> Say [t]o Kadašman-Enlil, the king of Karadun[i]še, my brother: For me all goes well. For you also may all go well. For your household, for your wives, for your sons, for your magnates, your horses, your chariots, for your countries, may all go very well. For me all goes well. For my household, for my wives, for my sons, for my magnates, my horses, the numerous troops, all goes well, and in my countries all goes very well (*EA* 5.1).

In a proposal of marriage sent by the Babylonian King Kadašman-Enlil to the Egyptian Pharaoh, we see a similar form of address:

> [Say] to Mimmuwareya, the king of Egypt, [my] brother: Thus [K]a[d]aš[m] a[n -En]il, the king of Kara[duniyaš]. For me and [m]y country all goes very [well]. For you, for [yo]ur wi[ves], for your sons,

---

speech acts. They are subject to rule-governed behavior, and occasional violations of the rules can produce quite effective rhetoric.

⁹ Moran AL, xxiii; W. von Soden, "Drei mittelassyrische Briefe aus Nippur," *AFO* 18 (1958) 369.

fo[r your magnates], your horses, your chariots, and your entire country, may all go very we[ll], (*EA* 2.1–5).

The above King addresses the Egyptian King on another matter but begins with the same greeting:

> [S]ay [to Nim]u'wareya, the king of Eg[ypt, m]y [brother]: [Thus Kad]ašman-Enlil, the king of Karaduniyaš, your brother. [For me all indeed goes w]ell. For you, your household, you wives, [and for you]r [sons], your country, your chariots, your horses, your [magn]ates may all go very well, (*EA* 3.1–3).

Another king of Babylonia by the name of Burra-Buriyaš, while extending an offer of friendship to the king of Egypt, addresses him in the same way.[10] While a letter, written by a princess, the daughter of the Babylonian King, who is perhaps destined for the Pharaoh's harem, uses the same form of address, adding at the same time some good wishes on the impending military expedition of the Pharaoh (*EA* 12.6–11). The letter of the Assyrian King Aššur-uballit contains a simpler address than that of the Babylonians:

> S[ay] to...[..., Great King], king of Egypt, my brother: Thus Aššur-uballit, king of [Assy]ria, Great King, your brother. For you, your household, and your country may all go well (*EA* 16.1).

All of the above writers follow the "Say to PN², thus PN¹" format in their address, assuring the addressée that the writer enjoys good health and that his country's affairs are in good order, wishing the addressee the same. The format changes when the addressée is a vassal, in which case he addresses his king/Lord by his name and title, to which are usually added various honorifics.[11]

When a relation through marriage is established, the correspondent often expresses his "love and affection" for the relative, adding, for example, good wishes in the formal address to the king for the king's wife who is at the same time the daughter of the writer (*EA* 19.1–9). In other instances while the relationship is mentioned, no specific reference is made to the wife of the King (*EA* 21.1–12). If a letter was addressed to the queen mother by a royal correspondent, the address usually follows the same pattern, with the name of the king being mentioned along with the wife or wives of the king, one of whom might be the daughter or perhaps sister of the correspondent (*EA* 26.1–6). When the correspondent is a high official

---

[10] Moran, AL, *EA* 11.1–4; 10.1–7.
[11] Moran AL, *EA* 83.1–6; 84; 85.1–5.

of the realm communicating with another high official of a country, the address form is simpler (*EA* 40.1–5). An older king would address a king who is his equal and his son-in-law at the same time as my "brother, my son-in law," while a young king, though equal in rank, would usually address another king as "my father, or grandfather, or your son." A prince would address a "great king" as "my father" while a vassal king would address his lord or lady in a more obsequious manner.[12]

The striking feature in the above letters is that their interpersonal relations are modeled on family patterns. Family metaphors are clearly evident in frequent use of terms such as "my brother," "my father," "my grandfather," "my mother," or "my sister"—some of them reserved for more aged partners, even though the actual practice of intermarriage among the royal families made some of the above terminology extremely abstract.[13] One can easily perceive that even when the nuclear family model is not the most suitable one for the king's external relations, the small community, the village, or clan is still the one which the individual kings seem to employ rather than that of the great state.[14] The prevalent model is that of the personal interaction that distinguishes neighbors, clans, or fellow villagers in their contacts to each. The interpersonal format is the one in use from the most trivial questions about the health of the partners and their families to the most demanding negotiations over inter-dynastic marriage alliances between kings. This state of affairs is characteristic of the patrimonial state belonging to the person and the family of the king who are closely identified with it.[15] *EA* 7 from the Babylonian king Burra–Buriyaš is a good example of such a format. The actual exchange of greetings normally perceived as pure formality is here of greater significance if Pharaoh did in fact know that the Babylonian king had been sick and failed to inquire about or respond to his illness. The distance of more than thirteen hundred miles seems to be overlooked in the complaint to his partner for not sending a message wishing him a quick recovery, something that would have been

---

[12] Moran AL, *EA* 12; 27; 28. The queen of a "Great King" was addressed as "my mistress," *EA* 26; A "Great King" who had given his daughter to a colleague addressed him as "brother and son-in law"; a prince addressed his father's colleague as "father" *EA* 44; a vassal addresses his king as "my Lord," *EA* 51–52.

[13] Moran, AL, *EA* 19; 23; 24; 27; 29 Liverani, "The Great Powers' Club," in *Amarna Diplomacy*, 18.

[14] Liverani, "The Great Powers' Club," in *Amarna Diplomacy*, 18.

[15] D. J. W. Wiseman, " 'Is it Peace?' Covenant and Diplomacy," *VT* 32 (1982) 317–22; Liverani, "The Great Powers' Club," in *Amarna Diplomacy*, 8.

perfectly appropriate for a social circle operating in the limited environment of a small town or neighboring states.[16] The problem of distance is raised in the same letter wherein both Egyptian and Babylonian messengers have to confirm to the whining king of Babylon that Egypt is indeed quite a distance away and that it takes days or even months to send and receive messages. Burra-Buriyaš, his complaints for some ulterior political reason notwithstanding, decided to put an end to the affair, apparently convinced of the excessiveness of his complaint when he officially accepted the messenger's testimony, something that he probably already knew. This type of omission might be typical of neighborly or small town relations where it might be viewed as impoliteness or even a violation of small town reciprocity but is rather intriguing when transferred to relations between distant courts. On the other hand, despite the Burra-Buriyaš' whining, the incident also manifests that the difficulty of communications in antiquity did not always hamper a distant king from knowing what transpired at a far away court, nor did distance necessarily diminish one's willingness to participate in a foreign colleague's social activities. The same peculiarity is to be found where the Babylonian king Kadašman-Enlil protests at not having been invited to a festivity at the Egyptian palace, while he himself, in spite of the social insult he has suffered, is inviting the Pharaoh to a feast at Babylon.[17] This failure to reciprocate and lack of regard is a frequent issue in a small-scale society, leading to misunderstandings and, occasionally, to feuds. Yet here it is transferred to interstate relations (*EA* 6.8–17).

MESSENGERS

The ancient Near Eastern states seemed to have had organized departments which dealt with a variety of foreign matters. As a result, messengers crisscrossed the area on a wide range of business. Amenophis III (*EA* 1), for example, responding to a letter received from the Babylonian King Kadašman-Enlil (c.1364–50), argues that the complaints expressed in his letter were not valid. Kadašman-Enlil had complained that the Pharaoh was asking for his daughter in marriage but had not provided information on his sister, who had also been married to the Pharaoh earlier, during his father's reign. The Pharaoh's refutation was that the messengers sent to him were men of "lowly" status who did not know the sister and could not identify her when she stood in front of them. He suggests that the Babylonian King

---

[16] Liverani, "The Great Powers' Club," in *Amarna Diplomacy*, 18.
[17] Moran AL, *EA* 3.13–22, 23–31.

dispatch a high dignitary who might know her and can identify her. Whether the messengers were of lower rank, as the Pharaoh contends here, cannot be ascertained since we only have the Pharaoh's statement.

A second point of dispute between the two was the report of the Babylonian messengers that no gift was given to them. Pharaoh countermands this report by asserting that of the messengers who go to him not a single one goes away without a gift of silver, gold, oil, or garment, and that in that respect he is generous in the extreme. The messenger(s) had given the same report to the Babylonian King's father, and to the reigning son himself, when he previously had sent them to Egypt. Since the messengers initially lied to their king about receiving presents, the Pharaoh decided not to give them gifts the next time they were sent to him. The inevitable conclusion of the Pharaoh from these instances as well as others is that the messengers of the Babylonian King were liars (*EA* 1.62–67).

The Pharaoh's response about the "lowly" status of the Babylonian messenger does not seem to be correct, if we are to judge from the general status of messengers. As a rule, messengers were considered to be professionally experienced and socially prominent. There are exceptions to the rule, however, as messengers may have been chosen according to exigencies of the occasion, but even in those cases, messengers were not generally "lowly." Untrained messengers may have been picked from the ranks if a royal needed someone to risk his neck on a perilous mission. On exceptional occasions, a king might be constrained to use someone as a special courier, since the enterprise might prove very risky, and a normal messenger would be unable to pass through the opponent's lines of siege. At other times, the sender would be unwilling to risk a beloved or experienced envoy for such an enterprise.[18]

The second complaint touched not only upon the truth of the statement but also upon the personal "honor" of the person to whom reference was made. According to the logic of interpersonal relations, correct and functional interactions among kings (that is the Great Kings) should express friendship and good relationships. The friendly character of these relationships becomes evident when supported by a constant and adequate flow of material exchanges in the form of gifts and warm greetings. Failure to extend the same courtesy to a king's messenger was an insult to the person of

---

[18] J. M. Munn-Rankin, "Diplomacy in Western Asia in the Early Second Millennium BC," *Iraq* 18 (1956) 99–100; S. A. B. Mercer, *The Tell El-Amarna Tablets* 1 (Toronto, 1939) 377.

the king himself. In cultures where a man's self-image is derived from gestures of this nature, failure to bestow a gift on his envoy was deemed an insult and had to be rectified. This insult violated the accepted code of behavior where equality among the kings prevailed. Even if the condition of equality did not exist, protocol still required the dispatch of a gift. Exceptions were often made, but they were understood because of prior stipulations between kings. Thus, in a treaty between Mursilis II and Niqmepa of Ugarit (c. 1300 BC), it was stipulated that "should it happen that a king's son or a noble goes from Hatti to Ugarit as a messenger, if it pleases the king of Ugarit to give a present to him, let him make a gift to him, but if it does not please him to give, he need not make a present. This is not an obligation."[19]

The Babylonian King had still another personal complaint for the Pharaoh, who was also his uncle. He noted that whenever his messengers visited other kings in the area of the Near East who were married to his daughters, these kings always sent greeting-gifts with the returning envoy. In contrast, the Pharaoh had failed to reciprocate (*EA* 1.52–62). The Pharaoh's response is puzzling, if not downright insulting. The Pharaoh countered this complaint with the hypothesis that the neighboring kings were rich and mighty. Because of their wealth, his daughters had acquired valuable items from their husbands. From this trove, they sent gifts to their father. Contrarily, the Babylonian King's sister, who was married to the Pharaoh, did not possess anything. If she ever did, the Pharaoh would send it to the Babylonian King. The Pharaoh then adds the rather strikingly odd statement that the Babylonian King married his daughters off in the hope of acquiring "a nugget of gold" from his neighboring kings.[20]

Pharaoh's statement regarding the riches of the other kings is strange because Egypt was the "super-power" in the Near East at that time, and the neighboring kings, including those in Assyria and Babylonia, often asked the Pharaohs for gold and other items because they believed the Egyptian kings were vastly wealthy. Pharaoh's statement that his Babylonian wife did not possess anything of value but that if she ever did, he would send Kadašman-Enlil what she acquired, is also intriguing because he does not explain the possible source of this acquisition, unless it was from the Pharaoh

---

[19] Zaccagnini, "The Forms of Alliance and Subjugation in the Near East of the Late Bronze Age," in *I Frattati nel Mondo Antico: Forma, Ideologia, Funzione*, Luigi Canfora et al. eds. (Rome, 1990) 63.

[20] Moran AL, *EA* 1.52–62 and notes 21 and 25.

himself, a point that the Pharaoh's statement does not address. Were the queens of Egypt receiving gifts or revenues from sources other than the Pharaoh which they could dispose independently of him? Pharaoh's answer does not elaborate.

In *EA* 2 and 3, messengers are sent by the Egyptian King Amenophis III to the Babylonian King Kadašman-Enlil to explore the possibility of a marriage proposal between the Egyptian King and the daughter of Kadašman-Enlil. In *EA* 2, the Babylonian King has no objection provided that the groom is of royal blood. In *EA* 3, the Babylonian King again has no objection, especially since the girl concerned has become of age. He only asks that an Egyptian delegation be sent to escort her to Egypt. Other issues, however, are raised which concern the fate of the messengers. Previously, when messengers were sent to Egypt, Amenophis would let them return fairly quickly, dispatching along with them a substantial greeting-gift. Now, whenever Kadašman sent a messenger to the Egyptian King, the latter detained him for six years, which implied that the Babylonian King had not received a greeting-gift for six years. To make matters worse, the gift was in the form of gold which contained a high percentage of silver, giving it a grayish cast. The gold was melted down in the presence of the Egyptian messenger Kasi, who carried it and thus became a witness to the low quality of gold, something that displeased the Babylonian King. Still another complaint, expressed in the same letter (*EA* 3) was that Kadašman-Enlil had received no invitation and greeting-gift when Amenophis celebrated his anniversary on the throne of Egypt.[21] The gift Amenophis sent did not amount to anything approximating the gifts that Kadašman-Enlil dispatched every year. Kadašman-Enlil had built a new palace, which the messengers of Amenophis had already seen, and he intended to invite Amenophis to its opening celebrations, contrasting his conformance to etiquette, hospitality, and attitude with that of his peer.

In a letter dispatched by Burra-Buriyaš to Amenophis IV (Akhenaten, c.1350–1334), Burra-Buriyaš (1349–23) describes some problems that stemmed from his ill-health (*EA* 7). Burra-Buriyaš explains that the Egyptian King's messenger arrived at the Babylonian court when the King was ill and unable to invite the Egyptian messenger to dinner. Long established custom required that the king welcome royal envoys to his table as often as

---

[21] It was a celebration on his thirtieth, thirty-fourth, and thirty-seventh years, Moran AL, *EA* 3. n. 8; Christian Kühne, *Die Chronologie der Internationalen Correspondenz von El Amarna* (Neukirchener Verlag, 1994), 254.

their rank demanded, furnish board and lodging, and bestow gifts upon them.[22] Because of his illness, the Babylonian King was remiss in honoring his obligations and made apologies. In corroboration of the validity of his assertion, the Babylonian King proposed that the Pharaoh use the Egyptian messenger as a witness (*EA* 7.8–13).

Further down in the same letter, the Babylonian King complains that his messenger had been detained unjustifiably for two years before he was finally permitted to return. This complaint was expressed to the Egyptian messenger who happened to be at the Babylonian court at that time. He furthermore elucidated that owing to the distance and the difficulties of the journey—hot weather and the lack of water—he was not sending many beautiful greeting-gifts. He reserved the dispatch of precious gifts for another time with another messenger when the weather would be better.

In *EA* 16, the Assyrian King Aššur-uballit notified his Egyptian counterpart of the happy arrival of his messengers, assuring him that as long as the messengers stayed with him, they would be viewed as objects of solicitude. The reference is to the care and honors commonly shown to messengers, implied by the alleged happiness mentioned in this letter. Such happiness and joy moved the Assyrian King to external expression.[23] Despite Aššur-uballit's joy, he does not hide his disappointment about the greeting-gifts the Egyptian King has sent. These gifts consisted of a beautiful royal chariot outfitted for him and two horses, a chariot not outfitted for him, and one seal of genuine lapis lazuli. White horses were highly prized in the ancient world, and in the classical world, they were valued for their color and their speed.[24] But Aššur-uballit was engaged in the construction of a new royal palace and was in desperate need of gold. Since he believed that gold was abundant in Egypt, he could not understand why the Egyptian was reluctant to share, and he urged the Pharaoh to send him enough gold to adorn the new palace. In support of his argument, he maintains that earlier Egyptian Kings had sent immense quantities of gold to his ancestors. The quantity the Egyptian King had dispatched to Aššr-Uballit did not justify or even cover the expenses of the mutual sending of messengers. In the letters,

---

[22] See *ARM* 21, pp. 506 ff.

[23] Moran AL, *EA* 16.6–8, n. 2; Joy moves, almost necessarily, to external expression, see Moses I. Finley, *The World of Odysseus* (New York, 1965) 132; Garry A. Anderson, *A Time to Mourn, A Time to Dance: The Expression of Grief and Joy in Israelite Religion* (University Park, Pa. 1991) 73.

[24] E. F. Weidner, *Bi. Or.* 9 (1952) 157 ff.; *ARM* 14, 40, 98; *Il.* 10.437; *Aeneid* 12.84; Horace, *Satires*. 1.7.7.

gifts obviously are requested and accepted but not always appreciated. The quality and amounts are often disputed, particularly Egyptian shipments of gold or gold items.[25] Although it appears here that the greatest emphasis is on monetary value, in actuality, according to gift-giving protocol, the dispute is framed in terms of pride and renown, namely the recipient's honor.

The messengers' positions in the court, their proximity to the king, and the frequent correspondence they carried back and forth made them invaluable and indispensable advisers to the king. In foreign affairs, they were often the only ones other than the king and his narrow circle who knew what had been exchanged between countries. Even the inner circle to the king might not know as much as the messengers because they were privy to the meetings between the kings and advisers in the countries to which they were dispatched, and had ample opportunity to observe their personalities. The tone of voice; movements of the hand, face, or eye; expressions of anger, placidity, sarcasm, and other gestures and features are part of the diplomatic game, which only those conversant with the opposite party can grasp and accurately assess. Thus Tušratta, the Mitanni King, when writing to the Egyptian Queen whose husband had recently died, acknowledged that she was one of the very few who knew of the affection the Mitanni King had for her husband and knew about the letters they had exchanged. His messenger, Keliya, and the famous Egyptian messenger, Manc, were the other two persons privy to the contents of the royal correspondence. The Egyptian Queen suggests, on the other hand, that the Mitanni King continue to send embassies, bringing her joy by receiving the brother king's greetings and no doubt at seeing the greeting-gifts that accompanied them.[26]

Similarly, when he sent a letter addressed to the Egyptian King, the son of the aforementioned queen, Tušratta emphasized that only a few people were privy to how he addressed the father of the reigning Egyptian King: namely, the Egyptian Queen Teye, Keliya, the Mitanni messenger and Mane, the Egyptian messenger of the deceased king. Likewise, no one except the aforementioned individuals knew of the words the former Egyptian King had sent to Tušratta. When the Mitanni King wished to have an account of the gold supply sent by his father to Tušratta he suggested that the Egyptian king should ask Haamašši, who had brought him the gold on behalf of his father.[27]

---

[25] Moran AL, *EA* 3.15; 7.69–72; 10.8–24; 20.46–59; 29.69–79.
[26] Moran AL, *EA* 26.7–18; 27.7–8.
[27] Moran AL, *EA* 27.55–58, note 12.

Elsewhere, in a letter that contains a long review of Mitannian-Egyptian relations, Tušratta describes how Nimmureya, the father of the reigning king of Egypt, viewed Tušratta's messengers:

> Just as when one sees [his] pee[r], he shows him respect, so Nimmureya showed respect to [my messengers as p]eers and as [f]rie[nds]. He sent back all my messengers that were in residence in(to?) the quarters that [were established] for Tadu-Heba, and there was not [a single one] among them who went in and [to whom he did not g]ive [something]. He gave Keliya's [in]got of gold weighing 1000 shekels, and Nimmureya gave [...sacks fu]ll of [gold] to Tadu-Heba. Tadu-Heba lai[d] them all out [before] my [messengers].

The long letter concludes with Tušratta's appreciation of the respect that the Egyptian King had always shown to Tušratta's messengers, whom the Egyptian King considered to be messengers, friends and peers, and unfailingly bestowed upon them presents before they started their return trip.[28] In an indirect way, Tušratta is telling the young king of Egypt how his father had repeatedly showed respect for Tušratta's messengers, thereby honoring Tušratta himself. He politely advises the Egyptian King to maintain the same respect for Tušratta's messengers, if he wishes to maintain the same good relations.

As part of their responsibilities, messengers often represented their king in criminal cases. Not only did they carry messages that demanded the arrest and punishment of violators, but they were also used as witnesses to ensure that the culprits were punished according to the customs of the time or the demands of the plaintiff. In *EA* 29, there is a request by the Egyptian King to the Mitanni King for the seizure of two criminals who had violated Egyptian law. The purported criminals were captured and eventually convicted in the presence of Tušratta and Mane, the Egyptian messenger who represented his king in this case. It appears that Mane's testimony convicted and put the two individuals into chains and fetters. Following their conviction, they were transported to a Mitanni border town, likely for incarceration, since their case evidently did not warrant execution. The Egyptian king himself did not write requesting the death penalty, nor did Mane, who was present at the trial, insist upon it. It appears that the Egyptian King's court did not give all the facts concerning the crime the guilty parties had committed, nor did Mane have all the facts. But as soon as the Egyptian chancellery heard of the Mitanni court's decision, most probably via Mane, the

---

[28] Moran AL, *EA* 29.32–37.

king expressed his dissatisfaction and demanded their execution. The Mitanni King consequently honored the Egyptian King's request, thereby evidencing that Mane not only carried out the wishes of the Egyptian King but also testified at the trial about the reputation of the accused. When the court reached a decision based on the facts Mane presented, Tušratta went so far as to suggest that the Egyptian King consult Mane regarding the fairness of the Mitanni court.

The trust and indispensability of messengers in the conduct of foreign affairs is also manifested by the case of Rib-Hadda, a Canaanite vassal of the Egyptian King (*EA* 117). He was in the habit of over-reporting to his lord to the point of becoming a nuisance, for which the Egyptian King chided him. Rib-Hadda excused his overindulgence by arguing that he did so because the other vassals in the area were not trusted to inform the king fully. Furthermore he claimed that he only trusted two of his messengers for his communication with the Egyptian court both of whom he had already sent to Egypt. Although he had made it clear to the king that he had no other trusty individuals to carry his tablets to the Egyptian palace, the palace did not quickly allow either of these two messengers to return to him. Consequently, he had no other confidants to carry his correspondence.

While the various kings employed certain trusty officials as messengers in the conduct of their foreign affairs, on some occasions they would opt to use certain high officials as messengers, as befitting the special nature of the occasion.[29] In special cases, kings would send their sons as messengers to underscore the gravity of the situation. How experienced these persons were compared to the "expert" messengers they employed cannot be known. But they must have been briefed as much as possible before they undertook their mission, and it is also safe to say, although our sources do not intimate so, that they were accompanied by more experienced persons. One good example is that of Rib-Ad[di], a vassal king of Egypt in the litto-

---

[29] Moran AL, *EA* 1.28–54. Since Kadašman-Enlil expresses doubts about his sister's well-being, the Pharaoh suggests that he send a special dignitary who knows Kadašman's sisters. Pharaoh's comments about the nonentities of Kadašman's envoys should perhaps not be taken very seriously. The custom of sending heralds or messengers is found also among the primitive tribes. In most instances these primitive diplomats returned as soon as they had performed their mission, but among the Indians of North America we also find occasional resident messengers, Ragnar Numelin, *The Beginning of Diplomacy, A Sociological Study of Intertribal and International Relations* (New York, 1950); J. Frazer. *The Aborigines of New South Wales* (Sydney, 1892) 41; K. L. Parker, *The Eahlayi Tribe* (London, 1905) 64.

ral of Palestine, who had been attacked by another vassal, a fellow mayor of another city in the area, and had been expelled from his city. His request for reinforcements from Egypt had fallen on deaf ears for reasons unknown. Exiled and desperate, Rib-Addi sends his own son, a measure indicative of the gravity of his situation, to ask for archers who would seize the area of Gubla and fight against his enemy (*EA* 137). The Egyptian administration did not take immediate action, and Rib-Addi complains (*EA* 138) that though four months had passed since he had dispatched his son to Egypt, the son had still not had an audience with the king. He therefore wants to hear the reason for the son's delay and detention in Egypt. Another king, King Ara[šš]a of Kumidu, similarly sent a request to the Egyptian King asking for some military help, for "I have neither horse nor chariot," (*EA* 198). The carrier of this message was the son of the king himself.

TREATMENT, DANGERS, ESCORTS

Hospitality and the good treatment shown to foreigners and guests were long established conventions in the Near East, though exceptions to this rule for a host of reasons were frequent. Officials representing kings, governors, or even minor personalities on official business expected fair treatment from their hosts. Not only did human customs demand it but divine law was supposed to protect them as well.

King Tušratta takes pride in writing the Egyptian King that he had honored his brother's messenger as well as the troops that accompanied Mane, treating them all with great distinction. Tušratta invokes the testimony of Mane himself when he had returned to Egypt, to corroborate whether or not he treats his guests as required (*EA* 20, 64–70). On a different occasion, the same king of Mitanni (*EA* 21, 24–32) claims that he exalted Mane the messenger and Hane the interpreter traveling with him, like gods. He bestowed upon them many gifts and treated them very kindly.

The same Tušratta exults at the way his Egyptian King and son-in-law treated his messengers when they took his daughter to Egypt as bride for the king:

> Just as when one sees [his] pee[r], he shows him respect, so Nimmureya showed respect to [my messengers as p]eers and as [f]riends.... As fa[r as] my [messe]ngers [were concerned], Nimmureya showed them respect with love [and evidence of esteem] (*EA* 29.32–44).

The king of Egypt wrote his vassal Aziru about the messenger he had sent to him and accused Aziru of hiding from him. Aziru apologizes for not treating the king's messenger as well as he would have liked explaining that he was absent in Tunip at the time of the messenger's arrival and had failed to give him the proper treatment. As soon as he heard of his arrival, however, he went after him, but failed to overtake him. He wished messenger Hani safe return, especially since Hani, upon returning to Egypt, would have the chance to explain to his lord, the king, how well he was provided on his return trip. The vassal's brothers and Bet-ili were placed at his service, and they provided him "with oxen, sheep and goats, and birds; his food; and his strong drink." In addition, Aziru supplied him with horses and asses for his journey (*EA* 161.11–22). The Pharaoh's strict reply in a letter seems to reinforce the suspicion that his vassal was double-dealing. In that letter the Pharaoh accuses the vassal of providing for the Hatti messenger, while failing to do so for the Pharaoh's messenger. The vassal does not protest Pharaoh's response; he simply seeks to mend his fences by stating that if the Pharaoh were to send his messenger back to him, he would provide him with food supplies, ships, oil, logs of boxwood, and other goods in order to prove his loyalty, *EA* 161.

Besides the regular messengers referred to here, kings and governors of the ancient world used other individuals in the capacity of messengers when circumstances did not require the presence of the customary messenger. When merchants were going to an area where the king intended to send a message of lesser importance, merchants were often charged with the responsibility of delivering the message. Burra-Buriyaš, the Babylonian King, complains in a letter to the Pharaoh that a caravan of Ṣalmu had been robbed twice. The Babylonian King even knew the culprits and reported them to the Pharaoh, since one of them was an Egyptian governor.[30]

The same Babylonian King alleges in another letter to the Pharaoh (*EA* 8) that, although the two kings had made a mutual declaration of friendship just as their fathers had done, his merchants and Aḫu-ṭabu, were detained in Canaan on their way to Egypt. Aḫu-ṭabu is ultimately allowed to leave but the rest of the men are killed and their money taken. The Babylonian King asks the Pharaoh for an inquest to determine the facts of the matter and impose the death penalty for the would-be culprits since Canaan, where the incident took place, is in the Pharaoh's domain. Burra-Buriyaš demands that the men be forced to make compensation for the lives and the money they had taken. Fear that they might kill again dictated that they should be condemned. If they killed again, it was possible that the

---

[30] Moran AL, *EA* 7.73–82, n. 24. For some of the problems with the name see W. F. Albright, *JEA* 23 (1937) 200, n.4; E. Edel, *JNES* 7 (1948) 24.

channels of communication between the two kings could be cut and that would be an even worse crime. In case the accused tried to deny their crime, the Babylonian King suggests that the two remaining witnesses who had escaped death testify so that the Pharaoh could establish the exact circumstances of the crime.[31]

The modern doctrine of diplomatic immunity, whereby a diplomat is not liable in the courts of the host country for certain illegal acts, is not attested to in ancient Near Eastern records, but the host king could ask his colleague for the punishment of an envoy for crimes committed in the host country.[32] In *EA* 29.173–81, for example, the Pharaoh demanded that the Mitannian king impose the death penalty on two of his diplomats who, the Pharaoh claimed, had committed unspecified crimes while in Egypt but who had since returned to Mitanni. The Mitannian king pointed out that he had already conducted a judicial inquiry in the presence of Mane, the Egyptian ambassador, apparently on the basis of an earlier demand, and that he had put the culprits in chains and transported them to the border. Nonetheless, he readily agreed to the Pharaoh's new demand, on the condition that proof be given of a capital offense.[33]

It becomes evident that messengers, whether they were royal officials or merchants operating as messengers of a king, functioned under constraints and were exposed to many dangers. Foremost among them was the distance and conditions of many of their journeys. The Assyrian King Aššur-uballit explains to the Egyptian King, in response to his complaint about the delayed return of his messengers, that the Suteans had pursued them on their way to Assyria and that at some point they were in mortal danger. Consequently, the Assyrian had detained them until the Suteans were captured and the area cleared. The Assyrian's only hope was that his own messengers would not be delayed in reaching him. Why, he asks, "should messengers be made to stay constantly out in the sun and so die in the sun? If staying out in the sun means profit for the king, then let him (a

---

[31] Moran AL, *EA* 8.8–42 and n. 2.

[32] Raymond Westbrook, "International Law in the Amarna Age," in *Amarna Diplomacy*, 33.

[33] Westbrook, "International Law in the Amarna Age" in *Amarna Diplomacy*, 33–34. Spy agents were sometimes sent by African tribes posing as itinerant merchants. In the Australian continent traders enjoyed special extraterritoriality privileges, like the envoys, A. W. Howitt, *Native Tribes in South Eastern Australia* (London, 1904) 714.

messenger) stay out and let him die right there in the sun, (but) for the king himself there must be a profit."[34]

There was always danger of seizure or death for a messenger at the hands of bandits or marauders, either for the sake of ransom or for the value of the goods and gifts they were carrying. Petty kings and chiefs also were not above plundering caravans of goods and holding the messengers for ransom. Because messages could easily be intercepted and the intelligence used by small kings, messengers are frequently provided with documents that differ substantially from their oral instructions in order to mislead the interceptor. In addition, messengers also faced dangers from wild animals, especially lions, which were plentiful and life-threatening.[35]

Pharaoh's vassal Rib-Hadda's comments on the prevailing insecurity in Canaan are also interesting. When he sends his man to Pharaoh, both of his horses and one of his men are taken. The tablet he carried from his king for the vassal never reaches its destination. Similarly, the king of Aziru notifies the Pharaoh that he sent his messengers to him but Yanhamu (another mayor or governor in the area of Canaan) had stopped them on the way, and "they have not got away" (*EA* 171). Tagi, another vassal of the Pharaoh in the area of Canaan, tries to assemble a caravan under the charge of his brother (probably a fellow-mayor) but barely escapes being killed and is not able to send his caravan to the Pharaoh (*EA* 264). Still another vassal sends a gift to the Pharaoh made up of a 5000 prisoners along with eight porters for the king's caravans, but they had been captured somewhere in the "countryside." Therefore, he wants to inform the Pharaoh that he is unable to send a caravan to the king (*EA* 287.53–59).

Like all other envoys in the Near East, Egyptian envoys enjoyed sacrosanctity, especially in times of peace. But the principle of sacrosanctity, though universally recognized, was subject to the whims of local leaders and their personal or state interests as they perceived them. Beyond this ambivalence, pirates, country robbers, and brigands in the countries through which envoys and messengers passed followed their own rules. Owing to the dangers inherent in being envoys and messengers, measures are often taken to protect them. Among such measures is the custom of assigning troop es-

---

[34] Moran AL, *EA* 16.37–55 and n. 16; *EA* 7.49 ff.
[35] Waterman, *ANET* 217, no. 1026; *ANET*, 205; *ANET* 10, no. 35. In Greek and Roman times ambassadors were not exempt from similar dangers, Aesch. *Pers.* 30.3; Dem. 12.4; Suda: Anthemocritus; Wolfgang Helck, *Die Beziehungen Ägyptens zu Vorderasien im 3. und 2. Jahrtausend, v. Chr.*, Ägyptologische Abhundlungen 5 (Wiesbaden, 1971) 442.

corts and guides for the countries through which the messengers were to travel. Similarly, they would ask friendly or neighboring kings and governors to protect messengers who journeyed through their territories and to provide them with escorts, provisions, and guides. Though in *EA* 7 the section of lines 49–62 is damaged, there is little doubt that what remains alludes to a request by Burra-Buriyaš to the Pharaoh to provide his messenger with a military escort. When Burra-Buriyaš complains that the Pharaoh sent only five chariots to escort his daughter to Egypt, he appears to be concerned with safety issues as well as proper respect for his stature.[36]

Another liability which would frequently befall messengers was the tendency of many kings to detain them for their own reasons. Such detentions could be limited to a few months or could be extended to years. Kadašman-Enlil, in his letter to the Pharaoh, complains that the latter detained his messenger for six years (*EA* 3.13–22). In the letter wherein Burra-Buriyaš announces the robbing and killing of his merchant-messengers (*EA* 8), he asks the Pharaoh to send off his messenger immediately to notify him about his actions regarding the assailants, urging him not to detain his messengers. In a like manner, Aššur-uballit tells the Pharaoh in a letter (*EA* 15.16–22) not to delay the messenger whom he had sent "to you for a visit." He should visit and then leave to return to Assyria. He should see what "you are like and what your country is like, and then leave for here." In letter *EA* 19.71–79, Tušratta states that he sent his messenger Keliya to the Pharaoh and asked that he not be detained. When Tušratta himself detained the Egyptian messenger Mane, he hastens to justify the reasons for this detention (*EA* 20.18–22). Similar justifications for detaining messengers are made in several other letters.[37] These justifications demonstrate that owing to personal whims of the host king or in the pursuit of policies considered beneficial to their personal and state interest, many kings were not above violating the universal principle of allowing the messengers to go when they wished to do so.

For their protection, Egyptian messengers were also accompanied by troops. In a letter to Tušratta, the Pharaoh expresses his dissatisfaction over the treatment of his messenger Haaramašši and his escort (*EA* 20.33–38). In the same letter, which is an obvious answer to Pharaoh's letter, Tušratta states that he has honored the Egyptian messenger Mane and all the troops

---

[36] Moran AL, *EA* 11.16–22 and on the reverse, 13–18.
[37] Moran AL, *EA* 7.49–62; 8.43–47; 29.166–172; 35.35–39; 38.23–26; 117.10–21.

that accompanied him to Mesopotamia. The same Tušratta, in a protest letter to the Pharaoh, cites the dispatch of his messengers Pirissi and Tulubri in posthaste along with a very small escort. Perhaps the small escort was intentional to facilitate the faster movement of his messengers to Egypt (*EA* 28.12–19). The same Tušratta requests the prompt return of his messengers and the dispatch of the Egyptian messenger Mane along with them. Upon the grant of this request, he promises to send his messenger Keliya along with a large escorting force (*EA* 29.166–172). In still another letter, a vassal notifies his Egyptian King that he made very careful preparations and personally escorted all the king's caravans as far as Busruna, while the independent king of Alašiya tells the Pharaoh to send him his messenger immediately along with the Alašiya messengers, for safe passage.[38]

MARRIAGE ALLIANCES

Several of the communications carried by messengers of the Near Eastern chancelleries concern political marriages. During the Egyptian supremacy in the Eighteenth Dynasty period, the Pharaohs included women of the highest rank from important kingdoms—if not always equal to their own—in their harems. One of the main reasons for several of these marriages was no doubt political. The Egyptian Kings, on the other hand, refused to reciprocate when it came to colleagues' requests for Egyptian princesses. Thus when Kadašman-Enlil asks the great king of the Eighteenth Dynasty Amenophis III for an Egyptian princess to marry as a token of brotherhood and amity between the two kings, the latter replies that it has been the practice from time immemorial not to give any Egyptian princess in marriage to a foreign leader. Yet, in another breath, Amenophis requests a Babylonian princess as a token of brotherhood and amity. Kadašman-Enlil considers turning down Amenophis' request as Amenophis had done to his, but in the end sends him his daughter. Kadašman-Enlil's decision in this matter is not entirely "charitable" inasmuch as he is engaged in the construction of a building and needed gold from the Egyptian King (*EA* 4.4–22).

Diplomatic marriage was, of course, already a well-known practice in Mesopotamia, occurring in both UR III and in the Mari texts before we encounter it in the Amarna Letters. The ancient monarchs had to rely upon

---

[38] Moran AL, *EA* 199; *EA* 35.16–18. Primitive Messenger, envoys, couriers, and heralds enjoyed a number of special privileges, among them inviolability, Frazer, *The Aborigines of New South Wales*, 37, 41; Numelin, *The Beginning of Diplomacy*, 150, 155, 157.

alliances with other powerful kings to maintain their international status. While in the beginning of Egyptian history there is evidence of marriage alliances as early as the First Dynasty (c. 3000 BC), by the time of the New Kingdom, the rulers of the Eighteenth Dynasty had decided to bar the marriage of kings' daughters outside the court, and this also extended to unions with rulers from other Near Eastern countries.[39]

On another occasion, it seems that the Babylonian Burra-Buriyaš agrees to provide the Egyptian King with a Babylonian princess as a wife. It appears that the girl promised to the Egyptian King in an earlier agreement had died, and there has been a delay in carrying out the offer of another girl (*EA* 11.7–8). Soon the Egyptian messenger Haamašši comes to Babylon together with an interpreter to "inspect" the prospective bride. They must like what they see because they proceed to pour o[il] on the girl's head as a sign of their acceptance of the prospective bride.

The Mitanni King also promises his daughter as a "mistress" to the Pharaoh, and the famous Egyptian envoy Mane comes to pick her up and take her to Egypt. Tušratta reads and rereads the message that Mane brings from the Egyptian King, in which the Egyptian probably explains that Tušratta's daughter is not going to be the official wife of Pharaoh, replacing Queen Teye.[40] From the tone of the letter, one can judge that Tušratta agrees with the arrangement and consents to carry out the wishes of the Egyptian. He then proceeds to notify the Egyptian King that he will dispatch the Pharaoh's bride-to-be in six months. To that effect, he detains Mane, who is supposed to return to Egypt along with Tušratta's messenger Keliya and a special greeting-gift for the Pharaoh.

---

[39] Pharaoh's daughters did marry foreigners later on in the first millennium during the declining days of the post-imperial times, the so-called Third Intermediate Period, J. A. Wilson, in *Before Philosophy: The Interlectual Adventure of Ancient Man*, H. Frankfort et al., eds. (The University of Chicago Press, 1946) 33. See also G. Robins, *Women in Ancient Egypt* (London, 1993) 30–36. The Romans during the Republican and Early Empire times exhibited the superciliousness of the Pharaohs, refusing to give prominent Roman women in marriage to foreign potentates. The Byzantines continued this tradition, at least during the apogee of their empire, with rare exceptions, Constantine VIII, *De Administrando Imperio*, G Moravcsik and R. J. Hemkins eds. and tr. (Washington, D.C., 1967) 70–72; R. J. Jenkins, ed., *De Administrado Imperio: Commentary* (London, 1962) ad loc.

[40] Moran AL, *EA* 20. n. 2. Tušratta's daughter was not going to replace Teye (*EA* 26) and Tušratta certainly knew it.

Although the Babylonians, the Mitanni, and others were willing to marry their sisters and daughters to the Egyptian Kings, even though the Egyptians did not reciprocate, agreement to such marriages is not always easily arranged. The Egyptian King had to ask Tušratta's grandfather for his daughter's hand seven times, applying all the pressure he could, before Tušratta's grandfather consented. Similarly, when another Egyptian King asks Tušratta's father for the hand of his daughter, Tušratta's sister, Tušratta's father ignores the Egyptian King the first four times. But when the Egyptian King asks for Tušratta's daughter, Tušratta consents the first time because he has a reason to befriend the Egyptian King, namely, the hope to receive special presents from him, as indeed he did.[41]

An important feature of the inter-dynastic marriage arrangement, probably an intense subject of negotiations, is the bride-price to be given to the family of the bride by the bridegroom. The Egyptian Pharaoh writes to his Babylonian future father-in-law that he intends to send him some furnishings he has already ordered before the bride arrives in Egypt. The new furnishings are destined for the new quarters the Babylonian is building. He will send them with the messenger of the Babylonian King who was accompanying the bride (*EA* 5).

Tušratta expresses his feelings of joy when he receives the marriage gifts from the Egyptian King. (*EA* 27.7–8). In the same letter, he describes the statements of the Egyptian King's father on a similar occasion:

> And your father, Mimmureya, s[aid] this on his tablet. When Mane brought the bride-price, thus spo[k]e my brother Mimmureya: 'These goods that I have now sent are nothing, and my brother is not to complain. I have sent nothing. These goods that I have now sent to you, I have sent to you with this understanding that, when my brother hands over my wife whom I have asked for, and they bring her here and I see her, then I will send you 10 times more than this' (*EA* 27.13–18).

In a message of Tušratta to the Egyptian King, which reviews Mitannian-Egyptian relations, Tušratta congratulates himself for replying in the affirmative to the Egyptian request for a bride. The reason for his self-congratulation is that he answers the Egyptian request for a bride in the affirmative and immediately, whereas his grandfather and father earlier had to be asked repeatedly before they consented to the Pharaoh's request.

---

[41] Moran AL, *EA* 29.16–27. Initial refusal to consent may not infer hostility toward the asker. Extended negotiations seem to have been the rule in inter-dynastic marriages.

Tušratta also explains that when the Egyptian messenger came for the second time, he poured oil on the girl's head and then delivered the girl's bride-price, upon which Tušratta handed the girl to the Egyptian messenger to be carried to Egypt. Tušratta's complaint against the Pharaoh in this instance seems to be that the bride-price is not worthy of the occasion and the promptness with which Tušratta responds to Pharaoh's request. In contrast, Nimmureya's bride-price earlier is considered to be beyond measure, rivaling in height heaven and earth, despite the slowness with which Tušratta's father Artatama answered Nimmureya's request for a bride (*EA* 29.16–27).

The Egyptian King informs the king of Arzawa that he has sent his messenger Iršappa to pick up Arzawa's daughter, who is to be his new bride, and that he has given him instructions concerning the bride-to-be. The messenger is to pour oil on the head of the girl and give the Arzawan King a sack of gold of excellent quality as a greeting-present. The Arzawan King wants to finish some business before he sends his daughter to Egypt, but the Egyptian King is anxious to receive the girl before this business was finished, perhaps for political reasons (*EA* 31.11–16). The practice of pouring oil on a would-be bride denotes approval by the messenger on behalf of the prospective groom. In this instance, it also denotes that the Egyptian kings often followed native customs when dealing with the Hittites and the Syro-Palestinian rulers. The practice of anointing a woman prior to marriage is found in many cuneiform tablets but not in tablets that concern Egyptian brides. As a result, scholars are inclined to believe that this was not an Egyptian custom. Rather, it was followed only where non-Egyptian brides were concerned and was intended to satisfy local demands: Levantine and Mesopotamian. On the other hand, the Egyptian refusal of matrimonial reciprocity is tantamount to an unofficial refusal of "brotherhood, or equality," the address-form of their correspondence with the other Near Eastern kings notwithstanding.[42]

Associated with the Near Eastern marriages was the habit of providing a bride-price. However, prior to the conclusion of the marriage agreement there were often minor problems that had to be resolved between the two parties as the following indicates:

> As to the things to be done that you wrote me about, ... First send back quickly your messenger and the messenger from me, and they must

---

[42] Moran AL, *EA* 4.4–22; *EA* 11.16–22; and n. 2; Meier, Samuel A., "Diplomacy and International Marriage," in *Amarna Diplomacy*, 167.

come. Then they will come (back) to you (and) bring along the bride-price for the daughter (*EA* 31.22–26).

Marriage agreements need some sort of confirmation. It is interesting that the idea of a marriage alliance was proposed by the Egyptian King to the Arzawan messenger Kalbaya. When Kalbaya broaches the subject to his king, the Arzawan king expresses doubts about the reliability of Kalbaya's message because it was not confirmed by the contents of the tablet. He suggests that if the Egyptian king really desires his daughter in marriage, he should also send his messenger quickly to him with a tablet on which the specifics of the proposal would be spelled out. Here Kalbaya's word has to be supported by a written statement, since the Egyptian King's orally-expressed desire to establish a blood relationship with the Arzawan royal family is a very serious matter indeed. The oral proposal does not completely satisfy Arzawa, who is willing to grant his daughter in marriage to the Pharaoh but needs a firm commitment in writing (*EA* 32.4–6).

Finally, in *EA* 4, Kadašman-Enlil barters his daughter for a quantity of gold, which he needs for the decoration of the building he is constructing. In the letter to the Pharaoh, he exhorts the Egyptian to send him in haste whatever quantity of gold was at hand with the messenger who was about to travel to Babylonia. If the Egyptian King sends the quantity of gold in the summer months,

> I will give you my daughter.... But if in the months of Tammuz or Ab you do not send me the gold and (with it) I do not finish the work I am engaged on, what would be the point of your being pleased to send me (gold)?

In other words, he threatens not to send his daughter unless the gold he needs is transported on time.

Besides the bride-prices and the greeting-gifts, the host rulers were in the habit of bestowing gifts upon the messengers who came to them. This was such a long-established custom that it is not usually mentioned each time a messenger went on travels, except on extraordinary occasions. The anticipation of presents from their host no doubt makes the idea of a journey more palatable to the messengers and, for most, these gifts were probably a source of personal wealth. The custom was so predominant that when the Babylonian messengers to the Egyptian King (*EA* 1) complain that the Egyptian failed to comply with this custom, the Babylonian King does not hesitate to take up the matter in his next communication with the Egyptian. The Egyptian King peremptorily dismisses the charge as a contemptuous lie, arguing that of all who came to Egypt, not a single one ever fails to receive a generous gift from the king, except Kadašman's messengers who were liars and scoundrels, and against whom he took the preventive action of not giving them a gift.

It seems that something goes askew in the relations of the two kingdoms since king Burra-Buriyaš also complains that the tradition of sending greeting-presents has been violated by the Egyptians not once but three times:

> Now, though you and I are friends, three times have your messengers come to me and you have not sent me a single beautiful greeting-gift, nor have I for my part sent you a beautiful greeting-gift.

This is clearly a tit-for-tat action since neither of the two withholds gifts because of scarcity of means. This admission points to the symbolism of the exchange of gifts and the idea that the necessity of gifts on these occasions is not dictated by need but by the maintenance of good relationships. A regular flow of gift exchanges provided the basis for good relations and reflected positive interstate contacts. A constant stream of comings and goings by messengers and caravans not only reassures the parties about the continuance of good relations but also implied the dispatch and arrival of material goods. Exchange of greeting gifts is the practical level of royal brotherhood, friendship, love, and so on, which becomes evident only if it supported by the constant chain of material exchanges. This fact is underscored by Burra-Buriyaš who reminds the Pharaoh that, since their states made a mutual declaration of friendship, they have been exchanging greeting gifts on a regular basis (*EA* 9.6–18). Kadašman-Enlil repeats a similar complaint to the Egyptian King who has not sent him a greeting-gift for six years, except for thirty minas of gold that looked like silver, nor did he send him an invitation in connection with the great festival he had recently celebrated (*EA* 3.13–22).

Though the fundamental norm today is that gifts, like hospitality, must be given, accepted, and appreciated, and not asked for, in Mesopotamia kings were in the habit of requesting gifts and when those gifts were not proportionate to the request or not given on time, they complained to the sender (*EA* 26.38–48). For gifts to be appreciated in the period of the Amarna Letters they have to correspond to the expectations of the receiver; otherwise they may be accepted but are not appreciated. The quality and amount of items received are often disputed, especially Egyptian shipments of gold or golden objects. Since the mistaken belief by the Asiatic kings was that gold in Egypt was as "common as dust" to be simply gathered up from the ground, unsatisfactory shipments of gold are frequently protested. Thus Tušratta did not consider it beneath his dignity to complain to Amenophis

III's wife Teye that he failed to receive all of the greeting-gifts that her husband had ordered to be sent to him. He further explains that he had specifically asked for statues of solid cast gold and for genuine lapis lazuli. Instead of the gold her husband promises him, Tušratta says that he received from her son only plated statues of wood. Nor did the son send the goods that his father was going to send him but a much "reduced" amount.[43] He cannot understand why the plates could not be of solid gold, a question that he repeats in *EA* 26.30–48. Similarly, Kadašman-Enlil's correspondence with the Pharaoh proclaims that the Pharaoh's gift is not equal to his gift which was sent on the occasion of the Pharaoh's house-opening. Though it is customary for vassals to send greeting gifts to their lords, the opposite was not commonly true. Yet on exceptional occasions, Lords did send gifts to trusted vassals. Because the Pharaoh is so pleased with the devotion of Tagi, his Palestinian vassal, he sends him a set of greeting-presents as evidence of his satisfaction (*EA* 265).

GIFT-SYMBOLISM

Beyond the real value of the gifts exchanged by kings in the ancient world, there is also the symbolic value of gifts, which plays a vital role in the relationships of alleged brotherhood, friendship, peace, and amity. Burra-Buriyaš mentions that the Egyptian King's father had sent much gold to Burra-Buriyaš' predecessor. The neighboring kings who hear of it say:

> The go[ld is much. Among] the kings there are brotherhood, amity, peace, and [good] relations (*EA* 11.19–23).

Symbolism plays a significant role on similar occasions. When, for instance, the Egyptian King sends troops to escort Burra-Buriyaš' betrothed daughter to Egypt, Burra-Buriyaš demonstrates his dismay that only five chariots are sent to accompany her to Egypt. This poor escort insults his honor; therefore he expresses his fear that the neighboring kings will disparagingly comment that the daughter of the king is being transported to Egypt in only five chariots! He reminds the Egyptian King that when his sister was transported for the father of the Egyptian King, there were three thousand troops accompanying her (*EA* 11.23–28). He worries that the neighboring kings will hear of it, and he will lose prestige. He consequently urges the present king of Egypt to send many more chariots and soldiers

---

[43] Moran Al, *EA* 7.63–72; 10.8–24; 20.46–59; 29.69–79; Liverani, "The Great Powers' Club," in *Amarna Letters*, 24–25.

and let only Haya, the Egyptian envoy, be the one "[to tak]e the princess to you." On the occasion of the "poor escort" Burra-Buriyaš grasps the opportunity to complain that the Babylonian dominance over the Assyrians is not duly respected by the Egyptian, something that disturbs him (*EA* 9).

Not unlike Burra-Buriyaš, the Assyrian King, compares his greeting-gifts from the Pharaoh to those received by Mitanni and finds them wanting.[44] In his desire to open up political relations with Egypt, Aššur-Uballit sends the Pharaoh a beautiful royal chariot which has been originally outfitted for him, two white horses also outfitted for him, a plain chariot, and one seal of genuine lazuli. His hope is that the Egyptian Pharaoh will respond with a shipment of gold with which Aššur-uballit intends to decorate his palace. The Pharaoh responds by sending him a messenger and obviously an unsatisfactory shipment of gold, something that attacks his honor. Aššur-uballit doubts that such presents are appropriate for a Great King and says that the Pharaoh should send him as much gold as he needs to adorn his palace. The shipment, he further contends, does not suffice for the expenses of his messenger's round trip to Egypt (*EA* 16.13–18).

Tušratta's humiliation at the Pharaoh's price-bride is equally great. Tušratta entered negotiation with the Pharaoh who had asked for Tušratta's daughter in marriage. In anticipation of the bridal gift, the Mitanni King gathers all his vassals to observe the auspicious occasion of unsealing a consignment which consisted of gold. To his dismay, the gold turns out to be debased. Instead of the solid gold statues which had been shown to Tušratta's envoys while they were in Egypt along with the other goods promised (*EA* 11.16–22, 19–23), the consignment contains wood statues plated with gold. Nor does it include all the goods promised to Tušratta. Obviously someone has played a trick on the Mitanni king, and Tušratta is greatly embarrassed in front of his friends. Fortunately, the Egyptian delegation, headed by the experienced Mane, reacts correctly: they appear also to be dismayed and break up in tears. Then with eloquent rhetoric, they defend their Lord's good intention, assuring Tušratta and his company that some mistake must have been committed which will be immediately corrected as soon as Mane and his company return to Egypt. Tušratta ex-

---

[44] Kevin Avruch, "Reciprocity, Equality, and Status-Anxiety," in *Amarna Diplomacy*, 162. The Assyrian king claims to be the equal of the Mitanni monarch. How did he know what the Egyptian had sent to the Mitanni? Either these kings advertised the gifts they had received for purposes of prestige, or their "intelligence" services kept track of what these kings exchanged.

presses his complete satisfaction with Mane, honoring him and his escorting troops.[45]

The Palestinian vassal Rib-Addi is equally humiliated when he sends a messenger to the palace who returns empty-handed and without an escort. Seeing that no money has been sent by the Egyptian King, the brothers and men of his house despise him, as his mayors had done earlier (*EA* 137.5–14).

The functional links between kings in the Ancient Near East are purported to have been practices such as friendship, love, and brotherhood, as these practices emerge from the Amarna correspondence, accompanied by the frequent and adequate flow of material exchanges of greeting gifts. This is constantly evident throughout the royal correspondence and failure to comply with this practice on any "important" occasion may draw censure from an offended colleague. In one of his letters, Burra-Buriyaš asserts: From the time his ancestors and the Pharaoh's ancestors made a mutual friendship, they sent beautiful gifts to each other and refused no request for anything beautiful (*EA* 9.6–18). Personal joy, national pride, and international prestige were likely to be transformed into distress and disrepute if foreign gifts failed to conform to the partner's expectations. Dismay and disillusionment are intensified if this failure is witnessed by a wider audience consisting of friends, vassals, or other high officials. This is exactly what happened when Tušratta assembled several of his friends to celebrate the opening of boxes of presents dispatched to him by the Egyptian King supposedly as tokens of the Egyptian's love. The gifts proved to be disappointing, and Tušratta feels humiliated. In a state of consternation, the guests burst out saying, "Are all of these gold? They do not look like gold." They further add the usual refrain about gold in Egypt being as abundant as the Egyptian sand. Embarrassed by the low grade of the gifts he has received, Tušratta confesses to the Egyptian in a letter that he could not say what he usually repeated about the Egyptian King, "My [brother], the king of Egypt, loves me very much," because if he really loved him, he would not have sent him such poor gifts (*EA* 20.46–59).

---

[45] Moran AL, *EA* 20.64–70; 8.49–62 says that provision for the escort of messengers was customary *EA* 30 n. 2; ARMT 21, pp. 509, 514. Escorts were not only customary in the Ancient Near East but also among primitive peoples. Bernhard Ankermann, *Ostafrika* in *Eigenborenenrecht*, E. Schultz-Ewert and L. Adam (Stuttgart, 1929) 48–50 ff. Envoys were hospitably treated, were given presents for their chief and usually furnished with a safe-conduct for their return journey.

It has been argued that these gift exchanges were symbolic of the relations between two states. Discontinuing exchange practices or delivery of inferior gifts was seen as a sign of souring relations between two states. Akhenaten's refusal to honor his father's promise to deliver solid gold statues to the Mitanni King symbolizes a deterioration of relations between the two states. Tušratta is expecting a tenfold better treatment than what Akhenaten extends to him, only to be deeply disappointed when he does not receive even what Akhenaten's father had promised him (*EA* 26.30–40). Tušratta's complaints regarding his colleague's purported parsimonious conduct clearly demonstrates, if indeed demonstration is needed, that the desire for recognition is a basic need central to our human sense of who and what we are. This desire assumes a greater dimension for those who are heads of state, especially monarchical states, since their own people or foreign leaders can interpret the presumed snub as an insult to them personally, their state, and their people as well.

In summation, despite the dangers they face and the obstacles in their way, messengers are able to carry on their duties even in the worst of times. They are able to do so in part because of the deference paid to them and their position, which contributes to the degree of stability the system enjoys even in the most hazardous times. The constant flow of comings and goings by messengers and their caravans reassures the parties about their friendships and also implies the dispatch and arrival of communications and goods. This regular exchange is a fundamental requirement for positive political interactions (*EA* 3.9–15).

Most international negotiations in the ancient Near East take place through representative agents who are authorized by their principals. These agents—messengers in the ancient Near East and diplomats in the modern parlance—are also of symbolic significance. The way they are treated reflects the status of relations between states. In his eagerness to forge friendly relations with Egypt, Tušratta points out that he has treated the Egyptian messengers "with great distinction," showing them "very great honors" and exalting them not only as peers but also "like gods" (*EA* 20.21). Tušratta makes it abundantly clear in his correspondence with Amenophis III that the selection of a messenger is of importance for both parties. In compliance with this diplomatic principle, Tušratta sends no less of a person than his chief and esteemed messenger, Keliya, together with Tuni-ibri, his chief-minister, when he makes his bid to renew his alliance with the Egyptian King (*EA* 17).

Among the various qualifications expected from prospective messengers is that they should be pleasing and friendly to whomever they are being sent and that these qualifications had already been manifest in the practice of their ambassadorial duties. Messengers well-liked by the kings to whom they are sent have greater possibilities of success in their mission. It is not adventitious that Near Eastern Kings are often asked for the dispatch of certain messengers, a request which is promptly granted, since the dispatch of well-liked messengers is also beneficial to the dispatcher's interest. Those who serve as messengers to a particular king or state more than once are often known to have established an excellent rapport, making their negotiations with the opposite side smoother.[46] From the *Amarna Letters*, it becomes immediately evident that international relations among "Great Kings" are modeled on the interpersonal relations of the family, neighborhood, or town relations, and the preference of certain messengers over others is the byproduct of this "familial" approach to envoys. Throughout the Amarna period, external relations are presented in the forms of hospitality, intermarriage, and the exchange of goods and services whereby the procedures of inner relationships in daily life take a slightly modified form in order to fulfill a wider purpose. The family metaphor is also immediately evident in the pervasive use of the personal address-form in which a partner is addressed or in the father-son metaphor on the occasions of age disparity between the partners. It is apparently used in the most trivial but socially meaningful situations: when asking news of health of the person addressed, his wife, his children, his household, or his property in general. In many ways, interstate relations reflect personal relations, and kings often copy relations familiar to them from the private sphere. As a result, the gamut of exchanges in both public and private relationships is in many cases very similar, if not the same. Even the frequent complaints between leaders take the personal form, which is perfectly appropriate for social interrelationships in the limited environment of small communities where closer personal relations exist. This may appear paradoxical to us today in long-distance epistolary exchanges among leaders of the Near Eastern states, yet behind this façade of ostensibly personal relations, one detects the official

---

[46] Primitive people employ respectable persons as envoys. These envoys are generally intelligent, knowledgeable, fluent in speech, and well-acquainted with the neighboring dialects. Some tribes usually choose a messenger who has a number of friends in the tribe to which he is sent. The envoys of Nahuas were men of much consequence and noble lineage. They were chosen on account of their courteous manners as well as their practical ability, Hubert How Bankcroft, *The Native Races of the Pacific States*, vol. 2. (San Francisco, 1886) 412, 419, 426; A. W. Howitt, *The Native Tribes of South-Australia* (London, 1904) 688.

capacity of the correspondence. These personal greetings include not only the personal household of the king but they also include things that touch upon the state, namely the officials, the armed forces, and the territory of the king. One is inclined to agree with R. Ragionieri's view that the contemporary actors tend to picture the unit of politics in terms of domestic society chiefly because states are thought of as synonymous with the ruler.[47] Yet terms such as "brotherhood," "father," "son," suggest for us a difficulty in thinking theoretically of external relations as an autonomous area of activity. In Egypt more so than the rest of the Near East, people identify the Pharaoh with what we understand as the state, and indeed earlier historians of Egypt have done so. Beyond these definitional difficulties, however, there is less doubt that the common interests of the Amarna Great Kings are much the same as at many other periods in human history: the maintenance of domestic stability, the protection of the borders, and the prosperity of the kingdom.[48]

In addition, political marriage is a vital Near Eastern tradition underpinning relations among kings. Associated with marriage agreements is the Near Eastern principle, which as we find frequently in the *Bible*, that a substantial bride-price gift be sent to the future father or brother-in-law.[49] Mutuality in marriage agreements is not always easily accepted, as the Egyptian Kings at the peak of their power in the New Kingdom period feign the existence of an immemorial Egyptian tradition that ostensibly prevents them from giving Egyptian princesses to foreign kings. Like the Romans and the

---

[47] Rodolfo Ragionieri, "The Amarna Age: An International Society in the Making," in *Amarna Letters*, 46–47 paints the Amarna Age as a society in the making, which implies that before it there was an interstate system but not an international society. His views depict our difficulties at conceptualizing what the contemporaneous people considered as a state, for the lack of a better term in describing the ancient Near Eastern states. One could also argue that in Egypt more so than in the rest of the Near East the Pharaoh was basically seen as the state.

[48] Raymond Cohen, *International Politics: The Rules of the Game* (London, 1981) 8.

[49] Moran AL, *EA* 27.13–18. Amenophis III sent a bride-price for the daughter of Tušratta, promising him even more when the daughter was sent. In his long review of Mitannian-Egyptian relations Tušratta states (*EA* 29.16–27) that when the Egyptian messenger brought to him the bride-price, which was copious "beyond measure," he sent his daughter to Pharaoh. The sack of gold of excellent quality, which the Egyptian sent to the king of Arzawa, seems to be a bride-price (*EA* 31.11–16). For the location of Arzawa to the west of Cilicia (Moran AL, 31.32) see Susanne Heinhold-Krahmer, "Arzawa: Untersuchungen zu Seiner Geschichte nach den hethitischen Quellen," *THeth* 8 (1977) 3–4; 50–55. Moran AL, *EA* 31, n. 2.

Byzantines later on, the "supercilious" Egyptians refuse marriage of their princesses to foreigners who they ostensibly view as of lower status, despite their frequent acknowledgements of brotherhood and equality.

Finally, a basic, traditional principle guiding the diplomatic relations of the Near Eastern kings is the reciprocity of gift-giving. This principle is almost as old as the history of the area since we trace it back to Mesopotamia in the third millennium BC. Greeting-gifts are sent with royal messengers on all or most of personal or state occasions while empty-handed messengers draw the censure of the host king. Gifts are also generally bestowed upon the messengers by the host king as a routine procedure—the violation of which displeases the sender as well as his messenger. Representations were made for such failures and explanations were as a rule offered, if good relations between kings were to continue.

3   Messengers in Western Asia

The history of Egypt begins around 3000 BC, when the ruler of the southern part united Southern and Northern Egypt and began the First Dynasty, ruling the country from its capital in the North. This period lasted close to eight hundred years and is known as the period of the Old Kingdom, ending with the decline and fall of the Sixth Dynasty and the beginnings of the First Intermediate Period. The great phase of the Egyptian civilization developed in the valley of Egypt in quasi isolation, since Egypt's borders were well insulated from the outside world on all sides. In the north, it was protected by the sea; there does not seem to have been any danger from that quarter so early in history. The same seems to be true of the eastern and western borders of Egypt, guarded as they were by the deserts. The nomads who lived scattered throughout the regions constituted no danger to Egypt's frontiers. This is equally true of the tribes in the area of Kush and farther south. The somewhat primitive tribes that lived scattered there would not pose a danger to Egypt until much later. During this period, they seem to have been the "borrowers" from the more advanced Egyptian civilization. It was in such safe geographic circumstances that the Egyptians set the basis of the magnificent and unique civilization of the Old Kingdom. As a result of their isolation, they came to believe that their civilization was superior to that of the other peoples in the Near East, with the concomitant notion that their ruler, the Pharaoh, from whom Egypt's safety and prosperity was believed to depend, was perceived as a god and protector of their land.

This Egyptian feeling continued through the period of the New Kingdom, roughly between sixteen hundred and one thousand BC, as is shown in the period of Amarna diplomacy, when the Pharaoh, despite his declarations of "brotherhood," exhibits a posture of superiority toward the other Near Eastern Kings. For the Pharaoh to treat foreigners on an equal basis was a remarkable compromise of centuries of condescension towards them.

Egypt was a culture where "the Egyptians were people," whereas foreigners were considered inferior.[1] This Pharaonic attitude shows up in the marriage policy of the Pharaohs who refuse to give Egyptian princesses in marriage to foreign potentates.[2] Nonetheless, the diplomatic practices between the Pharaoh and the other Near Eastern rulers continue to be principally "friendly," unaffected by marriage policies.[3] Messengers crisscross the Near East, expecting the application of traditional precedents whose roots probably go back to times immemorial. Because of the uniqueness of the Egyptian culture and the fact that this culture was the product almost exclusively of one people—the Egyptians, this chapter focuses on messenger customs and practices concerning the civilization of Western Asia and the Eastern Mediterranean littoral which, unlike the Egyptian civilization, was the product of multiple ethnic groups. From this standpoint, this chapter should not be seen as an exercise in repetition but as an effort to establish whether the same practices that prevailed among the Egyptians existed among these groups as well.

Again, the objective is not to treat all aspects of communication in which the messenger might be involved but only those which bear specifically upon his performance of the tasks that in today's parlance are known as "ambassadorial." If some examples seem repetitive, it is to illustrate a point. Some general features which have already been emphasized in earlier chapters, such as the exchange of gifts and the contraction of political marriage-alliances, may not need further elaboration but should be acknowledged as strongly present here as well. Since there is a frequent correlation between human practices and divine realm metaphors, with some exceptions, practices pertinent to divine messengers follow the known human pattern. Those examples are used to provide insight into perceptions of messenger activity.

It has been pointed out already that messengers were selected because of their trustworthiness, prudence, and dexterity in handling matters, as well as their high political standing. Without these qualifications, they would not

---

[1] J. A. Wilson, "Egypt," in Before Philosophy: The Intellectual Adventure of Ancient Man: An Essay on Speculative Thought in the Ancient Near East, H. Frankfort et al., eds. (Chicago University Press, 1946) 33.

[2] Egyptian attitude changed later during the bad times for Egypt; K. A. Kitchen, *The Third Intermediate Period in Egypt, 1100–650 B.C.E* (Warminster, Aris and Phillips, 1973) 178–80.

[3] Meier, "Diplomacy and International Marriages," in Cohen and Westbrook, *Amarna Diplomacy*, 168–170.

have been selected, and if they had been selected, they would not continue as messengers for very long. Ability, dexterity, wisdom, and tactfulness of some messengers were qualities recognized even by their interlocutors who often asked their colleague kings to send a particular messenger. Burna-Buriyaš of Babylon, for example, requests that Amenophis IV dispatch Haya to him—"Do not send some other magnate."[4] In contrast, there is Hattusilis' request to the Babylonian King to "send quickly another messenger," because he was displeased with the last Babylonian messenger's behavior.[5] In the same vein, King David requests that Uriah be sent to bear him news of the battle. A king's request for a specific messenger is not unusual and should not arouse great curiosity and suspicion (2 Sam. 11. 6–7). In certain cases, the Egyptian King felt it important that someone knowledgeable and of high social and official standing in the administration be sent to him as a messenger.[6] Some envoys were repeatedly in demand, so much so that they made a career as messengers in the royal service.

It was a gesture of honor for the recipient king to welcome messengers of some political standing, while at other times it was part of the contractual agreements between kings. In the Neo-Assyrian period, for example, a vassal apologizes to his king for being unable to lead an emissary to him, owing to illness, but informs him that he is sending his brother at the head of a delegation of ten nobles to Nippur to greet the king.[7] Something similar is made explicit in the Biblical literature as well (Num. 22.15). The sending of a king's or a vassal's son as messenger is also attested to in the first and second millennium. It was a sign of good will, an expression of devotion, or a measure of the gravity of his situation for a vassal to send his son as a messenger to his lord.[8] According to an agreement between the vassal state Kizzuwatna and the kingdom of Hatti, the vassal king was expected to pay visits of obeisance to the Hittite King whenever summoned to do so. In case the vassal was unable to do so, one of his sons, the one designated by

---

[4] Moran AL, *EA* 11, reverse side 13–18.

[5] *CTH* 172.1. Cases wherein the virtue of trustworthiness is emphasized abound in the Near Eastern documents, for example *ARM* 10, 32r.17–18; *AbB* 6, 57.5–6 and 6, 154.10; *LAS* 190.r11–15.

[6] Moran AL, *EA*, 24. §31, §17, § 18; 11, 5–8 and reverse 1–5 and 13–18. Keliya, Mane, Haamašši, Haya are a few of such names. In Homer, as we shall see, Odysseus, Nestor, the Trojan Idaeus served repeatedly on embassies.

[7] R. Pfeiffer, *State Letters of Assyria* AOS 6 (New Havern, American Oriental Society, 1935) 5–11; 123.

[8] Moran AL, *EA* 137; 138; 198.

the king of Hatti, should take the place of his father.[9] The Hittite prince Hishmi-sharruma may have been sent several times to Egypt on such trips. Though he is not specifically referred to as an envoy, we find him in the company of envoys traveling between Egypt and Hatti. At another time, Ramses requested that Hishmi-sharruma make the trip to Egypt on some state business. Equally, King Tou of Hamath sent his son Joram or Hadoram, loaded with gifts, to acknowledge David's victories over Hadadezer.[10] In a treaty between the King of Hatti and Paddatissu of Kizzuwatna, the King of Cilicia, there is a stipulation that if the Great King (of Hatti) sends either his son or his subject to Paddatissu, Paddatissu shall not harm him. And if Paddatissu sends either his son or his subject to the Great King, the Great King shall not harm him. Kings are sometimes scorned for the socially low individuals whom they were sending in place of high standing men or men of nobility.

Besides the special messengers so frequently dispatched on state business, merchants here as in the Amarna Letters are also employed as envoys to foreign kings.[11] The monarchs of this period identify such men as both "my merchants" and "my messengers" (*EA* 39.10–16). Diplomacy was intimately linked with trade, and it is not paradoxical that some diplomatic work was carried out by merchants who served also as envoys. The overlap of activities between the two roles is found frequently in the Near East as it has been seen already in the Amarna Letters. This overlap occurred fre-

---

[9] *PDK* 103.31–33; 101.67–68; *CTH* 26 1.

[10] *CTH* 165.18–20; 165.1.15–16; *Chron.* 18.10; 2 Sam. 8.10; F. M. Cross, "Two Notes on Palestinian Inscriptions of the Persian Age," *BASOR* 193 (1969) 21–24.

[11] C. Zaccagnini, "The Merchant at Nuzi," *Iraq* 39 (1977) 171–89; S. A. Meier, *The Messenger in the Ancient Semitic World* (Scholars Press, 1988) 21; Gary Beckman, *Hittite Diplomatic Texts* (Scholars Press, 1966) 12, 15; The use of merchants as envoys continues to the present. Aeneas Tacticus, who wrote rules to be followed in devising counter-espionage measures, warned that spies could come in the guise of traders and ambassadors, advising that contacts between them and the citizens of the states they visited should be subject to strict control, 10.6–10. The Byzantines frequently used merchants and so did the Italian as well as other states in the Renaissance and post-Renaissance period. Needless to say that merchants or business men are often used today. For Byzantine merchants see N. Oikonomides, "Byzantine Diplomacy, A.D. 1204–1453: Means and Ends," in J. Shapard and Simon Franklin, *Byzantine Diplomacy, Papers from the Twenty-fourth Spring Symposium of Byzantine Studies* (Cambridge, March 1990) 83. In early modern times merchants bearing the status of 'sub-ambassadors' were also used, Harold Nicolson, *The Evolution of Diplomatic Method* (New York, 1954) 34.

quently if for no other reason than that of trade, which was carried out extensively, and was an important subject of negotiations. Because of their frequent traveling in various parts outside of a king's territory and their meetings with a diverse number of people, merchants were wise in the ways of foreign peoples. Dealing with matters frequently intertwined with the interests of the state or the court, merchants were the obvious choice to double as diplomats, especially in the absence of a regular diplomatic service. In the Amarna Letters (*EA* 39), the ruler of Alašiya asked the Pharaoh to allow his messengers to leave Egypt without delay, for those men also served as merchants: "My brother, let my messengers go promptly and safely so that I may hear my brother's greeting. These men are my merchants."

These merchants are described by the king as "his" merchants, though the possessive pronoun may not imply that they worked exclusively for him. Trade was often conducted by "partnerships" or "societies" of merchants, each consisting of a number of traders who had invested money in the commercial activities conducted either by one man or several, themselves investors, or their representatives. Well-known merchant families also invested in the trade while several separate consignments, each led by its own personnel, formed groups which often traveled together in a sort of convoy for obvious safety reasons. Kings used these forms of merchants' associations to send or receive messages to and from vassals or fellow kings.[12] Like the regular messengers, merchant messengers were often summoned as witnesses. Atahna-Šamas, a high official of Sargon, perhaps a governor, called three merchants as his witnesses.[13]

For strictly personal business, servants and subordinates were frequently employed on missions for their masters. Thus there was a wide variety of individuals serving as messengers. Royalty would commonly select the most dignified and skilled representatives, while individuals of lower stature could be employed where prestige did not much matter. In some instances, speedy delivery of a message could determine the choice of messenger, though in this case serious negotiations might not have been in-

---

[12] M. T. Larsen, *The Old Assyrian City-state and Its Colonies, Copenhagen Studies in Assyriology*, vol. 4 (Copenhagen, 1976) 96; K. P. Veenhof, *Aspects of Old Assyrian Trade and Its Terminology* (Leiden, 1972) 103; P. Garelli, Marchands, Diplomates et Empereurs; Études sur la Civilization Mesopotamienne Offerts à Paul Garelli, D. Charpin et als. eds. (Paris, 1991) 189–191.

[13] Giovanni B. Lanfranchi and Simo Parpola, *The Correspondence of Sargon II*, (under the general title *State Archives of Assyria*) (*SAA*) vol. 5, p. 114, No. 150.

volved. In other instances, the affable qualities of the messenger, i.e., the ability to establish friendliness, no doubt, was a significant qualification for prospective messengers. Since the various courts often aimed at continuity of service, a vital criterion in the selection of a messenger could be the personal connection a messenger had already established with a particular court. Furthermore, those who previously had successfully dealt with a certain court were likely to be preferred for future service. As in the Amarna Letters, so in the Mari correspondence we read of some royal couriers and envoys, mentioned by name, as being especially trusted above all others. Zimri-Lim's man Ibâl-pî-El, for example, seems to have become very close to Hammurabi, who preferred to deal with him.[14]

References to a messenger's speed appear more frequently among Mari's narrative accounts, compared to the Egyptian records, since messengers are dispatched with the command to go quickly.[15] The speed with which couriers were able to carry messages depended upon a number of factors. Among them was the possibility of taking the shortest route and the need to detour either because of the physical conditions or because of hostile elements. Naturally, accidents on the road or equipment theft, the number of persons in the party, the type of equipage and what was being transported, the urgency of the message of the mission, and the question of secrecy were taken into consideration.[16] In other circumstances, dependability and reliability are the qualifications mentioned several times. The Subrian messengers, who carried certain tablets, were instructed to bring those tablets to the king to be read only by him. One of Sargon's governors received three men of the Kummeans who asked him to take them to the palace because their message was for the king's ear only since it concerned another country.[17]

Faithfulness is extolled as a great virtue in the literature of Mesopotamia from time immemorial. It is not rare that someone will request that a trustworthy messenger be sent on a mission, particularly if the requester had a bitter experience with an untrustworthy one. The complaint by Shulgi, in the bottom of the third millennium BC, reflects this particular concern:

---

[14] Alan D. Crown, "Tidings and Instructions: How News Traveled in the Ancient Near East," *JESHO* 17, (1974) 263.

[15] *ARM* vol. 1.39.17'r; 2.10.4'r; 1.93.11–17.

[16] Crown, *JESHO*, 17 (1974) 263.

[17] G. B. Lanfranchi and Simo Parpola, *SAA*, p. 46. No. 52; p.102, N.14, Subria, a country SW of Lake Van. Kummea was in Northern Mesopotamia.

The man whom you sent as a messenger is not dependable, he does not
Follow your instructions....[18] Let him send from among his servants
one who is trustworthy or send a trustworthy individual.[19]

There are also times when messengers are instructed not to tell the truth or to doctor their message to the expectations of the receiver. In Biblical literature, Ahimaaz is a classic example of the messenger who tells the person to whom he delivers the message exactly what that person wants to hear (2 Sam. 18.19–31). Shamshi-Adad I, in the beginning of the second millennium, after receiving a messenger from the Gutians, asks:

Who knows whether their words are trustworthy or treacherous? I questioned him, and he explained to me indications concerning those [the entourage] of Warad-Sharirm.

In this query Shamshi-Adad questions the validity not of the messenger's report but the reliability of the men who sent him. He proceeds to interrogate the messenger to determine the credibility of the messenger's report.[20]

Written tablets that recorded messages seemed to have removed some of the mistrust of oral reports. In the treaty between the Hittite King Muwatallis and the king of Kizzuwatna, the use of tablets becomes an issue of some importance. Muwatallis specifies, "if the word from the mouth of the messenger does not agree with the word of the tablet ... don't trust that messenger and don't take that word to heart."[21] Egyptian wisdom literature expresses the problem regarding truthfulness more explicitly, where it is said that a man of truth, sent by one great man to another, should adhere to the nature of him who sent him and should give the sender's message exactly as it was given.

It would have been ideal if a messenger could deliver his message verbatim as he received it, as the above recommendation implies. Indeed, literary and poetic depictions often paint pictures of messengers memorizing and reciting texts verbatim to the recipient. But that may not have always

---

[18] Meier, *The Messenger*, 24.

[19] *ARM* vol. 10, 324.17–18; *AbB* vol 57, 5–6; 154.10.

[20] J. Laessøe, *The Shemsharra Tablets* (Copenhagen, 1959). Ramses II's interrogation of two reputed Shosu messengers uncovered their treachery, for upon his asking where the tribal leaders are who sent them, they gave wrong information, A. Gardiner, *The Kadesh Inscriptions of Ramesses II* (Oxford University Press, 1969) 28–29.

[21] *PDK* 109.32–39. This is similar to the warning of the Egyptian Pharaoh, *EA* 32; Beckman, *Hittite*, no. 2. p. 20, paragr. 50.

been possible. Long messages carried over long distances might not always be reproduced verbatim, unless the carrier possessed a photographic memory. This being understood, the messenger was expected to deliver his message as closely to the language he received it or at least as closely to the meaning of the message.[22] Had verbatim delivery been a sine qua non requirement, one of the compelling qualifications of the messenger would have been his ability to memorize long messages and deliver them verbatim.[23] Though this qualification was occasionally required by the sender, the discovery of writing and the use of tablets in the Near East seem to have relieved the carrier of this stringent necessity.

From the discussion so far, it becomes clear that eloquence, tact, prudence, and dependability were the paramount qualifications in the selection of envoys; on the other hand, the ability to memorize though not always mentioned, must have also been on occasion an invaluable trait. When a king prefaces his oral message with the formula, "Thus says x to y," it is understood that the messenger has the obligation to relay his king's message as closely to the language he received as possible. In the above quotation, the recipient demands that the bearer deliver the message as his king gave it to him. In the cases that tablets were utilized for the delivery of a message, the envoy's role was not *ipso facto* minimized inasmuch as he was still expected to offer explanations over details that were not clear or clarifications on questions produced in the minds of the recipient by the written message. The messenger's explanations had to be consonant with the meaning of the written message; otherwise his mission was likely to be a failure.[24]

The significance of verbatim delivery becomes urgent in some circumstances. One such circumstance is illustrated in the correspondence of the Assyrian King Shamshi-Adad and his son Jašmah-Adad, who had notified his father that he had something to relay to him but did not feel comfortable putting it in writing. "These matters are not suitable to inscribe on a

---

[22] A. L. Oppenheim, "A Note on the Scribes in Mesopotamia," in *Studies in Honor of Benno Landsberger*, (University of Chicago, 1965) 254.

[23] *ARM* vol.1, 76.20–29; Beckman, *Hittite*, No. 2. p. 20. parg. 59.

[24] *ARM* vol. 1, 76.20–29; Meier, *The Messenger*, 166. The possibility remained that even a document could be so written as to be deceiving. The Assyrian king is warned that the bearer of certain letters is not only a liar but also that the letters he carried were untrue, R. Pfeiffer, *State Letters of Assyria*, *SLA* AOS 6 (1935) 194. Something similar happened with the Hittite king Suppiluliumas who mistrusted the Egyptian message of the Egyptian Queen asking for a groom from amongst his sons, *CAH* vol. 2, part 2, 18; 69; 84.

tablet," he explained. Shamshi-Adad responded with skepticism about his son's dilemma but in the end advised him to send a messenger with good memory:

> Why not? Have them inscribed on a tablet and sent to me! Otherwise, instruct a messenger who has a good memory and send him to me so that he can lay these matters out before me.[25]

When someone delivers an oral message, the cardinal feature of his task lay in the faithful reproduction of the sender's words—that is, delivering the hard core of the sender's central meaning. The task of clarifying the meaning of terms or phrases in the process of interrogation that might ensue moves the carrier from the level of simple messenger to the realm of the diplomat, where the focal task lay in responding to anticipated and unanticipated questions in a manner that would satisfy both the sender and the recipient. Such an occasion arose in *EA* 7.18–30, where the messenger rises to the occasion by answering questions of the asker in a pleasing, satisfying manner.

In the above situation the envoy becomes a resource person to whom one poses questions which the letter does not answer. Thus the envoy could be interrogated as to details omitted in the written document and is the person to ask for clarifications of nuances emerging from the issues discussed in the letter. We find an illustrative example in David's case a few centuries after the Amarna period. David's barrage of irate questions submitted to the bearer of a message suggests his thirst for details, and similarly points to the whipping-horse role messengers were often called upon to play (2 Sam 11.20–22). On some occasions, the sender of a letter wishes to relay to his correspondent information only if he asks for it, and for that reason, he does not set it down in writing. Instead, he authorizes the bearer of the letter to answer the questions when he is asked.[26] In this case, the initiative rests with the recipient to ask questions and to be informed about the issues that interest him. At other times, the sender informs the recipient that he can ask additional questions pertaining to the subject of the message from the bearer of the report.[27]

There are occasions when the letter-bearer is intentionally left in the dark about the contents of the message he carries, nor is he given any other oral instruction beyond the order to deliver the letter to the sender. Occa-

---

[25] *ARM* vol. 1, 76.20–29.
[26] *ARM* vol. 2, 241.4–11.
[27] *ARM* vol. 13.3224–30.

sionally, the instructions given to the messenger might have nothing to do with the contents of the letter. Such is the case in the fascinating account of the Bible where the messenger to David's general, Uriah, is ignorant of the contents of the letter he delivers, (2 Sam. 11. 14–15):

> And it came to pass in the morning, that David wrote a letter to Joab, and sent it by the hand of Uriah. And he wrote in the letter, saying, Set ye Uriah in the forefront of the hottest battle, and retire ye from him, that he may be smitten, and die.

Uriah's fate is a replay of a Sumerian story dated over a thousand years earlier, in which Sargon, not yet a king, is supposedly sent by King Urzaba with a letter containing the order that the bearer, Sargon, be put to death. In this case, the letter is apparently without a wrapping and ostensibly Sargon somehow learns of its contents.[28] In a badly broken inscription which is very difficult to make sense of, lines six and seven seem to advert to a messenger sent to the Assyrian King Sargon II from some governor with the suggestion that he dispose of the messenger after the message is delivered.[29] The message could only be written in such a way that its contents remained unknown to the carrier for the objectives of the message to be achieved. The circumstance of a messenger unknowingly carrying his own death-warrant is the motif of popular folktales which was not unique. It reappears from culture to culture.

The incident of Uriah is interesting because the message had to be in written form. In contrast, most of the communications in biblical literature were explicitly oral. In Biblical stories, messengers had to travel short distances in comparison with the long distances that separated the capitals of the large Near Eastern states. Often the personal nature of the Biblical messages made the oral delivery of messages possible as well as practical. No doubt, when messages were destined for the capitals of other Near Eastern states which were located at some distance, those messages were primarily written. The striking feature of narratives in Biblical messages is largely evident when they state, "And he sent messengers to PN saying:" Immediately following this introductory address, the oral nature of the communication is

---

[28] J. Cooper and W. Hempel, "The Sumerian Sargon Legend," *JAOS* 103 (1983) 76–77; Lanfranchi and Parpola, *SAA*, vol. 5, part 2, no. 128.

[29] Lafranchi and Parpola, *The Correspondence of Sargon II*, 5 vols., (Helsinki University Press, 1990) no. 197, p 138.

underscored, for the speaker says: "Thus shall you speak unto my lord Esau...." or "Thy servant Jacob saith thus, ..." (Gen. 32.40.).[30]

When Joab wished to relay information about the status of the war and the death of Uriah, the oral form of the message was underlined (2 Sam. 11.19):

> And charged the messenger, saying, "When thou hast made an end of telling the matters of the war unto the king…"

And then Joab said to the Kushite, "thy servant Uriah the Hittite is…dead." Elsewhere a group of messengers is commissioned in the place of a single messenger, but otherwise the pattern of the message remains the same (1 Sam. 11.9):

> And they said unto the messengers that came. Thus shall ye say unto the men of Jâ-besh-gil-e-ăd. Tomorrow by the time the sun be hot, ye shall have help.

In all the Biblical scenes above, the oral nature of communications is obvious. There is no hint of any type of written message.[31] In 2 Kings 14, for example, Hezekiah receives a letter from the "hands of the messengers." This written message along with Uriah's case are exceptions to the rule of the Bible in which most of the communications are in oral form.[32] By contrast, on many occasions, messages in Near Eastern states and Egypt are sent on tablets since oral communication, without authentication by written documentation, might be suspect. The overwhelming majority of oral communications in Israel points to the fact that oral commissioning, especially for short distances, was satisfactory. On these occasions, the message was to be relayed orally. However, the overwhelming majority of messages were put into writing. Written messages were, as a rule, enveloped and sealed with the official royal ring. The purpose was to protect the contents of the letter from unwanted eyes, but the seal also served as a certificate of authenticity and as a deterrent against clandestine breaking of the envelope.

---

[30] Meier, *The Messenger*, 42 mentions the existence of a Ph.D. dissertation on messengers written in Hebrew which remains untranslated.

[31] Verbal messages were used by primitive unalphabetic tribes whose messenger probably carried a stick marked by notches used as a means of fixing matter, *memoria technica*, in the messenger's mind which helped him to state his errand with the maximum accuracy, Eylmann, *Die Eingeborenen*, 422–24; Howitt, *Native Tribes*, 691; Franz Boas, *General Anthropolgy* (New York, 1938) 272.

[32] Meier, *The Messenger*, 42.

If there were any doubt as to the authenticity of the seal, the sender was immediately notified and verification of the contents was demanded.[33]

The royal messenger enjoys extraordinary status which entitles him to privileged treatment. There seems to be an accepted protocol for the reception of messengers and the granting of prompt audience. Naturally this protocol could be breached, with the messenger left cooling his heels, or he could even receive worse treatment. However, under normal circumstances, it would be unusual to keep a messenger waiting since such an act would be considered an offence to his master.[34] The envoy, especially of a friendly nation, is regarded as a guest of the host monarch, who is responsible for his housing and entertainment. The length of the envoy's stay is entirely at the discretion of the host king, whose permission is necessary before the envoy can depart.[35] Inordinate retention, nonetheless, would lead to protest, and unless a satisfactory explanation is proffered, the reaction of the messenger's master would be to retaliate against the violator by unnecessarily retaining his envoy whenever possible. In *EA* 29.155–61 we see the Mitanni King retaliating in kind for the detention of his messenger, or sending a lower-level envoy while, at the same time, appealing for cooperation and the avoidance of such unpleasant diplomatic practices (*EA* 28.19–20, 20–36).

Before the messengers deliver their message, they must identify themselves or submit their credentials.[36] Unfortunately, the issue of identification presents occasional difficulties as most of our evidence comes from incantation formulas rather than the messages themselves. In such cases the priest may say, "I am the messenger of the DN" or simply "DN sent me."[37] In Biblical literature, one may assume from the nature of the message that the messenger prefaces his message with the identification formula, "Thus

---

[33] *ABL*, No. 383; E. A. Budge, ed., *Cuneiform Texts from Babylonian Tablets in the British Museum*, (London, 1896) no. 53904.

[34] Pfeiffer, *State Letters*, 49.25; Crown, "Tidings and Instructions," *JESHO* (1974) 258; Grayson, *AR* I vol. 1, no. 11.

[35] Meier, *Messengers*, 229–45.

[36] Primitive tribes equipped their envoys with credentials to be presented to their host. The accreditation consisted mostly of a special staff which often enabled the envoy to travel through the territories of various groups unmolested, Sir Walter Baldwin Spencer, *Wanderings in Wild Australia*, vol. 1 (London, 1928) 328–331; R. G. Numenin, *The Beginnings of Diplomacy* (Oxford University Press, 1950) 167–169.

[37] E. Reiner, "Lipšur Litanies," *JNES* 15 (1956) 111; 128; Meier, *The Messenger*, 179; 181.

says PN." Accordingly, the Assyrian embassy to Hezekiah addresses Hezekiah with the formula, "Thus saith the great king, the king of Assyria," (2 Kings 18.19). According to Meier, all the literature employs self-identification statements, but it is particularly characteristic of Mesopotamia and rare among the West Semitic.[38] A question arises whether the messengers deliver their message only in the presence of the king. There is no clear-cut evidence on this point. What we have points to the delivery of the message in front of the king and the high officials of his administration or the nobles who made up his council. The Hittite King Tudhaliyas invites his former vassal Sunaššura to his palace to straighten out some thorny business between them. The King mandates that as soon as Sunaššura appears, the noblemen who surround the Great King should rise from their seats. Granted, Sunaššura is not a messenger but as a vassal king, the protocol, especially for envoys of the Great Kings, might not have been much different.[39] On the other hand, if the protocol regarding the acceptance of vassals and their envoys entails the presence of the king's council or nobles, one would conclude that the arrival of the great kings' messengers requires at least the same. After all, the arrival of a messenger of a great king would generally be considered a more "awesome" occasion.

MESSENGER HOSPITALITY

In the previous chapter wherein the institution of envoy hospitality is reviewed, the general principle emerges that envoys are welcomed and hospitality in the form of food, drink, and lodging is extended to them before they even explain the official purpose of their arrival. But there are also exceptions to the rule for various reasons. An emissary sent by Shulgi in the latter part of the third millennium BC writes back home that, "when he came to the gate of the palace, no one took notice of the greetings of my king: those who were sitting did not rise (and) did not bow down."[40] Clearly, not wishing to receive the message, the person for whom the message was destined avoids the messenger. Similarly, in the letter from Hattusilis III to Adad-nirari I of Assyria, Hattusilis admits that the messengers sent earlier to Hatti experienced difficulties and aggravations, but that the situation changed when Hattusilis took over the throne. In corroboration of

---

[38] Meier, *The Messenger*, 191.

[39] Beckman, *Hittite*, no. 2. p. 15. parag. 9.

[40] F. A. Ali, *Sumerian Letters: Two Collections from Old Babylonian Schools*, Ph. D. Dissertation (University of Pennsylvania, 1964) 32.

his treatment of the Assyrian messengers, Hattusilis suggests that the Assyrian King ask his messenger.[41] An important feature in this story is that the message was delivered in front of the king and those officials who constituted the king's immediate council. The king of Canaan, obviously a vassal of the Eyptian King, encounters a similar problem with the Pharaoh, who simply ignored the messengers sent to him, including the vassal's own son.[42] Hattushilis recounts how both he and Kadašman-Turgu once formed a united front against Egypt with the result that the Kadašman-Turgu combination prevented the royal Egyptian messengers from entering his kingdom. Hattushilis was consequently dismayed when the successor of the Babylonian King upset the alliance.[43] On another occasion, war ensued from the outrage Hanum displayed toward David's envoys. Hanum had half of the beards and garments of David's emissaries cut off before sending them back, thereby committing what is viewed as a personal offense against David (2 Sam. 10.2–5).

In special cases, messengers receive instructions from their lord forbidding them to eat or drink before they explain the reasons for their visit and receiving a response from the host, though admittedly instances of this nature are exceptional. Such an exceptional case concerns Abraham's emissary who was about to receive hospitality from Laban (Gen. 24.31–33). He refuses to eat until he explains the reason for his coming. His host went along with his wish, though he had earlier invited him to come in, wash, and allow those who were with him to do the same. On this occasion, the host is observing the established tradition by inviting the guest to food and drink before business is transacted whereas the guest turns down the invitation because he had been instructed to explain first the reasons for his visit. Refusal of the host's hospitality may not be interpreted here as a disregard of the norms or an insult to his host but simply as an indication of the special purpose of the emissary's mission. These exceptions to the rule notwithstanding, the custom of diplomacy no doubt having its roots in time immemorial, calls for the partaking of food and drink by the emissary at the table of the king and his council.[44] As representatives of their kings, royal

---

[41] *AbB* vol.3, 21.1032; Beckman, *Hittite*, No. 24B. p.140. parag. 5.

[42] Moran AL, *EA* 138.71–80.

[43] *CTH* 172, 71; Elmar Edel, "Die Abfassungszeit des Briefes" *Kbo* I 10; for the chronology of Ramses II *JCS* 12 (1958) 131–33.

[44] *ARM* vol.24, 65.15–20; II 25–30; vol. 75.5–11. Among primitive peoples etiquette was pretty strict most decidedly so where the reception of foreign messengers and envoys was concerned; R. S. Ashnti *Law and Constitution* (Oxford, 1929)

messengers enjoy certain amenities and privileges when on missions. Foreign envoys are even asked to be present in many important state public functions of the host country that happened to be held during their sojourn in the foreign court, and on occasion they are asked to put on special ceremonial vestments.[45] During the banquet, messengers could occasionally be made to feel humiliated by intentional or even unintentional comments. But these exceptions do not necessarily negate the long established principle that ample hospitality is due to envoys.[46]

While they are in the host country, envoys expected to be lodged at the palace, some other official residence of the host king, or at the residence of some other prominent host. Some Elamite messengers, for instance, do not seem to have been quartered in the palace of the Babylonian king, since there is a reference that, following their audience, the Elamite messengers were lodged "in the houses of their hosts" which were obviously different from the king's palaces.[47] It is not certain neither can it be ruled out that

---

91–95; A. A. D. Delobson, *L' Empire du Mongo-Naba* (*Institute de Droit, Comparative Ètudes*) 11, (1933) 107. In the Byzantine period the entertainment of envoys depended on the local authorities of the country they went through and the host country and the king they were visiting. Envoys who visited Constantinople were interned in conditions of extreme luxury in a special building, the *Xenodochium Romanorum*, where their movements, visitors, and communications were carefully scrutinized by a guard of honor composed of the secret police, Nicolson, *Diplomatic Method*, 26. In Republican Rome envoys were accepted by the Senate. In Imperial times the emperor presented envoys to the senate, thereby keeping Republican appearances, but in the second century circumstances changed. The pretension of presenting envoys to the Senate by the emperor ceases, especially since emperors were often away from Rome. Envoys now go wherever the emperor is. Hyginus, describing a model military camp in which the Imperial entourage was housed, mentions the *Questorium* which housed envoys of the enemy, Fergus Millar, "Government and Diplomacy in the Roman Empire during the First Three Centuries," *The International History Review*, 10 (1988) 345–47.

[45] *ARM* vol. 2, 76

[46] R. Whiting, "Old Babylonian Letters from Tell Asmar," *AS* 22 (Chicago, 1987)35, 14–22; M. Civil, "Enlil and Ninlil: The Marriage of Sud," *JAOS* 103 (1983) 43–66.

[47] *ARM* vol. 2, 7; Apollodorus. *Epitome* 3.28–29. It is obvious from the description of Apoll. that the envoys who visited Troy to demand the surrender of Helen (see Homer *Il.* 3.205 ff.; 11.138 ff.) were not lodged or entertained by Troy's ruling king but by the Trojan Antenor. This occasion would support the view of those Greek writers who maintain that the embassy came prior to the landing of the

foreign envoys on their way to a country enjoyed the privilege of staying and being re-provisioned at the special relay stations that had been constructed for the convenience of the host state's envoys. [48]

MESSENGER CREDENTIALS AND WELCOME

Even if it is not certain that foreign envoys did occasionally stay at these relay stations, it is nonetheless certain that they often passed through them. Bahdi-Lim, a Mari official commanding such a post regularly asked foreign messengers about their commission, expecting them to provide him with the requested information.[49] *EA* 30 reveals the possession of such passport, or letters of credentials, by a Mitannian envoy, whereas in *EA* 15.6–8 and n.2 the envoy's credentials are included in the Assyrian King's message of introduction. In the famous story of Wen-Amon, the envoy dispatched to Phoenicia by Heri-Hor, the high priest of Thebes and the virtual king of southern Egypt to fetch wood for the bark of Amon, Wen-Amon stops at one point at Tanis, the capital of northern Egypt. When the local Prince asks Wen-Amon for his credentials Wen-Amon read them in the presence of the prince and his wife. From Tanis, Wen-Amon sails on to Byblos where the city prince commands him to leave but reconsiders and allows him to stay. The Byblos prince then asks Wen-Amon how long he has been

---

Achaean army in the Troad or in Aulis. Hence, the envoys had to stay somewhere near Troy for a night at least. Be that as it may, the envoy practices here are similar to those of the Near Eastern practices. For some of the problems see note 1 to Apoll. text above (Loeb Clas. Library) and Kirk ad *Il.* 3.205 and 11.138. *Dictys Cretensis* 1.4.

[48] L. Casson, *Travel in the Ancient World* (London, 1974) 36; T. Jones and J. Snyder, *Sumerian Economic Texts from the Third Ur Dynasty* (Minneapolis, 1961) 293–302. A complete courier system was established throughout the empire of the Aztecs. At a distance of every six miles stations were built in the form of small towers whence one or more couriers were ever ready to set off with dispatches. It is very possible that guest couriers also stayed there on their way to the Aztec chief. This system of stations may not predate the Mesopotamian and Persian system but it does point out that other people, far removed from Mesopotamia had developed similar systems without copying one from another, Bankcroft, *The History of Mexico*, vol. 2, 413.

[49] *ARM* vol. 5, II 506; p. 101; Meier, *The Messengers*, 89–93; Pollux 8.94–95. In the Byzantine times credentials of ambassadors were of two sorts: letters of recommendation and letters containing instructions in which the extent of their authority was outlined.

in the land, and when Wen-Amon explains that he has been there hardly five months, the prince asks him for his credentials. Wen-Amon answers that he has lost his credentials owing to the misfortunes of his voyage, upon which the prince becomes extremely angry. He goes on to explain that when the Pharaoh sent somebody to ask for wood, he also sent several ships with him, carrying loads of goods as presents. In contrast, Wen-Amon arrives empty-handed, not even carrying his credentials with him.[50]

In the letters of recommendation supplied to their envoys, kings most often request the help, protection, safe passage and freedom of movement from the party through whose territory their messengers are to pass. They further ask for the billeting of the envoy and his retinue with a place to spend the night wherever there were no special inns available. Although credentials were an obvious diplomatic necessity, there is no evidence that such documents were legally required in every case as proof of an envoy's mission. Would the possession of credentials automatically translate into providing provisions, protection, or information to an envoy who passes through the territory of an official of a king? In cases where friendly relations among kings prevailed, this might have been true.

In the literature of the Near East, recipients of messages express their joy at receiving news and an envoy of a king, particularly when the envoy comes from a friendly country. Assur-uballit I expresses his joy upon the arrival of Amenophis IV's messenger and in a letter dispatched to the Egyptian King assures him that his messengers were entertained in his court with all due honor.[51] In a letter from prince Sutahapshap of Egypt to Hattusilis III of Hatti, found in the Hittite archives, the prince expresses his joy that Hattusilis has taken the time to inquire about his health. The same exuberance is contained in another letter from Ramses II to Queen Puduhepa of Hatti:

> When I saw the tablet which [my sister] sent to me, when I heard all the matters which my sister wrote me about, ... I was indeed overjoyed.

Elsewhere we read, "[The messenger] spoke the greeting ... and I rejoiced exceedingly and my heart was greatly pleased when I heard the greeting of my brother." The joy of the recipient is often exuberantly expressed. It is possible that the expression of joy is solely a social convention; on the other hand, one could argue that it may not be so since it is not a standard occur-

---

[50] *ANET* vol. 5, p. 27, col.1.
[51] Grayson, *ARI*, vol.1. no. 49.

rence for every piece of news and every envoy. In several instances, it is the sender's messenger who informs his lord about the joy with which he or the message was received. This latter case by an individual who was a witness to an event and in a position to understand the body language of his interlocutor affirms the view that there was spontaneity and sincerity in such expressions of joy. It is therefore easy to understand that expressions of joy upon the arrival of messengers are associated with abundant food and drinking and the eventual giving of gifts.[52] Gifts received by the kings were not simply a source of enrichment; they were also a matter of prestige or honor something equivalent to the Greek term (*timê*). They reflect the esteem a particular king enjoys among his peers. Thus, in an account of his career, Hattusilis boasts that his standing among his fellow kings is so high that they are sending him gifts. He makes clear that the prestige he enjoys among the other kings in the area when measured by the gifts they keep sending him is very high. The gifts they send had never been sent to his father or forefathers. The inevitable conclusion the reader is led to draw from reading Hattusilis' account is that he is the greatest king of the Hittites up to that time.

THE SIGNIFICANCE OF GIFTS

As in the Egyptian practices, so also in Mesopotamia and the Mediterranean littoral gifts appear to have been exchanged on various important occasions, since they constitute an effective medium of "nonverbal communication," conveying in a subtle way political points about the state of the relationships among the ancient kings. Sociologists often term this giving of gifts the "ceremonial or prestige dimension."[53] Gifts also serve as a congratulatory gesture or a form of recognition by a friendly king to an equal whenever a new king ascends the throne. The same thing is done by the king of a hegemonic power toward a lesser partner in his effort to keep the lesser

---

[52] Y. Muffs, "Joy and Love as Metaphorical Expression of Willingness and Spontaneity in Cuneiform, Ancient Hebrew and Related Literatures," in *Christianity, Judaism and Other Greco-Roman Cults*, J. Neusner, ed. (Leiden, 1976) 1–36; Beckman, *Hittite*, No. 22B, p. 123. parag. 3–4; *TCL* vol. 17, 34.6–8.

[53] M. Liverani, "Irrational Elements in the Amarna Trade," in *Three Essays* (Malibu, 1979) 27. The custom of giving gifts to the foreign ruler whom the envoys visited or to the visiting envoys by the host king continued in the Byzantine time. The recipient rulers frequently reciprocated by sending gifts to their opposites, Shepard and Franklin, *Byz. Diplomacy*, 84; 85; 100; 119; 140; 160; 162; 164. Gifts are also used today in diplomatic visits of presidents or prime ministers, and so on.

partner friendly. We have already seen that considerable quantities of gold flowed from Egypt to other members of the system during the period of the New Kingdom, a significant purpose of which was to keep the recipients friendly. The flow of gold constitutes a major source of Egyptian prestige and influence as well as a means to keep the expanded borders of the New Kingdom safe and peaceful. In addition, the distribution of gold constitutes an elegant form of commercial transactions disguised as a form of gift-exchange inasmuch as Egypt needed the import of certain foreign goods. For the recipient, the value of the gift is often a matter of prestige and international recognition, since some gifts are publicly exhibited and this exhibition elevates or depresses the political importance of the recipient in the eyes of his people and his political friends. In the letter that Išme-Dagan sends to Ishi-Adad, the latter criticizes the former for sending him only 20 minas of lead in return for his generous gift of two horses valued at 600 shekels of silver: "What will be said by those who hear of it?" Išme-Dagan complains. "Will they not compare us?" The obvious implication is that Išme-Dagan is treating Ishi-Adad as an inferior, not as a ruler of equal status.[54] That appearances were very important then as they are today is a subject that needs no belaboring. Kadašman-Enlil of Babylon asks for the hand of an Egyptian princess in marriage as a symbol of his equal standing to the Egyptian King who, in turn, is to marry his daughter. Having been told that the Egyptian Kings do not marry their princesses outside of Egypt, Kadašman is willing to accept a beautiful woman from the Pharaoh as long as the Pharaoh is willing to pretend that she is his daughter. Who is to say that "she was no daughter of the king?" Kadašman asks (*EA* 4 4–22). There could be no clearer description of the role of diplomatic symbolism than that the warmer the relationship, the finer the outward sign of esteem and, for an ally, the greater the prestige. Beyond the diplomatic value of gifts among the Great Kings such exchanges also have a commercial value, as was mentioned above. According to Liverani, the exchange of goods in the Late Bronze Age takes the place of international trade in high-value goods conducted under the guise of an exchange of diplomatic gifts. This aspect becomes clear from the evidence of the Amarna Letters and the

---

[54] *ANET* suppl. (1969) 628–29.

many requests by various kings from the king of Egypt for gold and other valuable items.[55]

Lastly, there is another type of exchange found in the Egyptian and the other correspondence of the Near Eastern kings: the frequent requests for scientists, specialists, or craftsmen. In a letter by Hattusilis (No. 22 G), Hattusilis asks the Pharaoh for obstetric assistance for his sterile sister. Ramses complies, although as a pragmatist, he realizes that no medical assistance can help his colleague's sister. He indicates that only a miracle from the gods will enable a woman of Matanazzi's age to conceive. When Hattusilis himself was suffering from an unknown illness, he asks Ramses for a specialist whom Ramses dispatches along with the pertinent medication.[56] Similarly, Shamshi-Adad, the king of Assyria, asks his son Jasmah-Adad to send him an architect along with brick-layers and masons whom he needs to finish the palace of Sabat-Enlil and some other houses or temples already under construction. When his son complies, Shamshi-Adad criticizes the architect for taking his time in arriving; in another instance, Shamshi-Adad asks for carpenters from one of his governors, Tabil-esarra, governor of Assur.[57]

TRAVELING, DANGERS, AND ESCORTS IN MESOPOTAMIA AND THE LITTORAL

As was explained in connection with Egypt there are many modes by which information can be carried from place to place. The principal means of transmitting information and instruction over a long distance was by special messenger or a merchant acting as a messenger. Envoys are recorded as traveling together with merchants in caravans. The ruler of Alašiya asks the Pharaoh to allow his messengers to leave Egypt without delay, for they are

---

[55] M. Liverani, *Prestige and Interest: International Relations in the Near East ca. 1600–1100 BC* (Padua, 1990) 205–82; Holmes, "The Messengers of the Amarna Letters," *JAOS* 95 (1975) 379–80.

[56] Elmar Edel, *Die Ägyptisch-Hethitische Korrespondenz aus Boghazköi in Babylonischer und Hethitischer Sprache. Vol 1. Umschriften und Übersetzungen*. Abhandlungen der Rheinisch-Westfälischen Akademie der Wissenschaften 77 (Opladen: Westdeutsche Verlag, 1994) no. 49 (E16) 53–57.

[57] *ARM* vol.2, no. 2; *SAA*. Vol. 2, no. 95, p. 81; Eric H. Cline, "Egyptian and Near Eastern Imports in Late Bronze Age Mycenae," in W. Vivian Davies and Louise Schofield, eds., *Egypt, the Aegean and the Levant* (British Museum Press, 1995) 52. col. 1.

also serving as merchants.[58] In the two Enmerkar tales, speed becomes the feature by which one type of messenger becomes known.[59] In the earliest period, running fulfilled this objective if the distance in question was not that long. Later on in the Assyrian and Persian empires speed remains an essential factor and for that reason, the system of relay stations is reorganized in order to facilitate speedy delivery and to provide lodging, food, and drink for messengers and traveling officials of the realm.[60] The messenger who reports the capture of the ark and defeat of Israel by the Philistines was such a great runner that he presumably covers a considerable distance in order to deliver his report on the same day in which the battle took place (1 Sam. 4.17). Two runners also bring news to David of the defeat of his son Absalom (2 Sam. 28.19–32). The Translation of the Seventy renders the adjectival description of the messengers with the word *kouphoi*, speedy or light.

It is clear that running speed was an effective means of transmitting communications in the Near East, as it is later among the Greeks. Where other means could be adopted for the transmission of messages quickly or comfortably, such means are frequently utilized. Mesopotamia was blessed with two rivers and Egypt with the Nile. In both places, boat travel is more efficient and comfortable. A messenger from Yamhad travels by boat down-stream and another is ordered by the king of Mari to take a messenger from Ekallatum to his destination by boat. Where topography allows, horse and chariot are used.[61] It is intriguing that we find some hosts furnishing a foreign messenger not only with provisions for his travel but also spare parts for his chariot.[62] The furnishing of parts by the host signifies the liabilities of the chariot, especially in poor terrain. In other cases in the second millennium, messengers are supplied solely with horses for their travel. The Neo-Assyrian couriers and escort-riders are associated with horses for their messenger activities.[63]

Before the messenger and his assistants depart, the dispatcher takes all imaginable measures possible for the protection and success of messenger

---

[58] *EA* 30. n. 5; *EA* 39–40; *ARM*. 5.11.

[59] Meier, *The Messenger*, 68.

[60] J. Klein, "Shulgi and Ishmedagan," in *Beer Sheva*, M. Cogan, ed. (Jerusalem, 1985) 7; 38; H. W. F. Saggs, "The Nimrud Letters," *Iraq* 21 (1959) 177.

[61] *ARM* vol. 3.56; 14.127.5–11.

[62] *ARM* vol. 23, 41.6–10; vol. 7. 161.9.

[63] J. V. Kinnier Wilson, *The Nimrud Wine Lists* (London, 1972) 57–61; 2 *Kings* 9.17–20; *EA* 161.23–24.

and mission. To insure the safe journey of the messenger, the protection of the gods is first invoked and religious rituals performed to ascertain whether the omens are favorable for the undertaking. The journey is almost always postponed when the omens turn out to be unfavorable.

> I investigated the omens about the welfare of the messengers and they were unfavorable. I shall do them again. When the omens are favorable, I shall send them.

Even when the omens are favorable, it is likely that prophylactic measures are taken to avoid mishaps. Besides the omens, people would perform all appropriate prayers to ensure that no untoward incidents befall their messengers during the journey.[64] Like the Egyptian envoys who encounter all sorts of difficulties while traveling from Egypt to the Mediterranean littoral or all the way to Mesopotamia, so envoys of other kings encounter similar dangers during their journeys:

> The envoy heeded the word of his master. By night he went just by the stars. By day he could go by heaven's sun divine.... He had to go up into the Zubi ranges, had to come down with it out of the Zubi ranges. Five mountain ranges, six mountain ranges, seven mountain ranges, he crossed over, lifted up his eyes, he was approaching Aratta.

As Meier remarks, this is a picture of the idealized messenger who never rests on duty. He ostensibly does not use the night as an excuse to rest. The mountain ranges signify the real effort required of a messenger.[65] Jašmah-Adad's messenger is slain by unnamed bandits along with fourteen others while traveling in a small caravan; some manage to escape, leaving behind ten donkeys and a horse.[66] Traditional inviolability and the norms established by society failed to protect messengers when they fell into ambushes of bandits, since they looked upon them as prized booty. How much bandits and rogues were affected by the invocation of curses and natural calamities called upon to overtake transgressors and malefactors is a very moot question. Nor did rogues and bandits discriminate between messengers of friendly and enemy states.[67] The same is sometimes true of state potentates who were supposed to accord diplomatic respect even to enemy

---

[64] *ARM* vol. 2, 97.5–11; E. Reiner, "Fortune-Telling in Mesopotamia," *JNES* 19 (1960) 27 and 33.

[65] Meier, *The Messenger*, 68.

[66] *ARM* vol. 22, 123.

[67] Pfeiffer, *SLA*, no. 25.12–14.

messengers. They would occasionally ignore diplomatic immunity. Diplomatic immunity in Western Asia was a traditional ideal but it was not always respected by all, especially during times of hostilities. The example of the Hittites who openly flout this tradition and encourage their allies to do likewise is widely known:

> If any one sends a messenger from a hostile land, don't hide him but seize him and deliver him to the king.[68]

Even if a messenger is not from a hostile land, he might find that his passage is blocked by hostile forces.[69] The literature of the Ancient Near East is replete with violence against envoys in spite of efforts to restrain abuse of envoys. Despite these dangerous conditions, even during the worst of times, envoys are as a rule able to transport messages. They are able to carry out their duties, in part, because of the deference paid to them and their position. This deference is an indication that the messenger system enjoys a high degree of respect in antiquity, in spite of occasional misdeeds against messengers. One could also venture to say that letters may also have reached their destination because the transportation system was well organized, operating quite successfully most of the time.

In response to dangers that messengers faced daily, they resort to alternative methods which helped minimize their dangers. One such method already mentioned is the messenger's attachment to a caravan of merchants in the belief that there might be greater safety in numbers. Other times they carry special documents that identify them as envoys in the service of an influential person in the hope that the name of the person may act as an impediment to trouble. Needless to say, useful though such documents might have been for the avoidance of bureaucratic delays, they would have had little influence on brigands.

For purposes of security, on their return trip messengers often travel with a messenger of the host country. An accompanying or escorting messenger very often has a larger task than merely providing safe-conduct for a colleague. Escorting messengers of the host country often carry messages from their lord to the king of their colleague. In that case the accompanying messenger's task is considered complete only when he finishes his round

---

[68] A. Kepinski and S. Košak, "Der Išmeriga Vertrag," *WO* 5 (1970) 193; A. Götze, "Madduwattaš," *MVAG* 32 (1927) 10–11.

[69] *EA* 114.33–43.

trip; thus, messengers are kept in constant motion.[70] Messengers could also serve as witnesses on behalf of fellow messengers or kings of the host country by testifying that his colleague speaks the truth to his master.[71] Thus, in several cases fraught with danger, two messengers are dispatched instead of one.[72] Escorts could serve as additional security or as guides through unfamiliar territory. Many times references to a single escort imply that this escort is accompanied by others, chiefly soldiers who are not always mentioned. Messengers on very significant missions are provided with a strong force to protect them.[73] Yet, despite this protection, messengers and their escorts at times fail to escape danger or death.

The common refrain with which the leaders closed their diplomatic letters in the first millennium is, "Quickly put the road at his feet," referring to those who function as their envoys. The same refrain appears frequently in the Old Babylonian period. "Let him come; don't hold him back," and other similar phrases.[74] The reason Tušratta uses for not releasing the Pharaoh's messenger has become proverbial: he would not return him until the Pharaoh let his messengers go. The Hittite king withholds the Assyrian envoy because the latter fails to send him gifts when he assumes the throne.[75] Queen Pudehepa complains to Ramses II in a letter that she has sent a messenger to Egypt who has not come back. Thereupon she sends Zuzu, charioteer and intimate of the Hittite King, but he too is delayed. Sargon II in the eighth century BC complains that even though he is kind to the fugitives from Elam, they in turn bind the messengers whom he has sent to bring greetings to them. When the Elamite chief sends Ashurbanipal insolent claims, Ashurbanipal holds the messengers to spite their lord.[76] In the same vein, Ramses expresses the complaint that the physician he has sent to

---

[70] *ARM* vol. 18, 59; 18.

[71] *EA* 7.8–32; Num. 35; 30; Deut. 17.6; 15; 19.

[72] *ARM* vol. 1,17, 39; vol. 2, 10.4–5.

[73] *ARM* vol. 24, 127; *ARM* nos. 105 and 123. We also find escort practices among the Byzantine and Romans. Strabo says that when Augustus spent a winter on Samos, an Ethiopian embassy sent by Queen Candace was forwarded to him there by the prefect of Egypt. The envoys had gone to Egypt asking for Augustus and the governor of Egypt. The governor of Egypt sent them on to Samos, providing them with an escort, Strabo *Geography*, 17.1.54.820–21.

[74] *NB* 19.27–29; 31.12–14; 119.14–15; 171.1–15.

[75] *EA* 28.17–19; *CTH* p. 173, 11–14; Götze, "Kizzuwatna and the Problem of Hittite Geography," YOS (1940) 30–31.

[76] Pfeiffer, *SLA*, No. 28, 5–15.

cure Hattusilis' sister of her sterility has not been sent back. Hattusilis answers apologetically that the good doctor has fallen sick, and that, in spite of Hattusilis efforts to save him, he has died. In support of his honesty, he invokes his former history in connection with the return of his guest-experts.[77] Hattusilis also adduces the case of his predecessor and brother, Muwattallis, who had formerly "borrowed" an incantation priest and a physician whom he detained. According to the story, Hattusilis expresses his disagreement with his "brother's" policy, maintaining that he had argued against their detention. In so arguing, he seeks to point out the injustice of Ramses' charge, claiming at the same time that he is not the type to detain Ramses' physician longer than necessary.

Generally, the information from Mari Letters and other Mesopotamian tablets lead to the inevitable conclusion that the diplomatic activities in the ancient world were constant and lively. As a rule, deputations from among the great centers of the fertile-crescent are composed of several members who are constantly on the move, entrusted with diverse undertakings. The Mari Letters provide details about diplomats participating in the diverse deputations, while still other details concern the customary practice of attaching to each mission a local representative of the people to whom the mission is sent, these persons acting either as escorts or guides or both.[78]

It is interesting that, in the literature of the Ancient Near East, we also meet gods and angels who serve as messengers of other, mostly higher and older, gods. Gods sent on missions are naturally pictured as traveling without escort. In the Biblical literature where there is only one God, angels serve as messengers of that God. Although angels were divine beings and stood in no mortal danger from bandits and criminals, while performing their tasks, on occasions of deep crisis we find them traveling in groups of two or three (Gen. 18.2; 19.1), a fact which may signal the gravity of the occasion.

ENVOYS AS INFORMANTS

Sundry references have already been made to intelligence information in the Near Eastern states. Among the topics the Amarna Letters touch on, albeit unsystematically, is that of the collection of intelligence in the Amarna age. The subject is very much a neglected dimension of the political and military

---

[77] Beckman, *Hittites*, No. 2.
[78] A. Malamat, "Hazor, the Head of all Those Kingdoms," *JBL* 79 (196) 13–14; Munn-Rankin, *Iraq* 18 (1959) 68–110.

history of the Near East. Thanks to the recent efforts of a number of scholars, there is now a much greater appreciation of the influential role of intelligence in foreign policy and military decision making.[79] A number of the letters, particularly from Egypt's Canaanite vassals, can be described as intelligence reports because they refer to intelligence issues. To correct confusion with modern intelligence, intelligence as described here is not synonymous with espionage, although some sort of primitive espionage is also perceivable in the reports of envoys. It is also true that the letters containing references to primitive espionage from the Ancient Near East can never be illustrative of the range of envoy activities in this department, since the greatest bulk of the information they transmit must be oral, and therefore unrecorded. Most of the intelligence material in the Amarna Letters flows from Canaan to Egypt and reflects the administration's need for information in that area, vital for the maintenance of the Asian imperial provinces. A fair example of an envoy-spy is the case of the Apophis envoy sent to the Kush allies, who is intercepted by Prince Kamose in the early part of the sixteenth century BC The message he carries suggests the creation of a pincher movement against Kamose from the north, the Hyksos, and the South, the territory of northern Sudan referred in antiquity as Kush. The messenger is caught; Apophis' plan fails; Kamose emerges the victor, throwing the occupier Hyksos out of Egypt. [80]

Canaan was the land bridge between Egypt and the other Great Kingdoms of the Ancient Near East. Troops, traders, messengers, Egyptians, and others, friendly and unfriendly alike, would have to travel through Canaanite territory and its harbors to complete their assignments. There, Egyptian governors were well placed to gather information of local or wider international concern. Merchants, caravans, travelers along the Levantine coast and along the main routes must have provided excellent morsels of

---

[79] R. Follet, " 'Deuxième Bureau' et information diplomatique dans L' Assyrie des Sargonides: Quelques notes," *Revista Degli Studi Orientali* 32 (1959) 61–81; M. Herman, *Intelligence Power in Peace and War* (Cambridge University Press, 1996); Cohen, "Intelligence in the Amarna Letters," in *Amarna Diplomacy*, 85–98.

[80] Elena Cassin, Jean Bottéro, Jean Vercoutter, eds., *Fischer Weltgeschichte*, vol. 2, part 1, p. 368. The Turin Royal Canon assigns this Hyksos to the fifteenth dynasty of Egypt made up of six foreign kings who ruled Egypt in the Second Intermediate Period, 1650–1540 BC. Their ethnic background still continues to be a subject of controversy, K. S. B. Ryholt, *The Political Situation in Egypt during the Second Intermediate Period*, (1997) 118–150. Some of Martin Bernal's comments in his *Black Athena*, vol. 1 (Rutgers University Press, 1989) about the Hyksos are off target.

news about events in far-flung parts of the Mediterranean world and the Fertile Crescent. Whether the Pharaoh and the other Great Kings ran spies on each other is not known. As Cohen appropriately remarks, it would have been surprising if they had not.[81] What is known is that messengers like Mane and Keliya often traveled together and most probably shared news. Diplomats, no matter how secretive, always exchanged and still exchange information. In addition to the Amarna Letters, the Mari archives which antedate Amarna by four hundred years provide first hand evidence of the extensive espionage activity of Ibal-pi-El, the envoy of Zimri-Lim, King of Mari at the court of Hammurabi.[82]

One should also bear in mind that the material in the Amarna pile reflects an arbitrary survival of the archives which may not represent all of Egypt's intelligence priorities. However, since the danger to the empire during the New Kingdom period was focused in the Levant where Egypt's access to the other major powers in Western Asia and vice versa lay, it may not be totally gratuitous that a great deal of the surviving intelligence information comes from the Levant area.

A sentence of Rib-Hadda's letter (*EA* 116.6–16) intimates that collecting and passing on intelligence was one of the duties of the vassal, "But give thought to the fact that I am your loyal servant, and whatever I hear I write to my lord." Instructions to the vassals to gather information on particular topics are also found in two additional places. In *EA* 145.22–29 the Pharaoh instructs Zimreddi, governor of Sidon, to collect intelligence on Amurru, "The word you hear from ther[e] you must report to me." Also in *EA* 151.49–58 Abi-Milku, ruler of Tyre, in a dispatch to Pharaoh, mentions the instruction given to him by the Egyptian King earlier: "Write to me what you have heard in Canaan," to which Abi-Milku responds promptly, giving him all the details that he knows about the developments in the area. In both places the key "marker" is "hear." In other instances intelligence reports are often prefaced by a variation of similar expressions such as "may the king, my lord, be informed," or "may the king know that," or "may the king, my lord, take cognizance," where we have intelligence exclusively about the internal affairs of the empire regarding events in the sensitive area

---

[81] Cohen, "Intelligence in the Amarna Letters," in *Amarna Diplomacy*, 87 and n. 7.

[82] *ARM* 2.26, 159–86. There is also an inkling of espionage by the Mitannis against Egypt in *EA* 29.

of Canaan. Similar hallmarks are used by governors and vassals for activities of adjoining states that impact the Egyptians.[83]

In *EA* 1.77–88 Amenophis III responds angrily to the Babylonian king's letter in which the latter quotes "sarcastically" a statement about the Egyptian King, "You said to my messengers, has your master no troops?" Taking this as an imputation on the quality of the information available to him, Pharaoh imperiously hints at his extensive intelligence capabilities. "Whether soldiers are on hand or not can be found out for me. What reason is there of asking about whether there are troops on hand belonging to you, whether there are horses on hand also belonging to you?" Amenophis implies that he had his own sources on Babylonian military forces and did not need to question Babylonian messengers on the subject. A second explicit reference to intelligence material is contained in *EA* 31.22–38 in a letter sent by Amenophis III to Tarhundaradu, the king of Arzawa, located in the the area of Cilicia, a neighbor at that time of the Hittite Kingdom. "I have heard," the Pharaoh says, "that everything is finished, and that the country of Hattussas is shattered." Pharaoh's phrase, "I have heard," serves as a marker for the quotation of intelligence material reported to the Pharaoh.

Similar practices are recorded among the Asiatic states either concerning internal or external affairs. We see that Joshua (Jos. 7.2–3) sends men from Jericho to Ai, which is near Beth-aven, east of Bethel, saying to them to go spy out the land. They do so reporting back to him that he does not have to send a strong army to Ai because the population of Ai is sparse. The same Joshua sends spies to Jericho before he captured it, the spies having been hidden by a harlot named Rahat. In recompense, when Jericho was captured, Joshua spared Rahat and all her relatives together with their households. The reported activities are in the whole or in part intelligence activities having as their main purpose the transmission of information for government use. The events contained in these reports are presented as a threat to Egypt's geostrategic interest in the Levant and include news of the neighboring great powers like Hatti and the Mitanni. *EA* 126 reports of the Hittite expansion, where Hittite and allied troop movements are depicted as threatening. As Cohen emphasizes, intelligence should not be considered synonymous with espionage. Without spies or the modern electronic

---

[83] Moran AL, *EA* 58.4–10; 68.7–11; 74.5–10; 75.6–14; 76.7–16; 78.7–16; 86.23–30; 90.1–7; 114.1–7; 170.19–35; 174.18–26; 175.14–20; 176.14–20 allude also to such possibilities of espionage, 177.287; 335; 363; 366.

means, it would have been impossible to gain access to the target's innermost deliberations. Much of the information was derived from open sources, be they travelers, diplomats, merchants or plain observers. Nevertheless, it must have helped to a degree the parties involved in these clandestine activities, otherwise they would not have been engaging in it.[84]

INTERMEDIARIES OF ROYAL MARRIAGES

Owing to their extensive travels and their exposure to diversified experiences, merchants were wise in the ways of foreign lands. Often acting on behalf of governors, princes, or kings, merchants were the obvious choice to double as diplomats in the absence of a regular diplomatic service. Like messengers, merchant-messengers served as intermediaries in marriages between their kings and foreign princesses. Diplomatic marriage is a widely practiced custom in the very early history of the Near East; the custom of dynastic marriages is in evidence in Mesopotamia as early as the third millennium BC, for the same purpose as utilized later, the building of political alliances. The Egyptian kings, while accepting foreign princesses in their harem, avoid giving Egyptian princesses to other kings in marriage, claiming rather falsely that tradition dictates their policy. Perhaps the air of superiority Egyptians foster toward foreigners during the height of their empire bars the marriage of the Pharaohs' daughters and sisters from unions with rulers from other Near Eastern countries; perhaps also political calculations prevail over pride. It is also very probable that the reason behind their refusal might have been the Egyptians' wish to protect themselves from family imbroglios outside the dynastic line.

A traditionally important custom associated with the institution of marital liaisons among the Near Easterners was the "bride-price" given by the groom, a type of gift different from the commonly exchanged gifts between kings on a variety of occasions. Ramses II quotes from a letter of Hattusilis, which had been sent to Pharaoh earlier, in which Hattusilis urges the Egyptian King to dispatch envoys who will pour oil on the head of Hattusilis' sister, and following this ceremony the envoys should lead the young bride-to-be to the house of Pharaoh.[85] From this letter we learn that Ram-

---

[84] R. Cohen, "Intelligence in the Amarna Letters," in *Amarna Diplomacy*, 86.
[85] Pouring oil on one's head was a common Egyptian practice bestowing sanctification on the individual on whose head the oil was poured as he entered into the Egyptian Royal family.

ses has accompanied his proposal for the hand of Hattusilis' sister with plentiful presents, which are enumerated in detail in the letter.[86]

In summary, this chapter underscores certain practices relating to the diplomatic usages of the second millennium BC among the peoples of Egypt and those of Western Asia. These practices bespeak of the envoy dispatches, their treatment, privileges generally accorded to them in the exercise of their missions, difficulties and dangers they faced in their travels, their qualifications, and the social and political standing in their native country. We also see the latitude given to them in the fulfillment of their tasks, measures taken for their protection, their carrying and receiving of gifts as tools of the diplomatic game, and more. All of these practices emerge as common features in Egypt as well as of the entire Mediterranean littoral. The royal messenger was a very important agent. He had to be an excellent and convincing speaker, alert and persuasive, sometimes an interpreter, acquainted with the geography of the foreign countries in which he was going, as well as the difficult paths and roads, the dangerous hiding places of thieves and bandits. For these reasons, some of these messengers were experienced, high civil officials or army officers familiar with the rulers of foreign lands, their customs and habits.

In modern times, the subject of international law usually applies to the states; individuals have no standing before its tribunals, with the exception of very recent times, when political and military individuals began to be pursued and judged by international courts for acts against humanity. These courts in essence are replacing the ancient divine courts in which the gods judged everyone, whether king or commoner, emperor or slave, and every individual within a state could seek direct recourse to divine justice through the invocation and appeal to the gods. For the individual, the gods were the residual and ultimate courts of appeal, tribunals that would punish those offenses that escaped human courts and where human courts could not or would not reach to provide justice. Even in disputes among kings, the divine tribunals were courts of first instance. There was no other super national authority to which state or individual might have recourse, except "Might" which individuals or rulers would exercise whenever that was expedient to them.

In times of good relations among the great Near Eastern powers, there was a continuous flow of messengers among the Near Eastern courts, a

---

[86] Elmar Edel, *Die Ägyptisch-Hethitische Korrespondenz*, no. 49, vol.1 (E 16)131–133.

regular chain of exchanges that provided the basis for and reflected positive international relations. A constant tempo of comings and goings by messengers and their caravans not only reassured the parties of their friendships but also implied the sending of material goods. Mari was one of the cities which had almost daily traffic of couriers and envoys and whose correspondence was deposited in special archives. The range of the Mari archives stretched westwardly to Crete, northwardly to Hattussas in Asia Minor, East to Gutium, southeast to Susa and Larsa, and southwest to Hasor in Galilee. A letter from Zimri-lim to Hammurabi speaks of gifts from Crete, while the archives mention copper from Cyprus. There are frequent reports of arrivals and departures of envoys whose destination or through-station was Mari. In these reports, some cities support permanent envoys (legations) in foreign courts either to be kept apprized of the intentions of their kings and avoid unpleasant or dangerous misunderstandings between their's and their host's courts.[87] The same frequency of traveling is described in the Amarna Letters. "[A]nd year by ye[ar] let my messenger to [into your presence], and, on you[r part], year by year, your messenger should come from [your] pre[sence] into my presence," wrote the king of Alašiya to Pharaoh" (*EA* 33.27–32). Another good example from the Amarna Letters is the complaint of Hattusilis III to the Babylonian King Kadašman-Enlil II. Ostensibly, the latter uses some flimsy pretext to cut off diplomatic traffic between their two realms. However, the principle that only if two kings are hostile do their messengers cease to travel constantly between them was not always correct, because the flow of traffic was not limited to friendly kings. In order for the recipient to be certain that the envoy was presenting his master's position accurately, the envoy was frequently given a written dispatch on a tablet. It is thanks to these tablets that we know about the Near Eastern diplomatic activities. What principally emerges from such tablets is that messengers in the ancient Near East were the vital tools of inter-state communication.[88]

Interstate communication was then as now perceived as conducive to the maintenance of peace and friendly relations among states. Traditionally, immunity of the envoy from local jurisdiction along with the duty of the receiving government to bestow special protection and treatment to his dignity and security constituted fundamental features of the interchange of messengers. Without these features, no system could function. This type of

---

[87] Elena Cassin, et al., *Fischer Weltgeschichte*, vol. 2, part 1, pp. 188–89.
[88] Beckman, *Hittite*, 5.

treatment extends not only to the person of the messenger but also to his entourage. Messengers were in principle free to depart whenever they pleased; in essence, tradition dictated that they were not to leave without the permission of their host. Although we find examples of resident envoys, these examples constitute the exception, not the rule; most of the envoys were not residents in the country where they were sent. In view of the primitiveness of the means of communication, even if envoys had been permanent, they would not have been as effective as modern ambassadors.[89] Nevertheless, envoys sometimes spent considerable periods at foreign courts for reasons beyond their control, but these compelling exigencies did not necessarily make an envoy permanent or semi-permanent. These unwelcome detentions at a host's place did carry an unexpected benefit: the messenger became more familiar with the conditions of the host country and inevitably gathered information during his residency, which later could prove useful to him and his master. One cannot ignore the recommendations to the Assyrian envoy in the letter of Ashur-uballit to the Egyptian Pharaoh, representing the first attempt on the part of Assyrian to establish diplomatic relations with Egypt. In this letter, the messenger is instructed to keep his eyes and ears open and report back to Assyria as quickly as possible.[90]

The investigation of the system of envoys thus far has provided us with irrefutable evidence of a quasi-fully fledged diplomatic system that had developed in the ancient Near East by the fifteenth century BC, especially considering the means in existence at that time.. This system evolved in the presence of a number of sovereign states in the area, the existence of a balance of power among them, a Pax Egyptiana, the strong motives of cooperation and conflict that prevailed, and their interdependent interests. Their members possessed a deep sense of society and maintained regular channels of communication, felt an intense need to conduct business among them and to maintain contacts. Many of these states shared the same strong, central system of government and a similar structure of society. As we have seen, the Near Eastern leaders used the family as a metaphor for political relationships; they shared the same conception of law as regards to contracts, marriage and crime, and all had the same ways of dealing with crimi-

---

[89] Cohen, *Diplomacy and Statecraft* 7 (1966) 257.
[90] Albert Kirk Grayson, *Assyrian Royal Inscriptions*, (*ARI*), vol. 1 (Wiesbaden, 1972–76) nos. 10 and 11.

nals.[91] Because of stature issues, they were also obsessed with the question of prestige, a key concept affecting their relationships and their position. Negotiations were absolutely central to this system. Everything was subject to negotiation, both the tangible and the intangible, such as status, prestige, and reputation. Like the European monarchs of the post-Napoleonic period, they considered themselves members of a brotherhood of great kings. They addressed themselves as brothers and appeared solicitous of each other's health, especially during normal times.

---

[91] Martin Wight, *System of States* (Leicester University Press, 1977) 33.

4 Homeric Messengers

Introductory Remarks

The Near Eastern and Egyptian documents discussed in the earlier chapters are official historical documents that express political, social, religious, and economic conditions mirroring their times. We know the courts that dispatched them, the purpose for which they dispatched them, and the approximate dates in which they were written. In contrast, the Homeric epics are primarily literary documents. We know roughly the time they were written and are fairly confident that as literary documents they must reflect the ideas of their age. The composition of both epics has traditionally been ascribed to Homer since antiquity but who this Homer is, and where and when he lived remains a mystery. It is not known whether he is truly the author of one of the epics or both or whether he composed them orally or penned them from the beginning. The above questions have "tormented" and bedeviled the minds of many scholars, who have adduced complex explanations not fully satisfactory to the scholarly community.

Unfortunately, the various facets of the fascinating debate of the Homeric epics cannot be unfolded here. Such an attempt would lead us far off the chartered course for this paper. Nonetheless, a few general remarks may be relevant to the discussion that will follow. Part of this overarching debate centers on how the Homeric poems eventually became fixed texts as well as how the status of the textual variants produced in antiquity found their way in various written sources. Suffice it here to mention that one school of scholars maintains that the fixed text developed after a long period of rhapsodic recitations and that the textual variants are reflections of the process of recitation and addition, characteristic of oral performances and orally-derived poetry. As such, these textual variants represent the multiformity of poetic transmissions. Another school proposes an early date for a fixed text through oral dictation by a singer to a scribe, and the attempt to recover the archetypal texts provides the criterion of assessing the correctness of the textual variants. Considerable disagreement prevails between those who support the theory of continuity and their critics who support the opposite, though almost all agree that the epic tradition embodies the transmission of multiple, often conflicting, versions of poetic material.

Still another school deals with the literacy or illiteracy of the archetypal singer. Even earlier than Parry's days, scholars have articulated views about the development of oral tradition that argues mostly, if not wholly, in favor of the view of an illiterate, oral poet. On the other side, a considerable number of scholars maintains that this theory is wrong, arguing that the archetypal singer was literate, though his tradition may have been oral.[1] Others still believe that Homer was "oral-derived," meaning that he may have sung, written, or dictated his poems, but that even if he were literate, his poetry was composed in the manner of oral poetry.[2] As disparate as these theories are, all agree that as poetry the Homeric epics abide by the rules of its genre. The question has also been frequently asked whether Homeric poetry reflects historical reality as poetry often does and, if so, to what extent. These questions become much more difficult since the Homeric epics are the earliest texts we possess—barring the Linear B Tablets—and the only extensive early sources that describe life and society during and prior to their written composition.

The question further emerges whether it is possible to utilize the legendary material contained in the epics, at least on a limited scale, in the study of the period that preceded the Homeric epics, namely the Mycenaean epoch, or reject this opinion altogether. Both views have won support among modern scholars. In the 1930's Martin P. Nilsson argued that the outlines of the great mythological cycles that we possess about early Greek history originated in the pre-Iron Age and attempted to elucidate the his-

---

[1] Samuel Bassett, *The Poetry of Homer*, new ed., by Bruce Heiden (Lexington Book, 1003) ch. 1 in which Basset argues for the orality of the epics but is also critical of Parryism; Adam Parry, ed., *The Making of Homeric Verses, The Collected Papers of Milman Parry* (Oxford University Press, 1971); M. Parry, "Studies in the Epic Technique of Oral Verse-Making. I. Homer and the Homeric Style," *HSCP* 41 (1930) 73–147; M. Parry, "Studies in the Epic Technique or Oral Verse-Making. II. The Homeric Language as the Language of an Oral Poetry," *HSCP* 45 (1932 1–50; M. Parry, "Whole Formulaic Verses in Greek and Southslavic Heroic Song," *TAPA* 64 (1933); G. P. Shipp, *Studies in the Language of Homer*, 2nd ed. (Cambridge University Press, 1972).

[2] M. P. Martin, *The Language of Heroes* (Cornell University Press, 1989) 146; 205; Joseph Russo, "The Formula," in *A New Companion to Homer*, Ian Morris and Barry Power, eds. (Leiden, 1997).

torical content of many of the major legends.[3] More recently Stubbings has maintained the theory that it is legitimate to use legends.[4] According to him, the Greeks of later times inherited an immense body of legends and traditions, often confused or contaminated by myth and folktale, but valid in their main sequence.

The reader should be aware that the material of the Homeric epics is the type of material that invites varying forms of interpretations.[5] Ever since the rise of the modern study of history in the early part of the nineteenth century, there have been two broad schools of thought about the Homeric epics and the Trojan War. One school accepts that the epics contain much in them which reflects real events. Those who belong to it believe that the Trojan War really happened and that there is a substantial kernel of historical truth in Homer. For that reason this school is often referred to as the "positivist" school.[6] The positivists came to prominence since the excavations of Schliemann in Troy in the latter part of the nineteenth century and have remained very vocal through the mid-twentieth century.

In contrast, the second school dubbed as the "skeptics" maintains that there is no truth in Homer and that the Homeric story is nothing more than a beautiful fairy tale. The excavations of Troy in the 1930's pointed to a small and unimposing location, not the grand city imagined by earlier scholars as painted in the *Iliad*. The skeptics have managed to pick holes in the ancient texts that were supposed to provide written confirmation of the truth of Homer's tale. Perhaps the catastrophes and the bitterness that emerged after World War II rendered unfashionable heroic actions as those described in Homer. In the second half of the twentieth century the greatest

---

[3] M. P. Nilsson, *The Mycenaean Origin of Greek Mythology* (New York, 1962) passim; Geoffrey Kirk, *Myth: Its Meaning and Function in Ancient and Other Cultures* (University of California Press, 1970) 32; 241; 247; Carol G. Thomas, *Finding People in Early Greece* (University of Missouri Press, 2005) 83.

[4] F. H. Stubbings, *CAH* 3rd ed., vol. 1, part 1, 240–42; 245.

[5] Machteld J. Mellink, ed., *Troy and the Trojan War*, (Bryn Mawr, Pa. 1986) and a special issue of the journal *The Classical World* 91 (1998) issue 5 is dedicated to the subject. See also Hans Günter Jansen, "Troy: Legend and Reality," in J. M. Sasson, ed., *Civilizations of the Ancient Near East*, 2 vols. (New York, 1995) 1121–34;

[6] D. L. Page, *History and the Homeric Iliad* (University of California Press, 1959); J. V. Luce, *Homer and the Heroic Age* (New York, 1975); T. B. L. Webster, *From Mycenae to Homer* (New York, 1964) constitute important examples in support of the theory that there really was a Trojan War and that Homer's narrative reflects the Bronze Age.

advocates of the "Skeptic" theory were M. I. Finley and his sympathizers. Linguists and students of inscriptions followed suit by a concerted attack upon positivism and the reexamination of ancient texts that supposedly provided written confirmation of the truth of Homer's tales.[7]

Recently the pendulum has been swinging in the opposite direction once more, as a younger generation of scholars is inclined to think that skepticism was carried to unjustifiable extremes by its proponents. This revisionist approach is doing to the "skeptics" what they did to the positivists with the formulation of new interpretations of the extant literature. They are also providing a "more" careful reexamination of the older archaeological findings and new material data, among them the results of new excavations at Troy since the middle of the 1980's.[8]

---

[7] Moses I. Finley, *The World of Odysseus*, rev. ed., (New York, 1978) who argues that there is in Homer mostly Iron Age material; also his "The Trojan War," *JHS* 84 (1964) 1–20; or "Lost: The Trojan War," in his *Antiquity: Discoveries and Controversies* (London, Penguin, 1991); see also several of the essays in J. K. Davies and L. Foxhall, eds., *The Trojan War: Its Historicity and the Context—Papers of the First Greenbank Colloquium* (Liverpool Classical Press, 1981); Ian Morris, "The Use and Abuse of Homer," *Classical Antiquity* 6 (1986) 81–138; Finley, "Myth, Memory and History," in *History and Theory* 4 (1965) 288; Michael Ventris and John Chadwick, 2nd ed., *Documents in Mycenaean Greek* (Cambridge University Press, 1973) 156; 190; John Chadwick, *The Mycenaean World* (Cambridge University Press, 1976) 80–81.

[8] Joachim Latacz, *Troy and Homer: Towards a Solution of an Old Mystery*, transl. by Kevin Windle and Rosh Ireland (Oxford, 2004); Eric H. Cline, *Sailing the Wine-Dark Sea: International Trade and the Late Bronze Age Aegean* (Oxford: Tempus Reparatum, 1994) favors the positivist view; Cline, "Archaeology and the Iliad: Did the Trojan War Take Place?" (Modern Scholar, 2006); Carol G. Thomas and Craig Conant, *The Trojan War* (Westport, 2005); Ione M. Shear, *Tales of Heroes: The Origins of the Homeric Texts* (New York, 2000); G. S. Kirk, in his *The Iliad: A Commentary*, especially vol. 2, Books 5–8 (Cambridge University Press, 1990). W.-D. Niemeier, "Greeks vs. Hittites: Why Troy is Troy and the Trojan War is Real," *Archaeology Odyssey* 5 (2002) 24–35; Trevor Bryce, *The Kingdom of the Hittites* (Clarendon Press, 1998); Bryce, *Letters of the Great Kings of the Ancient Near East* (Routledge, 2003); Bryce, *The Trojans and Their Neighbors* (London, 2006); all three of Bryce's books examine the relationship between Hittites and and Ahhiyawans; N. Fields, *Troy c. 1700 – 1250 BC* (Osceola, Fla.; 2004) A. Ünal, "Two Peoples on Both Sides of the Aegean Sea: Did the Achaeans and the Hittites Know Each Other?" in *Essays on Ancient Anatolian and Syrian Studies in the 2nd and 1st Millennium B.C. Bulletin of the Middle Eastern Culture Center in Japan* 4 (1991) 22–24. Edzar Visser, "Formale Typologien im Schiffskatalog der Ilias: Befunde und Konzequenzen" in H. L. C. Tristram, ed., *New Methods in the Research of Epic* (Tübingen 1998) 30. Today the equation of the Ahhiyawans with the

The latest epigraphical research increases also the likelihood of *Ilion* being the city the Hittites called Wilusa. It also supports the theory that the people whom Homer refers to as Achaeans are really the Mycenaeans referred to as Ahhiyawans in the Hittite texts. More and more scholars are inclined to accept that the Mycenaeans expanded from the mainland to the eastern and southern Aegean islands and that their ships carried them as far afield as Cyprus and the Eastern littoral of the Mediterranean. Others, aware of the strength of the Ahhiyawan-Achaean theory, hesitate to join ranks with the champions of that theory without undeniable proof that will absolutely convince them the Ahhiyawans were indeed Achaeans.[9]

After all, archaeological and epigraphical material is subject to the reevaluations and limitations of almost the same order as literary or historical material. For that reason, Mortimer Wheeler said once that we need to use human imagination in recreating the past because of the evidence at our disposal, and historians must do whatever they can with the material vouchsafed to them, in full consciousness of its incompleteness.[10] It should be borne in mind that any picture of the past recaptured from the available fragmentary evidence and analyzed by our often inadequate techniques cannot be more that a rough approximation of the historical truth. That the Homeric poems are real and objective as poetry is readily admitted. Whether or not we should accept them as historical facts—making them into yet another type of "documentation" is an arguable point. This paper

---

Mycenaean Greeks, whether on the Aegean Islands or on the Greek mainland, is accepted by many scholars including Mycenaean specialists and Hellenists, Bryce, "Ahhiyawans and Mycenaean," 307; Dickinson, *The Aegean Bronze Age*, 234–56; for the impact of the Ancient Near East on Homer see M. L. West, *The East Face of Helicon* (Oxford Clarendon Press, 1997).

[9] J. D. Hawkins, "The End of the Bronze Age in Anatolia: New Light from Recent Discoveries, in Çilingirroglu and D. French, eds., *Anatolian Iron Ages* 3 (British Institute of Archaeology at Ankara, 1994) 91–94; W.-D. Niemeier, "Miletus in the Bronze Age: Bridge Between The Aegean and Anatolia," *Bulletin of the Institute of Classical Studies* 46 (2002–03) 225–27; Niemeier, "The Mycenaeans in Western Anatolia and the Problem of the Origins of the Sea People," in S. Gritin, Amihai Mazar, Ephraim Stern, eds. in Honor of Prof. Trude Dhoheim, *Mediterranean Peoples in Transition, Thirteenth to Early Tenth Century BCE. Israel Exploration Society* (Jerusalem, 1988) 17–65; Thomas and Conant, *The Trojan War*; R. E. M. Wheeler, *Alms for Oblivion* (London, 1966) 115; Ruth B. Edwards, *Kadmos the Phoenician* (Amsterdam, 1979) 205.

[10] R. E. M. Wheeler, *Alms for Oblivion* (London, 1966) 115; Ruth B. Edwards, *Kadmos and Phoenician* (Amsterdam, 1979) 205.

argues that the Homeric epics reveal significant historical facts using as example the scrutiny of Homeric messenger practices as evidence.

CONTINUITY VS. DISCONTINUITY

The utilization of the Homeric poetry in support of Mycenaean messenger practices follows the syllogism that support of proposition B, namely the Mycenaean messenger practices (Introd., p.5) through proposition C (Homeric practices) places the contemporaneous Mycenaean world at a disadvantage for a number of reasons. Homeric poetry may not be seen as providing a true reflection of Mycenaean life and history in the social, political, economic, or religious arenas, since it began to take form years after the purported "collapse" of the Mycenaean civilization; as a result, some suggest that it may reflect life and institutional practices in the Dark Age Greece. Furthermore, archaeological evidence needs the support of historical evidence to be securely interpreted, but this evidence is often unavailable. The question posited in this paper is whether these epics reflect aspects of the institutional practices of the Mycenaean period or whether they simply mirror life in the Dark Ages of Greece and the age of Homer. Many scholars in the past have supported the former; recent scholars have argued in favor of the latter.[11]

According to the earlier view, inasmuch as all elements of the Bronze Age Mycenaean culture were virtually erased, the second millennium civilization of the Mycenaeans could have had no major "influence" upon the culture that succeeded it. Thus the *Iliad*, while retelling the war between Greeks and Trojans during the Bronze Age, is in essence describing the Dark Age world, an age that had caused a clean break with the culture of its preceding age. It must then be asked whether it is realistic to strip the Bronze Age of any influence on its subsequent age. Before we arrive at a conclusion, it might be advisable for us to review the opinions of selected modern scholars, since these modern views are intimately intertwined with the basic thesis of our examination.

Modern archaeologists take the view that the Aegean Bronze Age was a recognizable geographic unity with an admirable degree of internal coherence in the sequence of Greek development, that is, that society had inherited much from its Neolithic and Bronze Age predecessors which in turn

---

[11] C. G. Starr, *The Origins of Greek Civilization, 1100–650* (New York, 1962) 46–47; 67;109; Finley, "The Trojan War" 84 (1964)1–19; Finley, *The World of Odysseus*, rev.ed., passim; Carol G. Thomas and Craig Conant, *Citadel*, their Introduction.

transmitted it to that of the succeeding Dark Age from which Archaic Greece developed. The theories of northern invasions which had previously been widely held have largely lost their momentum and plausibility. Not only do they rely upon tendentious interpretations of generally scanty archaeological material, most of it discredited, they also fail to offer sound rational motivation for such movements. To take an example: why Dickinson asks, referring to Bernal's theory, should Egyptians whose life-style and culture depended upon residence along the Nile show any interest in a mountainous region of such a completely different nature? What reliable evidence do we possess for the theory of the northern invasion of Greece by allegedly mounted people who came from afar? The only rational hypothesis is that sometimes farming groups would move into adjacent unpopulated or sparsely populated areas which provided the movers with better land than theirs. Under normal circumstances early farming populations possessing decently productive land could have no valid reasons to be constantly on the move.[12] It has been argued that moving peoples were often displaced by others who came and occupied their lands, but modern research has discredited this view since we possess no reliable evidence for its support.

Even Thucydides, who bequeathed to us the story of movement among the early inhabitants of Greece, is not specific, and his ideas lend themselves to overgeneralizations. Aside from his description of times of turmoil and movements from north to south, he seems to know of nothing comparable to our concept of a Dark Age. His description of migratory movements might be nothing more than a memory of a remote age common in the stories of his time, but, since he does not seem to be clear as to whether these movements were tantamount to a general catastrophe, we cannot be certain about his exact meaning. True, Thucydides speaks of civil strife following the Trojan War which frequently forced cities to relocate to new locations, but are these stories sufficient evidence that he is painting an accurate picture of the Dark Ages?[13]

Indeed, it is very difficult to accept that the decline of the Mycenaean world implied *ipso facto* the disappearance of that world; monuments can be destroyed but ideas, customs, practices, and institutions as a rule persist

---

[12] Dickinson, *The Aegean Bronze Age*, 295; S. Diamant, "Mycenaean Origins: Infiltration from the North?" in E. B. French and K. A. Wardle, eds., *Problems in Greek Prehistory* (Bristol Classical Pres, 1988) 153.

[13] Thuc. 1.12.3–4; Thomas and Conant, *Citadel*, xviii-xix.

unless the population which practiced them is totally eliminated. But this did not happen with the decline of the Mycenaean civilization. Houses and monuments were built anew, but the people who survived the transition continued to live as they did before, adjusting to novel situations which likely changed the economic and social status for many of them. How radical the changes generated by the decline of the Mycenaean civilization were we do not exactly know. In some places and for a number of people, the changes might have been more radical than others. In others, as for example Attica, the changes could not have been abrupt. Generally, many of the customs that dominated everyday life must have continued, despite the purported occasional movement of new groups, particularly since the new groups probably possessed the same or similar culture. Anthropologists have noted that ethnic or cultural minority groups frequently assimilate rapidly into larger local communities.[14] Even the modern villagers of Greece still follow practices and customs that have their roots deep in the very distant past, despite the overwhelming catastrophes that have visited the area in the last two thousand years, the arrival and settlement in Greece of new groups, and the introduction of the Christian religion. This view is so widely accepted to those who have studied the history of medieval and modern Greece that there is no need to belabor it. A rather mirthful little incident to which I was an eye-witness in the latter part of the 1940's highlights my point.

The Swedish Count Folke Bernadotte visited the Greek city of Patras in 1948 to lay the foundation stone for a children's "Prevantorium," a sanatorium for the prevention of tuberculosis in children who had suffered from malnutrition during the German occupation and the guerrilla warfare that followed. Bernadotte had been appointed the UN mediator in the Arab-Israeli dispute and on his way to Palestine, he stopped to lay the foundation stone for the hospital on behalf of the Swedish Government, which footed the bill. A brief ceremony was held during which a priest read some prayers and blessed the ground on which the hospital was to be founded; following the ceremonies Bernadotte delivered a very short speech

---

[14] F. Barth, "Ethnic Groups and Boundaries," in *TAPS* 57, (Philadelphia, 1969) pt.8; George de Vos and Lola Rumanusci-Ross, eds., "Ethnic Pluralism: Conflict and Accommodation," in *Ethnic Identitity* (New York, 1991) 376–77; O. Dickinson, *The Aegean Bronze Age*, 298; P. R. S. Moorey, "On Tracing the Cultural Transfers in Prehistory: The Case of Egypt and Lower Mesopotamia in the Fourth Millennium B.C." in Michael Rowland, Mogens Larsen, and Kristian Kristiansen, eds. in *Center and Periphery in the Ancient World*, (Cambridge University Press, 1987) 44.

and proceeded to lay the foundation stone. At the end of the ceremony, a member of the small crowd brought forward a rooster and tried to pass it on to Count Bernadotte. Utterly befuddled, Bernadotte asked his interpreter about the meaning of the gesture. The interpreter himself asked the man who brought the rooster. He said that Bernadotte should slay the rooster on the foundation stone for the good luck of the building about to be erected. Bernadotte refused to slay the bird and asked that it be taken away. A few years after this incident, as a student of ancient history, I learned that it was a common practice in the Near Eastern and Aegean cultures to slay a rooster on the foundation stone of the building to be constructed for the building's good luck. Thus, a very ancient custom common among the peoples of the Eastern Mediterranean had survived also in Greece for thousands of years, in spite of the efforts of several Church leaders to "free" the Christian religion from "contamination" by ancient pagan superstitions and magical beliefs. Their efforts often came to naught, which may not have been a bad development. The great Greek Religion specialist Nilsson has wisely pointed out that if anyone wanted to find out how the ancient Greeks celebrated their festivals all he had to do was to attend the celebration of a modern religious Greek festival.[15] Other similarities can be adduced about other Greek customs. It is the advent of modern industrialism, technology, and the overwhelming spread of modern urbanism in Greece which slowly but steadily cut off people from their rural roots and traditional customs.

It has also been argued that continuity persists in other facets of ancient Greek life such as in building construction. Fortunately, archaeology comes to our aid as it documents for us that not only ideas but also excavated buildings show the same pattern of construction dating occasionally all the way back to Chalcolithic times. The make up of these buildings consists of mixed material, including wood, stone and clay blocks. Wood was widely utilized in construction, and even when buildings were made of clay blocks or stone, wood was widely used to bind the building in the construction of floors, doors, roofs, and internal ladders.[16] A building 50 by 10 m. in size unearthed in Lefkandi of Euboea, in a place called Toumba, was internally supported by wood. According to the Greek archaeologist Orlandos, the types of material and the techniques of construction used by the ancient

---

[15] M. P. Nilsson, *Greek Folk Religion* (Harper Torch Books, 1961) 100.

[16] Anastasios Orlandos, *Ta Ylika Domês tôn Archaiôn Hellenôn kata tous Syggrafeis, tas Epigrafas, kai ta Mnêmeia*, vol. 1 (Athens, 1955) 81.

villagers in Greece continued into the period of Turkish occupation and even into the modern times.[17]

The above is one example drawn from the area of archaeology. There are other examples in the area of diplomatic practices that point to the connections between the earlier and later times in Greece. The differences between the two areas not withstanding, such as the tighter organization and greater sophistication of the Near Eastern states, there are also fascinating similarities in the use of diplomatic rules. True, the diplomatic methods of the Near East are institutionalized, stemming from documents. In contrast, our information about diplomatic activities in the Greek Bronze Age derives not from any official documents of the Mycenaean chancelleries but from the literary works of Homer. Despite the obvious weakness in our evidence, Homer provides us with information that cannot be overlooked, first because it is the only information we possess, and secondly because the information Homer provides for us is very valuable.[18] The very meager information regarding longer distances covered by envoys in the *Odyssey* is sufficiently indicative of Greek diplomatic practices for a reasonable comparison with the Near Eastern practices.

The salient impression given by the Aegean world in the Mycenaean times is that this world was largely homogeneous and politically united, and that Mycenae in several ways seems to have been the leading center.[19] The

---

[17] Orlandos, *Ta Ylika Domês*, 81; Hara Papadatou-Yiannopoulou, "E Diasôsê tês Archaias Ellênikês Oikodomikês Paradoseôs stên Lefkada," *Sixth International Panionian Congress*, vol. 3 (Athens, 2002) 318; M. R. Phopham, M. R. Touloupa, and L. H. Sackett, "Further Excavations of the Toumba Cemetery at Lefkandi," *BSA* 79 (1982) 80–81; 213–48.

[18] The Mycenaean palace society is not fully known to us, but we may presume fairly safely that the size of the Mycenaean centers with their surrounding area was larger as a rule than most of the later city-states. One may perhaps call them "district" states. Despite our limited knowledge of the Mycenaean centers, the Pylos texts do imply that Pylos was of a far more developed nature, closer to the system of those of the Near Eastern civilizations than those centering on individual chieftains or aristocratic households, which have been deduced from Homer, and the same might be true of Thebes, see Latacz, *Troy and Homer*, 130–31, 244–46, 239, 240–42.

[19] O. Dickinson, *The Aegean Bronze Age*, 306; J. C. Wight, "From Chief to King in Mycenaean Society," in P. Rhehak's *The Role of the Ruler in the Prehistoric Aegean*, Aegaeum 11 (Liège, 1995) 63–85. Even Carol Thomas, who had argued against the notion of Mycenaean hegemony some years ago, is ready to admit now that in the last centuries of the Mycenaean period a single authority was succeeding in concen-

palace society was headed by an established hierarchy whose leading man was the *wanax* with *lawagetas* as another functionary who shared some responsibility with the *wanax*.[20] It is very plausible that a skeletal administrative machine below the *wanax* operated certain service departments sharing some weaker similarities with those of the Near East.[21] These officials were either the typical aristocrats from whose class they were drawn or land owners by virtue of the fact that they had been given land in compensation for their services. This question is difficult to decide, but there are signs pointing to the existence of a major land-holding class from which the officials could have been drawn.

Below the *wanax* and the *lawagetas* were officials in charge of certain services in the Homeric world, such as Odysseus' herald Eurybates, Eumaeus, Odysseus' chief overseer of his herds, a man of noble extraction who had deservedly earned Odysseus' trust through his hard work, his zeal for his master's household, and his unconditional faithfulness. Euryclea, the daughter of Ops, is another important and trusted official who served him from childhood as Odysseus' female personnel. Someone must have been in charge of agricultural activities which Laertes himself supervised in his old age in Odysseus' absence. There were also officials serving as advisors who, like Eurybates, probably doubled on occasion as envoys. The Mycenaean royal houses consequently possessed an efficient, if skeletal, organization that assisted in the performance of state business. Indeed no state can function without a variety of functionaries.

Another picture relating to Bronze Age wars also arises from pre-Trojan War references as attested to in the epics. There are several scanty mentions of wars and embassies in which envoys have been used. Wars are also mentioned in connection with the Ahhiyawans, but to what degree the Ahhyawans are connected with the Greeks remains an unsolved question in the history of the Eastern Mediterranean.

Much ink has been devoted to the question of the provenance of the Ahhiyawans and their relationship to the Hittites in the Late Bronze Age. References mention kings, persons, and deities of Ahhiyawa, and insofar as

---

trating power, "The Components of Political Identity in Mycenaean Greece," in *Politeia, Society and State in the Aegean Bronze Age, Proceedings of the 5th International Aegean Conference*, vol. 2, Aegaeum 12 (Université Liège, 1995) 354.

[20] Klaus Kilian, "The Emergence of Wanax Ideology in the Mycenaean Palaces," in *OJA* 7(1988) 291–303; O. Dickinson, *The Aegean Bronze Age*, 306.

[21] J. Whitley, "Social Diversity in Dark Age Greece," *BSA* 86 (1991) 341–65; O. Dickinson, *The Bronze Bronze Age* Aegean, 306.

they are datable, they span the period between 1400 and 1200 BC. At least one of the Ahhiyawan kings was ranked as a 'Great King,' and thus the equal of the Hittite and Egyptian King. Unfortunately, the location and identification of the Ahhiyawans remain highly controversial. Their identification as Achaean (Mycenaean) by Forrer in the 1920s has been much disputed. Some scholars have sought to locate Ahhiyawa on some of the Eastern Aegean islands or on the Western Anatolian mainland. Rhodes and Miletus (Millawanda) are the most commonly mentioned places, yet the identity of the Ahhiyawans still remains elusive. We seem to have a people with no definitive locations, and possibly Ahhiyawan places like Rhodes and Millawanda without the exact identity of the people who resided in them. Arguments in favor of Rhodes, Miletus, and southwestern Asia Minor have been gaining ground lately, buttressed by the increasing presence of Mycenaeans finds in Western Anatolia.[22]

These arguments emphasize principally the improbability that the Hittites with their interest in western Anatolia should have failed to mention the Mycenaeans in their records, but we have no way of knowing. Be that as it may, the identity of the Ahhiyawans and their relation to the Mycenaean people cannot be a topic of discussion in this paper. Suffice it to mention that whatever the political organizational structure of the Ahhiyawans might have been, it cannot be readily assumed that it was closely analogous to those of the contemporary Near Eastern kingdoms with their complex vassal states under the immediate control of local rulers. A closer comparison to them is probably possible for only the latter part of Ahhiyawan history, a century or so before the Ahhiyawan collapse. But since our knowledge of them is limited, our judgment on this subject must remain suspended.[23]

---

[22] Barry Strauss, *The Trojan War, A New History* accepts the theory of the Ahhiyawans being Greeks.

See p. 19 and his reference on it in pp. 201–202; Trevor Bryce, *Letters of the Great Kings of the Ancient Near East*, 123; Dickinson, *The Bronze Age Aegean*, ch. 4; Trevor R. Bryce, "Ahhiyawans and Mycenaeans—An Anatolian Viewpoint," *OJA* 8 (1989) 306; Visser, *Homers Katalog der Schiffe* (Stuttgart and Leipzig, 1998) 30–41. In the light of the latest research by Bryce and others many scholars are inclined to accept the Ahhiyawans as the Homeric Achaeans. Yet, not all scholars have been entirely convinced.

[23] H. Güterbock, "Hittites and Akhaeans: A New Look," in *Proceedings of the American Philosophical Society* 128 (1984) 114–122; Bryce, "The Nature of Mycenaean Involvement in Western Anatolia" *Historia* 3 (1988) 1–21.

The above discussion has touched on few of the vast number of problems that bedevil those who dare scout the Mycenaean and the Iron Ages. In spite of the insurmountable problems and pitfalls surrounding the subject, one should nevertheless attempt to tackle the question of Homeric diplomatic practices by utilizing the information Homer has provided for us by focusing particularly on such traditional institutional practices that are related to those discussed so far in the area of the Near East.

PRE-TROJAN WAR STORIES

A basic cause of friction among some of the communities of the Pre-Trojan War period relates to the stealing of cattle, a custom which seems to have continued in the post-Trojan period, indeed almost down to the present time in many of the rural areas of Greece. In his quarrel with Agamemnon in the beginning of the *Iliad*, Achilles explains that he has no quarrel with the Trojans on his own account because they have done nothing to harm him. They never harried his kin or horses nor did they ever lay waste his grain (*Il.* 1.154–56). The common response by the victims of such razzias would be to organize a counter-stealing foray which was perceived not only as a retaliatory response but also as a preventive measure against similar future forays. It is fairly certain that such forays also provided a diversion for the participants from the "boredom" of everyday life. In some cases these activities resulted in a localized war or feud, as Achilles' statement signifies, and no doubt this sort of war was settled by some satisfactory arrangement in the eyes of the victors or became the source of a vendetta that might have lasted for a number of years. In the negotiations over the arrangement, messengers must have been dispatched as representatives of their kings. Nestor cites a localized incident that occurred in his youth which led to a war between Pylians and Epeians. The cause of the war was the stealing of Pylian cattle by the Epeians. Nestor mentions with pride how the retaliatory raid of the Pylians netted for them many flocks of sheep, droves of swine, many droves of goats, fifty herds of kine, and one hundred and fifty chestnut-colored mares with foals at the teat.[24]

---

[24] Livestock loomed large in the Late Bronze lists of booty. Egyptian, Mesopotamian, and Hittite texts often portrayed it as a coveted prize, John Wilson, "The Asiatic Campaigns of Tutmosis III: The Battle of Megiddo" and "Subsequent Campaigns," in Pritchard, *ANET*, 234–41; Wolfgang Heimpel, *Letters to the King of Mari* (Winona Lake, Ind., 2003) 27; 112, p. 449; H. A. Hoffner, Jr., "Deeds of Šup-

Nestor, Neleus' youngest child, who survived Heracles' attack on his brothers, claims to have distinguished himself during the hostilities by "single-handedly" defeating the Elians during the Epeian massacre (*Il.* 11.670–93).[25] Since the purpose of the narration was to illustrate Nestor's heroism, no details are mentioned regarding a final settlement between the two sides. Homer describes the military actions' quasi-epic proportions. In essence, cattle-rustling was a common occurrence in Mediterranean life as other cases show (1 Sam. 12.3). Among the Greeks, raiding cattle, horses, and sheep was at times honorable. Heroes themselves guarded herds, and the action that Homer describes constitutes a typical epic subject prevalent in the Bronze Age. When Attarisya (Atreus) attacks the kingdom of Madduwatta in southwestern Anatolia around 1400 BC, for example, he targets cattle and sheep. Homer mentions various wars in Greece fought over cattle-thieving, and it was not unusual for noblemen to die in the process. We know that Helen's brother Castor was killed in such a raid.[26] It would not be too daring to presume, nonetheless, that the rustling stories are not simply saga but instead are indicative of the activities that must have been frequent among the Bronze Age Greeks. In Nestor's story, some effort toward a final settlement—perhaps a truce agreement for the collection of the bodies—must have taken place, plausibly involving envoys, if we are to judge from similar stories in Homer (*Il.* 7.400–04).

There are two other major pre-Trojan polemic stories, one relating to the incident of the Seven against Thebes and the significant role that Tydeus, Diomedes' father, played in it. We learn that Tydeus had gone as a messenger (*angelos*) to the Thebans and that his enemies try to ambush him.

---

piluliumas," in W. W. Hallo, ed., *The Context of Scripture*, vol. 1, pp.185–92; Bryce, *Life and Society*, 104–107.

[25] The names of Nestor's brothers listed in *Hesiodi Theogonia, Opera et Dies, Scutum Fragmenta Selecta*, R. Merkelbach and M. A. West eds. (Oxford University Press, 1970) fr. 33. ll. 9–12. Beyond the references to the pre-Trojan hostile activities between Greeks there is the widely accepted view regarding the invasion or occupation of Crete by the Achaeans in the fifteenth century BC. Unfortunately, the sources for this occupation are primarily archaeological. We have no mention of messengers or envoys and their possible activities.

[26] Castor was killed by Lynceus in a quarrel over cattle. Lynceus in turn was killed by Castor's brother Polydeuces, *Cypria* fr. 15 PEG I; Pind. *Nem.* 10.60ff.; Apollod. 3.135 f.

Tydeus fight backs valiantly, killing forty nine of the ambuscaders.[27] The second incident is mentioned in the embassy to Achilles (9.534–605); it is the story of the hero Meleager that refers to the feud between Calydonians and Kuretes. In Meleager's genealogy, Homer describes the feud of Meleager as having preceded the Trojan War by two to three generations, though the origins of the story may lie even deeper in history.[28] Such events must have been rather common in the Mycenaean communities, providing the basic material for later sagas, enriched and dramatized by the various narrators with the passage of time.

MESSENGERS IN THE *ILIAD*

We find various persons serving as messengers in the *Iliad*, though the format of the embassies may differ from case to case depending upon the special circumstances of the embassy. In Book One, we notice already a form of embassy (*Il.* 1.11–42). Although this occasion is not a typical embassy scene, nonetheless, it gives us an idea regarding messenger activities and treatment. It also entails aspects relating to peripheral but important personal matters of prestige issues on the part of those who received and heard the envoy's case. Chryses, the envoy, is not a delegate of an independent state but an important person, a priest and father, acting as delegate on be-

---

[27] *Il.* 10.285–94; 14.114; 4.376–78, 392–97; 5.802–08; Kirk, *The Iliad* ad loc. The story of the end of the Theban war heroes was in the *Thebaid*, which probably ended with the funerals of the Seven outside of Thebes. Variations of details are given by several Greek and Latin authors, Theocr. 16.104; Pind. *Ol.* 14.4 with scholia; Strabo 9.414; Paus. 9.34.9; 35.1.; 38.1; Aesch. *Seven against Thebes*; Soph. *Oed. Tyr.* and *Oed. at Col.*; *Antig.*; Eur. *Phoen.*; Apollod. 3.57 ff.; Hyg. *Fab.* 70 ff. A striking part of the story relates how upon his arrival at the Cithaeron Adrastus did not immediately proceed to attack his enemies but sent instead Tydeus as his herald with the proposal that Eteocles should resign the throne in favor of Polyneices. Only when this proposal was rejected did Tydeus challenge the Theban chieftains to a single combat. For this practice see Thuc. 12.1–2; *Il.* 3.205–08. There was another embassy much earlier upon the abduction of Helen. At that time Priam denied knowledge of Helen's abduction and was unwilling to pursue the subject. The embassy from Tenedos shows that the ancient Greeks wanted to exhaust all chances of reconciliation before they resorted to war. See also Hdt. 1.3; *Cypria* quoted in Proclus's *Christomathy* 1; Apoll. *Epitome* 3.6.

[28] Merkelbach and West, *Hesiod*, fr. 135; Apoll. 1.8.2; Hyg. *Fab.* 171; Stesich. Fr. 179 (II). For some of the problems of the parallel situations made at this point between Meleager and Achilles Meleager and Bellerophon, Hesiod 43a82.

half of his daughter. He goes to the Achaean camp as a messenger-suppliant, carrying with him extensive ransom-gifts as remuneration for his daughter's freedom. In his hands, he holds the fillets of Apollo on a staff of gold to show his messenger sacrosanctity, hoping that he will command the respect of the Achaeans. He begs all, especially the two Atreids, to respect Apollo and accept the ransom-gifts, crowning his appeal with wishes to the Achaeans for the success of their enterprise against Troy.

The Achaeans' response to Chryses' request is overwhelmingly positive. They applaud him heartily and urge Agamemnon to respect the messenger-priest, accept the generous ransom-gifts he offers, and deliver his daughter to him. Unfortunately, Agamemnon chooses to ignore the priest's appeal and the advice of the Achaeans. He orders the priest, instead, to leave his camp, accompanying his command with the caveat that if he catches him loitering around the Achaean camp again, he will not respect his staff or his fillets. His daughter, he asserts, is destined to remain as his concubine, and Chryses had better understand it. Scared and dispirited, Chryses leaves the camp silent and heart-broken, resorting in his desperation to the only weapon left to him: prayer to his patron Apollo.

Apollo's response is immediate as well as devastating. For nine days, an epidemic grips the Achaean camp. It starts with the mules and the dogs and then spreads to the men. The Achaeans start dying in droves, while the beach of Troy is crowded with funeral pyres. No doubt, the smoke and the smell of bodies lying across the Trojan plain make the Trojans fearful of contagious diseases, even as they cried tears of joy.[29] The Greeks, like the Near Easterners, suspect that the plague is divine punishment for some sin of theirs but fail to connect it to Chryses' treatment (*Il.* 1.64–65). Consequently, on the tenth day Achilles calls an assembly on the beach by the hollow ships, and it is there that the famous quarrel breaks out. The Achaeans resort to mantic, asking Calchas to provide an explanation of their misery (*Il.* 1.72–91).[30] The prophet, no friend of Agamemnon, makes a

---

[29] For a Near Eastern analogy, see Kemal Balkan, *Letter of King Anum-Hirbi of Mama to the King of Warshama of Kanish*, (Ankara, 1959) 8, 16.

[30] The Spartans found themselves in a similar situation and for a long time they could not get good omens from their sacrifices, owing allegedly to Talthybius' anger over the Spartan's killing of Darius' envoys by throwing them into a well. Talthybius opted for the traditional sacrosanctity of envoys over localism and for that reason they would let the Spartans have good omens, until two distinguished Spartans volunteered to deliver themselves to the Persians in an act of atonement. Hdt. mentions something similar about the Athenians, Hdt. 133–34.

terrible announcement. Apollo has sent the epidemic to punish the Greeks for having turned a deaf ear to his priest, who serves at the shrine of Apollo Smintheus in the southern Troad. The episode typifies Bronze Age religious ideas in Anatolia and Greece where people were used to the connection between gods and pestilence.[31]

Full and welcome attention has been paid to the skill and subtlety of the presentation of the actions and character of the protagonists in the feud, both seriously concerned to protect or increase their honor in different ways, through different ways and varying types and levels of emotions. On the other hand, the quarrel between Agamemnon and Achilles exhibits the poet's skill and complexity in the highest degree. The quarrel is patently about honor and time, though the issues and reactions are complex. The underlying tension between the two men is rooted in their different temperament and their different claims to time. Agamemnon feels his overall command threatened by young Achilles' readiness to criticize openly, and welcomes the chance to take action to demonstrate his superiority (*Il.* 176 and 185 ff.). Achilles feels that his unquestioned primacy as a warrior is not adequately appreciated and resents the fact that Agamemnon compounds his leadership privileges by an unfair defense of his claims to the major share of booty (*Il.* 1.149–71). In the later books he will recur constantly to the feeling of deep and burning rage at the dishonor done to him. The participle ephybrizôn (*Il.* 9.368) serves to underline that the act of removing his prize (*geras*) is patently a sinister insult that is in fact precisely performed with the intention of inflicting a public humiliation upon him and a demonstration to all present who is the better man of the two (*Il.* 9.367–72).

The surface problem in this ugly exchange may have appeared to be the division of loot, but the real issue, as in many instances of the Near

---

[31] In Anatolia the local war-god Iyarri was also the god of pestilence being designated as "Lord of the Bow" with a name similar to Apollo of the "glorious bow." In the area Iarry was worshipped as Apollo Smintheus, a god of mice and place. A shrine to him stood near the city of Chryse at least as early as 700 BC, possibly in the Bronze Age too. Hallo, ed., *The Context of Scripture*, vol. 1, (Brill, Leiden, 1997–2000) 201; Maciej Popko, *Religions of Asia Minor*, trans. Iwana Zych (Warsaw: Academic Publications Dialog, 1995) 93; Strauss, *The Trojan War*, 103. For kings prone to blame the messenger for the bad message see also the Hittite King Hattusilis, who exploded at the men who reported that their battering ram had broken during a siege. He cursed them by saying that the Storm God would wash them away! Garry Beckman, "The Siege of Uršu Texts," (*CTH* 7) and *Journal of Cuneiform Studies* 47 (1955) 25.

Eastern kings is really the question of honor. In the end, deeply concerned about the safety of his troops Agamemnon opts to return Chryseis, in the hope that the plague will end. The messengers proposed to return Chryseis are among the most prominent in the Achaean camp; the individual finally chosen to lead the embassy is Odysseus, accompanied by twenty rowers (*Il.* 1.309–11).

The circumstances surrounding this delegation are somewhat unusual in the history of ancient embassies. On the surface at least, the delegation visiting Chryses ends up playing the role of host instead of vice versa. It is also the visiting delegation which provides the victims of the hecatomb for the doxological sacrifice upon the occasion of the delivery of Chryseis, not Chryses. The customary dinner that follows the sacrifice is given by the Achaeans, not Chryses who, as host, would have the customary obligation to offer entertainment to the envoy and his attendants (*Il.* 1.438–44). In this reversal of roles, the balance of host-visitor is now obviously restored by the contrite attitude of the visitors and their suppliant status. In all other aspects, the feast is sumptuous, with hosts and guests feasting the entire day until night falls. Following the celebration, the envoy and those who accompanied him retire to their quarters at the beached ships.

The choice of a single envoy is interesting on this occasion. Embassies in the *Iliad* are often made up of more than one person, the main negotiator and another person in an auxiliary role, along with their escorts and guards. In this instance only, one person is the envoy. Why one envoy is selected out of the four originally proposed is not known. The fact that Chryses is not a head of state but a priest may have something to do with it, but Homer does not elaborate. Perhaps Agamemnon, still fuming over the incident with Chryseis, decided to select a single envoy, not wishing to "honor" Chryses with a regular embassy. That no negotiations take place beyond the simple delivery of Chryseis may also have something to do with the single envoy make-up of the embassy.

Another unusual feature associated with this embassy is that upon the embassy's return, Odysseus and his crew scatter among their ships. The most fitting, traditional, and logical procedure would have been for Odysseus to report either to Agamemnon, or to Agamemnon and the council of the Achaean leaders. Neither of the two seems to have occurred; if it did, Homer fails to report it, a failure that seems puzzling. Be that as it may, this is not the final phase of the thrilling episode that began with Chryses' visit.

Personal Honor

In the feud between Agamemnon and Achilles, both commit gross political, social, and religious errors since both allow themselves to fall victim to their irascibility. Achilles should have known that Agamemnon, as commander-in-chief and a "senior" officer, would be insulted by strong language and that he would be bound to react violently to the insults hurled in front of the other kings and the army. Consequently, in the prevailing climate of personal relations, there is no doubt that Achilles errs seriously by embarrassing the supreme commander with his unpalatable comments. Achilles could phrase his guarantee of Calchas' protection in a less offensive and combative manner. Regrettably, youthful Achilles' irascibility, fanned by his physical prowess, precludes such an approach. On the other side, Agamemnon's attack upon young Achilles' honor is something equally intolerable for the young king who must defend his damaged honor at all cost, fearing that he will otherwise fall into dishonor (*atimia*). He is bound to insist upon reparation. Agamemnon, in his turn, equally protective of his seniority and his superiority as a commander, threatens to engage in a counter-offensive of self-compensation for the loss of Chryseis by depriving Achilles of his prize Briseis, thus adding insult to injury to Achilles' pride and honor. When that occurs, it proves to be the straw that breaks the camel's back. It leads the two chiefs to a fateful and dolorous rift whose resonance is still celebrated in the form of thousands of books, literary articles, and discussions and whose end will likely never come for as long as humanity remains in existence. The immediate effect of this feud is that Achilles leaves the battlefield and the Greeks pay for his absence with many dead and wounded. In a society that prizes personal honor (*timê*) and respect for the divine (*eusebeia*), Agamemnon must expiate these sins by returning Chryseis, and compensating Achilles abundantly for the damage done to his honor, if he ever expects Achilles to return to the fight. Equally, if the offended god has to be placated, analogous sacrifices have to be offered. The hecatomb Agamemnon offers to Apollo is therefore tantamount to a request for forgiveness and the restoration of the disturbed divine balance of things by Agamemnon's ill-advised behavior.

Shame and honor experienced in the above incident are dominant and recurring themes in Homeric society. Prior to the beginning of the duel between Menelaus and Paris, Priam asks Helen to identify for him the various Greek leaders. Helen appears for the first time in the *Iliad*, and while providing the information she is asked, her eyes search for her two brothers, Castor and Polydeuces. Not seeing them among the Achaeans, she imagines that they are hidden among the troops or that they might not even have come to Troy, owing to her shaming her family's honor. Demonstrating Helen's extraordinary sensitivity, Homer does not portray Priam as asking Helen about Menelaus, nor does he describe Helen's feelings when she sees him in the plain readying himself to encounter Paris (*Il.* 3.172–76, 243–44). Helen knows that all the other women in Troy perceive her as the cause of their misfortune and is gravely embarrassed by it. Beyond the good-hearted Priam and the knightly Hector, the other relatives, particularly the women, barely tolerate Helen's presence. It is not strange that, in the entire *Iliad*, Homer does not present Helen as speaking with Hecuba or Andromache, or any other woman. Only at the end of the *Iliad* do we see her mourning the dead Hector, in tandem with Andromache and Hecuba (*Il.* 24.748–60). Actually, the image of Helen appears in similar fashion in both Homeric books. Although she shows the same strong character that elevates her above her somewhat fickle husbands, Menelaus and Paris, in both epics she acknowledges her self-inflicted shame and recognizes her deep responsibility in her dishonorable love affair.

The themes of shame and honor recur everywhere in Homer, as in the games at the funeral of Patroclus (*Il.* 23.257 ff.). Cultural activities like singing, oratory, and dramatic performances are competitive exhibitions performed in honor of the gods or heroes and the glory of the winners. To be the best and superior to others sums up the heroic code. With this form of counsel, Peleus sends his mighty son to fight with the Achaeans in Troy, and in the same spirit Hippolochus sends his son Glaucus to fight on the opposite side (*Il.* 6.208; 11.783). With great pathos, Hector confesses to his wife that he would be ashamed before the Trojan men and women if he did not fight in the front ranks of the Trojans (*Il.* 6.441ff.); the same sense of shame keeps him facing Achilles in their final duel (*Il.* 22.238). Odysseus, finding himself in a tight spot, says "that only cowards retreat; a man who wants honor in battle must stand fast and kill or die" (*Il.* 11.408–10.). The winners' prize is honor, the public acknowledgement of their superiority, and honor is usually compensated by material tributes and gifts. Agamemnon, as commander-in-chief, has the pick of booty (*Il.* 1.166–67), and Achilles is honored for his valor in battle by a gift from the army (*Il.* 1.276). The honor a hero achieves endures forever after his death. If Achilles stays and fights at Troy, his glory will be everlasting (*Il.* 9.413), an idea that Hector stresses earlier. (*Il.* 7.87–91). Sophocles, in his *Aias*, portrays a hero of the Homeric kind who ends his life because he fails to win the honor he desires. Aias' choice of death is further emphasized as the hero meditates aloud before his audience and then kills himself when his claim of honor is denied and his revenge frustrated. The quest for honor is the result of the wider principle of ensuring that others recognize one's proper status.

In the *Iliad*, two are the great heroes who die, one Greek and the other Trojan: Patroclus and Hector. When Patroclus falls fighting Hector, the Greeks, though getting the worst in the battle against the Trojans in a vicious conflict, regroup hurriedly and with great difficulty, snatch Patroclus' body from the hands of the Trojans. They know that they must try their utmost, no matter what the cost, to retrieve his body, for otherwise Patroclus' body will not escape the dishonor of being eaten by dogs.[32]

So prominent are the concepts of honor and shame in the Homeric community that they are portrayed as extending beyond the humans to the most beloved animal of the Homeric heroes, the horse. They talk to them as if they are humans, with a human heart and human honor. In *Il*. 23.403–13 that describes the contest during Patroclus' funeral, Antilochus urges his horses to outrun Menelaus's horses. "Strain to your utmost; overtake the horses of the son of Atreus and be not outstripped by them lest shame comes upon you by Aethe that is but a mare."[33] He even threatens them with death, if through their heedlessness or laziness rider and horses end up with a prize below their status.[34]

The graceful way whereby the hero endeavors to stir up the love of honor (*philotimon*) of his horses is humorous. It would be a shame if, male horses as they are, they are defeated by a female horse. The contempt of the male for the female here is carried over from the human community to the community of the animals. In a different but similarly graceful manner, Hector, while being chased by Nestor and Diomedes, urges his horses to honor him by outrunning their horses:

> Xanthus, and you nobly-born Podargus, and you Aethon and goodly Lampus, Pay me back now for the rich care with which Andromache, the daughter of great-hearted Eetion, fed you with honey-hearted wheat,

---

[32] Though it was dishonorable to mistreat a rival's body, the Greeks, like the Hittite and Egyptian generals, often mistreated their enemy's corpse. Billie Jean Collins, "The Ritual Between the Pieces" in Hallo, ed., *Context of Scripture*, vol. 1, 160–61; Collins, "the Puppy in Hittite Ritual," *JCS* 42 (1990) 211–26; J. Wilson, "The Asiatic Campaigning of Amen-hotep II," in *ANET*, 247–48.

[33] *Il*. 20.220–29; 23.406–413; John Kakrides, *Homeric Themes* (Athens 1981)109. Aethe was Agamemnon's mare which he had loaned to his brother Menelaus.

[34] *Il*. 8.185–91; Kakrides, *Homeric Themes*, 109–10. Many of the horses of heroes are gifts from gods and heroes.

mixing it with wine for you to drink before she fed me, her stalwart husband.[35]

As often happens in similar Near Eastern circumstances, when the received message is unpleasant for the receiver, the welcome of Agamemnon's envoys is cold, even fearful. Fearing Achilles' wrath, the two herald-messengers do not address any word to their purported host but stand in front of him, silent and terror stricken. Aware of their predicament, the host addresses them coldly but kindly by saluting and acknowledging them as messengers of Zeus and men. Noticing that they stand somewhat distantly, he bids them draw near and seeks to soothe their obvious anxiety with assurances that he does not consider them responsible for their sinister mission; their master is to blame for it. There is a tepid welcome here for the messengers but no invitation to enter Achilles' quarters and no request to stay for dinner, as we have frequently witnessed in the investigation of the Near Eastern embassies. Achilles instead proceeds immediately with the

---

[35] *Il.* 23.295.Kadrides, *Homeric Themes*, 110. Kakrides points to the similarity between these Homeric verses and some contemporary Greek demotic songs of an unknown Greek poet which leads him to assert that both Homer as well as this unknown poet, who is doubtful whether he new Homer's poetry, derived some of their poetic ideas from unknown predecessors. From all the horses of the hero in the demotic poem one only shows itself bold enough to save its lady, who is being led away to a loveless marriage, though it carried on its body forty wounds.

Ἐγώ εἰμ' ἄξιος κι ἀπότορμος νὰ φθάσω τὴν κυρά μου
Γιατὶ μ' ἀκριβοτάγιζε κριθάρι στὴν ποδιά της,
Γιατὶ μ' ἀκριβοπότιζε μὲς σ' ἀργυρῆ λεγένη.

(I am the worthy and daring one to reach my lady
Because she fed me in her apron with expensive barley
Because she watered me lovingly from a silver bowl)

For the above simile, as well as for other poetic techniques, it is certain, Kakrides says, Homer relied on his unknown forerunner(s), when using the same themes as they did and not unlikely similar verses. At the same time, he cautions us not to forget that whatever Homer gives us in his poetic creation, even when he borrows the idea from somebody else, whatever elements he uses, old, foreign, contemporary, or demotic inventions, he has to make them first his own, to have worked them out in advance, to have recognized their value before he thought them worthy to utilize them himself.

business at hand. He orders his friend Patroclus to fetch Briseis and deliver her to the messengers, who remain standing, silent, and fearful, since any effort at an explanation on their part might aggravate the already tense situation and jeopardize their mission and their lives.

The above story points to the three arbitrary decisions with which the *Iliad* begins, all three offensive to the contemporaneous social mores. The first is the mistreatment of Apollo's suppliant and the offense to his patron god; the second, Agamemnon's refusal to accept Chryses' generous gifts as ransom for his daughter; and the third, the disregard of the *vox populi*, which dictates respect of the priest and return of the girl.[36] As if to make the difficult situation more complex, Agamemnon seeks to compensate himself for the loss of Chryseis by seizing Achilles' spear-prize, Briseis. Agamemnon's last act is understandable only in the sense that failure to proceed with the execution of his threat might appear to be an empty boast. On the other hand, by so doing, Agamemnon makes his insult to Achilles' honor even worse. Following Briseis' delivery, Achilles invokes the two heralds as witnesses to Agamemnon's perfidy and takes an oath not to participate in future combats against the Trojans, even if the Greeks are driven to ruin.[37] All the while the heralds, using their discretion and judgment, choose to remain silent lest they provoke Achilles' irascibility.

In a culture where man's image depends greatly on the opinion of others, the loss of honor is an unbearable burden for any person to carry and he must defend it at all cost; otherwise, he is likely to fall into dishonor and disrepute. Consequently, Achilles must restore his honor by insisting on an analogous rehabilitation. Agamemnon's insults, and the taking of Briseis, deeply wound Achilles' pride and shame his honor to the point that he has no other viable option but to retire from the coalition of the Achaeans. Another alternative would have been the killing of Agamemnon, which Achilles temporarily meditates but is dissuaded from by the intervention of the goddess of wisdom, Athena. His frustration is so intense, however, that after Briseis is taken from him, Achilles sits on the beach and cries like a baby, tears of both rage and loss.[38]

---

[36] For the significance of the *vox populi* even in tyrannical regimes, Karavites, *Promise-Giving*, 127–56.

[37] *Il.* 1.338–44; Kirk, *The Iliad* ad loc.; W. A. Camps, *Introduction to Homer* (Oxford University Press, 1980). 5.

[38] Plato and other philosophers who followed him censured Homer for making his heroes cry. But in doing so Homer was following the pattern of Bronze Age poetry. Both the Mesopotamian Hero Gilgamesh and the Hittite and Anatolian

THE ROUTE TO RECONCILIATION

In the meantime, finding himself in a situation without palatable options, being torn by the responsibility for the fate of his army, and feeling that he has treated Achilles shabbily, Agamemnon calls the council of the Achaean elders to deliberate about the Achaeans' next measure of action. This act shows that Agamemnon makes mistakes and that he also responds to the circumstances, being a good general, admitting error, and swiftly switching course. He has the courage to apologize and make amends for his mistakes.

The withdrawal of Achilles' elite corps and the repeated Greek setbacks on the battlefield demoralize the rest of the Greek army and corrode its confidence. In the nearly two weeks that have passed since Achilles' withdrawal, the military picture has become gloomier by the day. In view of this desperate predicament, the top commanders gather in Agamemnon's headquarters. Here the best imported Thracian wine is served along with superb food as the council members seek to devise a way out of their terrible demise. This is only the first of many sumptuous dinners for the gathering of kings that night. The many dinners may or may not be an epic exaggeration. In the Bronze Age, Aegean hospitality was standard at any gathering under another man's roof and meals were as much a social as a nutritional occasion.

In the council deliberations, Nestor speaks frankly, rebuking Agamemnon for having ignored the council's advice and insulting Achilles' honor. He foresees a hopeless impasse unless they convince Achilles and the Myrmidons to come back into the war. That can happen only if Agamemnon makes an immediate move to reconcile with Achilles. Nestor could have saved his words because Agamemnon has already reached a similar conclusion. He accepts their criticism by ascribing his former conduct to blindness, *Atê*.[39] Now that he can look at the military situation with

---

storm god Tešub cry in their respective poems; so does the Canaanite epic hero Kirta (c. 1300 BC), the Egyptian Wenamun and the Philistine prince Beder of Dor in the Egyptian tale of Wenamun (c. the 11th century BC); E. A. Speiser, "The epic of Gilgamesh," in *ANET*, 87; West, *The East Face of Helicon*, 231–32; for Tešub, "The Song of Hedammu," and "the Song of Ulikummi," in H. A. Hoffner, Jr., *Hittite Myths*, 2nd ed. (Scholars Press, 1998) 51–52; 6; for Kirta, see "Kirta Epic," in W. W. Hallo, ed., *Context of Scripture*, vol. 1, 33; for Wenamun Miriam Lichtheim, " The Report of Wenamun," in *Ancient Egyptian Literature: A Book of Readings*, vol. 2 (University of California Press, 1976) 229; for Hattusilis I see Amelie Kuhrt, *The Ancient Near East*, vol. 1, 238.

[39] W. F. Wyatt, "Homeric Atê," *AJPh* 103(1982) 147–76.

a cool mind, he is ready to make amends not merely by returning the young woman and sending his apologies, but by adding gifts worthy of a king whose property is already great. He proposes that the Achaeans send forth envoys to Achilles to apologize on his behalf and explain that he is ready to pay abundant recompense toward the restoration of Achilles' honor. As in the case of Chryses, the restoration of the offended party's dignity involves a transfer of valuable objects, the social mechanism of restoring the disturbed social balance.

In a fascinating scene reminiscent of the Near East, Agamemnon proceeds to enumerate the gifts in front of all the members of the council who are to be the witnesses to his sincerity and generosity. Agamemnon's gifts include highly valued items, namely horses and slave women skilled in handiwork and surpassing most women in beauty. Agamemnon is further prepared to swear an oath that he never even as much as touched Briseis, another indirect admission that he has acted unfairly when he took her from Achilles in the first place.

By his generous gifts to his rival, Agamemnon not only seeks to compensate Achilles for the wrong he heaped upon him but he is simultaneously expressing his deep concern for the plight of the troops. In another way, by placing the army's interest above his ego, he is indirectly reaffirming his responsibilities as the supreme commander. In addition to the many presents Agamemnon is ready to bestow upon Achilles, he promises to give him many more prizes upon the seizure of Troy. To stress his sincerity, he tops his offer by proposing a marriage alliance between their two noble families, being willing to endow the marriage with a rich dowry made up of seven Peloponnesian cities, whose residents would honor him like a god.[40] The only thing he asks in return is the respect due from a younger to an older person, a conduct that will restore Agamemnon's own personal honor

---

[40] These cities are not listed in the Pylian entry of the catalogue of ships (*Il.* 2.591–602), V. Burr, Νεῶν Κατάλογος, *Klio Beiheft* 49 (Leipzig, 1944) 60–61 discounted by D. L. Page, *History and the Homeric Iliad* (University of California Press, 1959) 165–66; R. Hope Simpson and J. F. Lazenby, *The Catalogue of Ships in Homer's Iliad* (Oxford University Press, 1970); Adalberto Giovannini, *Étude historique sur les origenes du catalogue de Vaisseaux* (Bern, 1969); Giovannini's theory is rejected by E. Visser, *Homers Katalog der Schiffe* (Stuttgart-Leipzig, 1997) 746. As in the Near Eastern customs, Odysseus here mentions the plethora of expensive gifts Agamemnon was ready to bestow on Achilles as a recompense for his earlier conduct *Il.* 9.260–282. The same counting off of gifts was made earlier by Agamemnon himself in front of the Achaean kings.

and position among the Achaean leadership. Agamemnon's offer does not simply constitute opportunistic palm-greasing diplomacy. It is simply a part and parcel of traditional Near Eastern and Aegean diplomatic practices toward a dishonored king.

Irrespective of this council's historicity, the description of the council's deliberations reflects what is likely to have transpired in the royal councils of the Mycenaean kings in circumstances when major state decisions were to be made. If poetry often takes its cue from actual life, Homer's account may prove illuminating here. The discussion in the council has its analogy in royal decision-makings which were practiced in early historical times, if the Epic of Gilgamesh and the use of the purported deliberations of the councils in that epic are of any historical value. The use of gifts to maintain alliances or to acquire friends, on the other hand, was not unique to the Bronze World. The practice was widely spread in the Near East, and it seems to have continued among the Greeks into the Classical times.[41] The reference of Agamemnon to a marriage alliance is reinforced by similar practices among the Near Easterners and the Greeks of the archaic age inasmuch as marriage liaisons among the early royal families were a customary practice, something to which we shall return in the course of the present investigation.[42]

In pursuit of Agamemnon's proposal in the royal council, Nestor proposes that a delegation of the highest rank, befitting the equality status of the two kings, be sent to Achilles to negotiate the dispute (v. 167). His suggestion entails the dispatch of two royal members of the council, not simply heralds. Another interesting but "puzzling" proposal by Nestor is that the royal envoys be accompanied by Phoenix, Achilles' mentor and subordinate who, for some mystifying reason, is present at the deliberations of the council. As Achilles' mentor he will now lead the way and plead the Achaean cause before Achilles (v.168). Obviously, Phoenix's return to Achilles' quarter is cleverly combined by the poet with the dispatch of the envoys. This combination of the two envoys and Phoenix is intriguing because it is reminiscent of the common Near Eastern practice of combining

---

[41] Thuc. 2.40.4; Arist. *Rhet.* 1.9.2; *Eth. Nic.* 9.7.1; 1167b16; Plut. *Flam.* 1.1–3.

[42] A category of prestigious goods—indeed the most prestigious—was that of foreign princesses of Greek kings for whom international marriages were concluded. This practice represented a true cornerstone of Eastern as well as Homeric interstate relationships. It continued in the post-Homeric world among the aristocrats who ruled the Greek poleis. It took a downward trend during the dominance of the democracies in Greece, to be revived in the Hellenistic world.

the return of the guest envoy with a host envoy. Is this case a remnant of a Bronze Age practice that Homer reproduces here? Is Phoenix to serve here as a quasi-support witness to Agamemnon's sincerity as envoys in the Near Eastern diplomatic delegations used to do? Homer does not say; consequently, the presence of Phoenix in the Achaean camp as well as his accompanying of the delegation to Achilles remains a puzzle. But nothing can be excluded here. Phoenix' presence at the deliberations of the Achaean kings and his speech at Achilles' quarters in support of Agamemnon and the Achaean council's decision tempt one to think that Phoenix had gone to the Achaean council on official business. If this inference is true, it reminds us of the role of the "host-envoys" in the Near Eastern documents. There is no other logical way whereby Phoenix could have gone to the Achaean council. Unfortunately, Homer does not even provide as much as a hint to this paradoxical presence of Phoenix in the Achaean council and forces us to hypothesize, and one hypothesis at this point is as good as another. One thing seems certain: Homer would not have placed Phoenix in the middle of the Achaean council at a time when there were no communications between Achilles and Agamemnon. If Phoenix went to the council, he must have done so with the knowledge and approval of Achilles. Could there have been another reason for his presence in the council beyond some sort of official business?

The two envoys selected for the embassy are Odysseus and Aias Telamonius, both dear to Achilles, one a clever speaker, the other a highly respected warrior and a relative of Achilles. The two delegates are to be accompanied by the heralds Odius and Eurybates, Odysseus' herald (*Il.* 9.169–79). The picture that emerges from the council deliberations is that the two envoys are not given absolute freedom to improvise arguments designed to persuade Achilles, notwithstanding Odysseus' well known speaking talents. Instead, Nestor, speaking on behalf of the council members, instructs Odysseus as to the arguments he is to use and the manner in which he is to deliver these arguments, accompanying his instructions with many attendant glances at the envoys, especially to Odysseus, the leader and main speaker of the delegation. As soon as Nestor finishes his instructions, water and wine are brought, which the heralds pour over the hands of the delegates, while youths hand out cups for the customary libations. The libations are coupled by a prayer to Zeus, imploring him to bless the work of the mission. Upon completion of the libations and prayers, the envoys depart. The picture presented here by Homer corresponds closely to the procedure preceding the departure of Near Eastern embassies.

When the envoys reach Achilles' quarters (*Il.* 9.197), the latter welcomes them and, unlike his reception of the herald, he leads the envoys into his headquarters. Subsequently, he orders Patroclus to bring cups and wine for all to drink and to prepare meat for dinner in honor of the guests. From these preparations, it becomes clear that the delegates stay at Achilles' quarters a considerable length of time (*Il.* 9.210–17). Only when the envoys have eaten and tasted the wine of their host does Aias nod to Phoenix, a signal which prompts Odysseus to begin his explanation of their visit.

Aias' nod to Phoenix is another puzzling development. Have the delegates been instructed by Nestor to wait for Aias' nod before Odysseus begins his speech? Does Aias nod to Phoenix on his own initiative simply because he feels that Phoenix, as the eldest, should speak? Is his not simply the signal that Odysseus is waiting for to begin the discussion? Does Odysseus begin because he feels that, as the leader of the delegation, he is the one commissioned to do so? Homer is a bit murky on this point, though the text seems to favor the latter interpretation, with the statement "and noble Odysseus took notice" (*Il.* 9.223). A number of viewpoints have been proposed since antiquity regarding Phoenix' role in the embassy but despite the great variety of views, skepticism prevails.

THE SPEECHES IN ACHILLES' QUARTERS

Achilles' sumptuous hospitality provides Odysseus with a splendid opportunity for his clever introduction into the topic of the envoys' visit. He points out emphatically that the Achaeans' stand in imminent danger from which only Achilles can save them. In his beautifully composed speech, Odysseus appeals to Achilles to set aside his justifiable anger and help the Greeks in their hour of need, warning him in a semi-prophetic manner that if something dreadful were to happen to them, Achilles would certainly be the first to be sorry, but that his grief would be too late to rectify the situation. He proceeds to remind Achilles of Peleus' parting advice to him to curb his irascibility, a defect of his character already known to the Achaeans from Achilles' previous encounter with Agamemnon. He emphasizes Agamemnon's deep regret for his earlier improper behavior and cites his deep repentance for that incident and his wish for reconciliation. He highlights Agamemnon's sincerity by pointing out the many precious gifts Agamemnon is ready to confer upon Achilles and many more upon the capture of Troy. To top it all, he punctuates Agamemnon's sincerity by stating that he has even refrained from sleeping with Achilles' concubine, while he also adds that Agamemnon would be glad to give any daughter of his to Achilles as a bride. Odysseus finally adds what he probably feels is a strong appeal on behalf of all the Achaeans who were innocent of Agamemnon's offense: that if Achilles does not care for Agamemnon, he should at least try to help for the sake of the rest of the Achaean army who consider him equal to a god. By helping the rest of the Greeks, he will also have the opportunity he has sought all along: to slay Hector and thus achieve great honor and glory (*Il.* 9.300–306).

The artistry with which Odysseus crafts his speech notwithstanding, Achilles rejects Odysseus' argument, claiming that action in Troy so far has brought him dishonor instead of honor (*Il.* 9.315–36). He even intimates something he is mulling in his mind, that is, his impending return home. He further explains that Agamemnon's gifts leave him indifferent (356–77), since no imaginable treasure can compensate him for the dishonor and grief Agamemnon has caused him. In a statement foreshadowing Archilochus' Age, Achilles acknowledges that all of Troy's and Delphi's treasures are not sufficient to justify risking his life, because there is nothing as valuable as life itself (401–05).

Since Odysseus' brilliant argumentation fails to melt Achilles' anger, his speech is followed by an equally well-crafted speech on the part of Phoenix. With unparalleled adroitness, Phoenix elaborates points that Odysseus had omitted. Achilles, he argues, has a right to be angry for his mistreatment by Agamemnon, but once the latter recognized his error and apologized publicly by offering overgenerous gifts in compensation and restoration of Achilles' honor, it would be unwise for Achilles to persist in his wrath. Inasmuch as even the gods bend their minds (v. 497), for humans to persist in their anger is dangerous, because stubbornness can easily lead to disaster, another prophetic statement. Is not, after all, *hybris* ordinarily punished by the divine? Unfortunately, Phoenix' hard-hitting argument fails to bend Achilles' mind. On the contrary, it elicits Achilles' caveat that as his man Phoenix ought to take Achilles' side.[43]

---

[43] F. E. Brenk, "The Speech of Phoenix and the Tragedy of Achilles," *Eranos* 84 (1986) 77–86; Ruth Scodel, "The Autobiography of Phoenix: Iliad 9. 444–95" *AJPh* 103 (1982) 128–36; *Il.* 9.401–09 and Kirk ad loc for the sole reference to Delphi in the *Iliad*; Charles Segal, "The embassy of the Duals of Iliad 9.182.98," *GRBS* 9 (1968) 101–114; Adolf Köhnken, "Die Role der Phoinix und die Duale im I der Ilias," *Glotta* 53 (1975) 89–113; Gregory Nagy, *The Best of the Achaeans: Concepts of the Hero in Archaic Greek Poetry* (Baltimore, 1979); Rismag Gordesiani, "Zur Interpretation der Duale in 9 Buch der Ilias," *Philologus* 124 (163–74); A. Thornton, "Once Again, the Duals in Book of the Iliad," *Glotta* 56 (1978) 1–4.

In the face of Achilles' obduracy, Aias unexpectedly and angrily decides to enter the discussion with a short but poignant speech of his own. He castigates Achilles' callousness and indifference to the fate of the Achaean army and expresses his shock that the emissaries from the whole army, holding out a hand of friendship and kindness to Achilles, should have been so harshly snubbed, especially since they have been welcomed and entertained royally by Achilles (v. 640). Aias, the simple and unselfish warrior, cannot believe that Achilles would treat his friends and guests in such an appalling manner in his own house (vs. 643–55).[44]

Admittedly shaken by Aias' brief, simple, spontaneous, straightforward, and angry outburst, Achilles counters with the promise that he will not depart for home. He even goes a step further by making the important concession that he will enter the fighting, if Hector dares come near the ships of the Myrmidons. With these concessions, Achilles signals the end of the meeting with the remark "go and relay my message" (v. 649). Before the envoys depart, however, they take a cup, pour libations, and then leave, with Odysseus leading the way (v. 597). As soon as they reach their impatiently waiting colleagues and the formalities of welcome are finished, Agamemnon is the first to ask Odysseus for his report on the results of his embassy. Odysseus announces the failure of the embassy's overture and in confirmation of his truthfulness he calls upon Aias and the two heralds to be his witnesses.

Once again, the above embassy may not have been a real historical event but part of the Trojan saga found or concocted by the composer of the *Iliad*. As an imaginary description of an ambassadorial event, however, its form fits very well with our knowledge of the Near Eastern ambassadorial missions and the circumstances the poet is outlining. If poets take their inspiration from historical events, then this description is very likely mirroring real practices and procedures existing in the material, oral or written, out of which the poet composed his epics and depicted the diplomatic practices as followed during the writer's time or before his time. Since these practices bear close resemblance to diplomatic practices in the Ancient Near East, the reader is led to the reasonable conclusion that such practices were known in the contemporaneous Aegean Dark Age world and were most probably inherited from the Mycenaean world, notwithstanding the fact that no direct evidence is left to us regarding the diplomatic procedures of

---

[44] *Il.* 9.401–405, 643–55; Kirk ad loc.; Adam Parry, "The Language of Achilles," *TAPA* 87 (1956) 17; Scodel, "The World of Achilles," *CP* 84 (1989) 91–99.

the Mycenaean states in the Writing B tablets unearthed by modern archaeologists. The alternative would be to hypothesize that the similarity in practices was the product of borrowing by the inhabitants of Greece in the period between the Dark Ages and the time the epics were synthesized, sometime in the latter part of the eighth century. This seems a less tenable hypothesis. It is not so easy to accept that the Mycenaeans living adjacently to the Near Eastern states had no diplomatic practices similar to them, or that the immediate descendants of these Mycenaeans borrowed wholesale their diplomatic practices from the Near Easterners. There is no convincing proof that the inhabitants of Greece lacked diplomatic practices, even basic ones, though they had conflicts—before the advent of the twelfth century—the age that archaeologists and earlier historians have labeled as the Dark Age. It is difficult indeed to accept—it is a question of supposition here since no pertinent written evidence has survived—that a highly sophisticated civilization like the Mycenaean with a six hundred year history left no trace of diplomatic practices behind. Nor is it easier or more logical to accept that the alleged catastrophe c. 1200 BC was so total and complete that the inhabitants of Greece resorted to wholesale borrowing of their diplomatic practices from their Near Eastern neighbors. Since the Homeric epics allude to pre-Homeric hostilities, logically it would be impossible to admit that the pre-Homeric societies had no customary practices pertaining to their autonomous inter-community relations, however primitive those relations might be imagined to have been. On the contrary, it is easier to accept that practices of the Homeric epics' point to the existence of such customs in the Aegean Bronze World.

PRIAM'S EMBASSY

The next major occasion in the *Iliad* which necessitates the dispatch of messengers is the death of Hector. The story of this embassy begins with the killing of Hector by Achilles and the desecration of Hector's corpse. It is viewed as a matter of course that in serious duels one would kill his opponent and be declared the victor and that the victor would treat the dead man's body with respect. However, Achilles' hatred for Hector, following Patroclus' death, is so intense that Achilles' thirst for revenge is not satisfied with Hector's death. Achilles' unacceptable treatment of Hector's body displeases the gods, who feel revulsion at this barbarous act. Zeus, articulating the consensus of the divine community, decides to put a stop to this sacrilegious act (*Il.* 24.77 ff.). After all, Hector is a noble and valiant warrior as well as a devout and pious man. Zeus, therefore, asks one of the other gods to have Iris come to him. In reality, Zeus, like a human king, does not call

Iris directly, though she is nearby, but lets another of the gods do so on his behalf. When Iris comes, he charges her with the responsibility of finding Thetis in her watery home, and notifying her that she is wanted by Zeus. Iris dashes off immediately to fulfill Zeus' command.

Upon arrival in Thetis' domain, Iris finds her surrounded by the other goddesses of the sea. Drawing near, she relays Zeus' message.[45] Thetis puts on a dark-colored veil and sets out to meet Zeus, with Iris leading the way. Again we see in this scene that Iris, Zeus' envoy, is accompanying Thetis on her way to Olympus, a pattern typical of the Near Eastern messenger format. As soon as Thetis sits down, Hera places in her hand a fair golden cup and addresses her in cheerful tones (101–02). Only when Thetis finishes her drink does Zeus impart his message to her. He addresses her in a courteous tone, reassuring her that he will continue to honor her. Following this brief introduction, he goes into the reasons for which he has invited her to Olympus (vs. 104–112). Finally, Zeus asks her to inform her son speedily that the gods are angry over his treatment of Hector's body and his refusal to give it up for burial. She should inform her son that he must release Hector's body, and that Zeus means to dispatch Iris to Priam to bid him go to the Achaean ships in order to ransom his son's body. She is also expected to tell Priam that he should bear such gifts that would appease Achilles' heart.[46]

Thetis darts down to Achilles' headquarters to transmit Zeus' message. She finds him groaning ceaselessly and, sitting close to him (v. 126), strokes him gently with her hand. At first, she sympathetically reminds him that mourning should have its limits and that he should slowly return to his normal human activities; then she comes to the real purpose of her visit: the message from Zeus (Διός δέ τοι ἄγγελός εἰμι, *Il.* 24.133). Achilles does not object, if such is the gods' desire. Whoever brings the ransom can bear away the corpse, if this is the wish of the Olympian Zeus (vs. 139–40). With the delivery of her message, Thetis' task is completed, although this is not true for Iris.

Iris' next errand is to visit Priam to tell him that he has to go to Achilles' quarters with rich gifts of ransom, urging him not to be afraid because Hermes will be his escort. When Iris hastens to Priam's house, she finds him weeping and wailing; stopping near Priam she addresses him very softly

---

[45] On the typical form of such divine messenger scenes see Arend, *Scenen*, 54–71.

[46] *Il.* 24.115–19; 19.12–14.

to avoid alarming him. As she starts to speak, Priam's limbs begin to tremble. To instill courage in him, Iris explains that she is Zeus' messenger and that she has come with good intent because Zeus cares for him and pities him. She subsequently proceeds to elaborate on the purpose of her arrival: that he should go ransom his son, bearing copious gifts to please Achilles' heart. Just as the poem began with a ransom scene in which the suppliant is rudely rebuffed, it ends with a similar scene in which the suppliant is treated with great courtesy. The scene shows that Achilles, the killer of so many of Priam's sons during the war, is also human and has respect for human traditions. Priam is to be accompanied only by an elderly herald to help him guide the wagon with which Priam will bring back his son's corpse. For the duration of the trip, Hermes will guide and protect them both until they reach Achilles' quarters. When he arrives there, neither Achilles nor any other will harm him, since Achilles does not lack wisdom, nor is he a malicious individual. On the contrary, Iris stresses Achilles' nurtured respect for the tradition regarding suppliants and messengers.

It is paradoxical that Priam fails to repeat Iris' promise about the divine escort when relaying her message to his wife (vs. 194–99), notwithstanding the fact that Hecuba is understandably frightened by the idea of her husband's perilous journey to the Achaean camp and strongly advises him against it. Skepticism about prophecies, religious omens, or divine apparitions is a frequent occurrence in epic poetry and later Greek literature. It is not at all illogical that, in her grief and anxiety for her husband's security, Hecuba refuses to place any faith in the divine message. Yet, in view of her husband's insistence to carry through his mission, she would rather rely on some personal assurance by a divine vision that will corroborate her husband's trust in the divine apparition. If no visible, favorable omen appears before her husband's departure, Hecuba will advise him against going. The omen that Hecuba advises her husband to seek from Zeus appears in the form of an eagle and disarms her of her objections to Priam's mission. Priam then goes to the storage room whence he chooses bounteous presents for Achilles in recompense for his son's corpse. In the earlier case of Agamemnon, Homer does not merely refer to the presents for Achilles; he goes to the trouble of counting them off and commenting on their extremely precious value. Homer does something similar here with the exception that the witnesses to the enumeration are his listeners, not any kings or allies. The only other witness is his wife Hecuba, who does not seem to be interested in their value or number.

Before her husband departs, Hecuba comes carrying in her right hand a golden cup filled with honey-hearted wine so that the travelers will offer the necessary prayers and libations to the gods for their safe trip. Priam is asked to pour a libation to Zeus, praying to him for a bird of omen which may appear on his right hand-side as a sign of his safe return. Priam feels that lifting up one's hand to Zeus in prayer is a good thing and complies with his wife's wishes. As soon as Priam completes his prayer and libations, Zeus' eagle appears (*Il* 24.302–316).[47]

In the meanwhile, Zeus commands Hermes to accompany Priam to the ships of the Achaeans, remaining visible only to the duo. Hermes has not been active in the *Iliad* up to this point. Now he is commanded to undertake the role of escort rather than messenger, since he has the power to lull men to sleep or wake them up by means of his wand.[48] This may be the reason that the term Homer uses for Hermes in this instance is *diactôr*, not *angelos*, the term for messengers (v. 339). Upon receiving the order, Hermes dons his sandals and takes with him the wand, which combines the functions of the shepherd's scepter, the herald's scepter, and that of a magic wand. Disguised as a young man, Hermes is depicted in a delightful scene between himself and the aged Priam where the contrast of youth and old age produces a moving feeling of sympathy and grace that leads to a lively conversation. Pretending to be the son of the Myrmidon Polyctor, Hermes volunteers some information regarding the immediate plans of the Achaeans for the purpose of making his plausible story persuasive. Irrespective of the validity of Hermes' information, this is the type of information messengers ordinarily pick up from other travelers, merchants, or various people they meet while traveling on their missions through alien lands, and often turn out to be useful to them or their masters.

The next scene describes the arrival of Priam at Achilles' quarters. Priam is not only a messenger but, like Chryses, he is also a supplicant. As

---

[47] *Il.* 24.308–16. Priam goes against his wife's advice but yields to her on the question of prayer for the appearance of an omen. When the omen appeared Hecuba reluctantly yielded. Hecuba's skepticism about omens reminds us of Thomas' skepticism in the evangelical pericope.

[48] Escorting envoys was a frequent practice in the Near East. Not so strangely we find it at this point in Homer. Besides Homer it is found in Greek mythology ostensibly referring to times earlier than the Trojan War. King Lycus, grateful for the news the Argonauts brought him when they touched his coast, offered his son Dascyllus to guide them on their journey along the Pontic coast, see also Apoll. Rhodius 2.803; *Argonautical Orphica*, 279 ff.; Hyg. *Fab.* 14 and 18; Apollod. 1.9.23; Menelaus was ready to escort Telemachus throughout Hellas if the latter wanted to travel there in pursuit of his father's news (*Od.* 15.80–82).

supplicant, he falls to his knees before Achilles and kisses his hands. It is a humiliating gesture but in so doing Priam is engaging in a classic gesture of prostration and self abasement by kissing Achilles' hands.[49] Just as an enemy king might signal his surrender by offering valuable gifts, so Priam comes laden with a trove of gifts.[50] As soon as the two meet, Achilles ushers Priam into his quarters in the traditional fashion and offers him hospitality. Priam, on the other hand, is not ready for the customary hospitality, being overeager to get Hector's body and return to Troy. He can think only of seeing the body of his son, but Priam's haste triggers Achilles' wrath (*Il.* 24.559–60). Frightened by Achilles' angry reaction, Priam decides to comply for fear that he may jeopardize his mission and his own safety. In the meantime, Achilles gives orders to his lieutenants to wash, cleanse, and clothe the corpse in robes from the ransom Priam brought so that dead Hector will not be insulted in his death by lying clothed in his enemy's cloths. When the preparations are finished, Achilles explains that Priam can take his son's body and depart for home but not before he accepts Achilles' hospitality. The meal provides a temporary relief to Priam's mourning, because Achilles might have been angered if Priam continues his lament over Hector's corpse. In this scene, Homer wants to show the wisdom of controlled grief; something about which Thetis had also admonished her son earlier. The emphasis temporarily shifts from Priam's feelings to those of Achilles. To dramatize the depth of Achilles' emotions, the poet has the hero himself lift the body of his enemy onto the bier with an apology to his dead rival (*Il.* 24.594). By so doing, Achilles symbolizes the beginnings of Hector's funeral rites. On the other hand, by asking Priam to participate in a meal, Achilles not only invites Priam to fulfill the standing traditional obligation of a host to guest and messengers but persuades him by the paradigm of Niobe, who

---

[49] Priam is engaging in a classic gesture of prostration and self-abasement by falling to his knees before Achilles and kissing Achilles' hands. And just as an enemy of the Hittite king might signal his surrender by offering valuable gifts, so Priam came laden with treasures, Moran, AL, *EA* 64; 151; 314; Houwink ten Cate, "The History of Warfare According to Hittite Sources: The Annals of Hattusilis I, (Part II)" *Anatolica* 11 (1984) 66–67.

[50] *Il.* 24.228–37 and Kirk, *The Iliad* ad loc. Again in a typical Near Eastern fashion Homer here enumerates the many gifts that Priam took with him for Achilles, as Agamemnon did earlier in his effort to make amends to Achilles for insulting him. The enumeration format is repeated many times in the *Iliad* and the *Odyssey*, Agamemnon-Achilles, Odysseus-Achilles, Menelaus-Telemachus, Nestor-Telemachus, Alcinous-Odysseus, and so on.

thought of food when worn out by weeping (613). The poet chooses the myth because of the parallel of Niobe's many children killed by Leto's two children, just as Priam's many sons have died at the hands of Peleus' only son. In an indirect way, it is also a reminder to his mourning guest that the host regulates the timing of departure. As the rules of hospitality protect the messenger during his stay abroad, they also prevent him from leaving without the host's consent.

No washing of the hands is mentioned in this section, though Priam's hands have been befouled with dust during his days of grief and his travel to Achilles' quarters. This silence about the hand washing may be due to Priam's condition of continued mourning. It becomes a reminder to the reader that Achilles, too, in his grief refuses to wash before his feast with Agamemnon (*Il.* 23.38). There is no prayer, no libation, no conversation recorded over dinner; instead the poet has the two of them gaze silently at each other in admiration.

Following the meal, a bed is prepared on the porch for Priam to rest. The same arrangement is made for young Telemachus in Menelaus' elaborate palace, the arrangement being presumably normal in guest or messenger visitations (*Od.* 4.296). In the case of Priam, there is a special reason for the choice of the porch. Achilles explains that some Greeks may come to talk with him inside his dwelling and report Priam's presence to Agamemnon. The location of Priam's somewhat remote sleeping quarter becomes also convenient for another reason Achilles could not have foreseen: Priam's later unobserved escape. Achilles' mention of Agamemnon reminds us of the unchanged background of the war, and the participle *epikertomeón* may be intended to convey that he and Priam, though united in a hospitable meal, remain formal enemies.

At the end, the timing designated by Achilles for Priam's departure has to be changed. The gods, fearing complications in view of the hostile sentiments among the Achaeans, advise Priam through Hermes not to wait for the morning but to depart under the cover of night. On this occasion, we will never know whether Achilles intends to assign a special escort for Priam's safe conduct, as often happens among the rulers in the Near East. Yet it is not far-fetched to argue that following the customs of the time, Achilles would have assigned some sort of escort for the safe return of the elderly duo. This likelihood is supported by 1) the drift in the meaning of Zeus' message to Thetis; 2) the "miraculous" arrival of Priam at the Achaean and Myrmidon lines through so many dangers, an impossible task indeed that even Achilles attributes to divine intervention (vs. 562–70); 3) Achilles' advice to the old man that he should sleep in the outer section of

Achilles' quarters to avoid detection by any unexpected night visitor (vs. 654–55); and 4) Achilles' promise to Priam of an eleven day-truce for Hector's funeral. All of the above militate against an opposite view which would have been incongruous with traditional practices (v. 667). The possible assignment of a human escort to guard the guests and the corpse during the return trip is not even discussed owing to Priam's abrupt departure. His nocturnal departure at the gods' advice provides an easy solution to the problem of Priam's return, freeing Achilles at the same time from a possibly thorny problem with the rest of the Achaeans.

OTHER MESSENGER CASES

Other messenger cases in the *Iliad* are not as important as the one noted above; nonetheless, they too provide us with inklings into the ambassadorial customs practiced in the pre-Homeric world. In Book Three of the *Iliad* it is Hector himself who is the messenger for his brother Paris. Hector had previously berated his brother for acting irresponsibly during the war, even though he was the cause of it. Paris feels the sting of his brother's reproach deeply enough to suggest a solution to the war in the form of a duel between himself and Menelaus. In sympathy with Paris' suggestion, Hector undertakes the role of messenger-conveyer to the Greeks in the hopes that Paris' suggestion may provide a satisfactory resolution to the protracted conflict. According to Paris' proposal, the winner of the duel will take Helen and her possessions, while the rest will swear friendship and offer oaths of faith accompanied by sacrifices to authenticate the agreement.[51] Acceptance of the agreement entails friendship between the parties that is a mutual defense treaty for the two sides.

Accordingly, Hector goes into the middle of the Trojan army holding his spear by the middle, thereby indicating a pacific intention, which the Achaean troops fail at first to recognize. Agamemnon first notices it and

---

[51] φιλότητα καὶ ὅρκια τάμωμεν, seems to have been one of the standard formulas used by Achaeans and the Near Easterners which Homer continued. For similar standard phrases see *Il*. 2.234, 339; 3.73, 94, 105, 252, 256, and so on. The phrases denote an agreement in which animals were sacrificed as part of the ceremony of cementing an agreement. Although the expression may be metonomized into the oath taking itself, it applies to two separate acts involved in the searing: first the cutting of hair from the victim's head, which is then distributed to the participants (273 ff.), secondly, the cutting of the victim's throat following the pronouncement of the oaths (292). See B. C. Fenik, ed., *Homer: Tradition and Invention* (Leiden, 1978) 19–40.

stops the troops from shooting. The reference of the agreement to possessions (*Il.* 3.70, 72) refers to Helen's possessions, which Paris has carried with him from Sparta, as well as whatever else belonged to Menelaus. Agamemnon further adds a clause for the recompense of Menelaus' honor (*timê*) which is not mentioned in Paris' proposal, but which Agamemnon and the Achaeans cannot easily ignore.[52] As the dishonored person, it is reasonable that Menelaus would insist on payment of that portion of honor taken from him, something that Agamemnon, as his spokesman, now does for him. The inserted compensatory clause makes it clear that the compensation has to be commensurate to the offense committed; otherwise the Greeks will not comply with the agreement but will stay and fight to the end. Agamemnon's addition is a gloss on v. 3.286, which Hector accepts without demur. The agreement is sealed by a sacrificial ceremony during which the names of certain gods are invoked as guarantors. Appropriately, some of the magic elements associated with the history of sacrifices and the swearing ceremony have their correspondence with Near East Eastern elements. The Greek *Helios* is associated with oaths, as is the Mesopotamian sun-god Shamash. Burkert points to the oriental and later Greek parallels for the conjunction in oath invocations to the sun, earth, rivers, and underworld deities. At *Il.* 15.36 ff., we remark that Hera herself swears by Gaia and Ouranus and the river Styx, as well as by Zeus' holy head and their marriage bed. The similarities between the Homeric Dark Age have Near Eastern parallels whose history goes back to the Bronze Age and supports the view of commonality in the swearing practices between the two adjoining areas.[53] At the end, the duel fails to come to the anticipated resolution because Aphrodite abducts Paris at the point when Menelaus is readying to

---

[52] *Il.* 3.286–291. Agamemnon appends an additional term to the agreement to cover the honor of the Argives, τιμὴν δ' Ἀργείοις, not only Menelaus, which he felt would be considered fair by the participants in the war but also by the future generations as well, Kirk, *The Iliad* ad loc.

[53] Walter Burkert, *Greek Religion*, 377–79; Nilsson, *GDGR*, 3rd ed., 129; Kirk, *The Iliad* ad 3.286–91.

Burkert has pointed out the oriental character of the oath formulas. In reality it is nothing but correspondence between the Near Eastern oath and Greek oath. Nowhere do we have explicit and irrefutable evidence of borrowing by the Bronze Age Greeks from the Near Easterners. We can only speak of sharing similar religious ideas. In this instance Burkert may not be right when he speaks of borrowings.

finish him off. The Achaeans blame the Trojans for the non-resolution of the duel, while the Trojans ascribe it to powers beyond their will.

Just prior to the duel, Iris comes to Helen in the likeness of Helen's sister-in-law, Laodice (3.121), and finding her in the palace weaving a purple web, urges her to go watch the duel between Alexander and Menelaus. Homer does not say if Iris is sent by Zeus but the expression "she came as a messenger" (*angelos êlthen*) is a pat expression signifying her dispatch by Zeus whose messenger (*angelos*) she is. Iris does not normally act on her own will. Only in *Il.* 23.198 ff. does she seem to have acted on her own initiative and then in a completely different context.

In the fight that follows Menelaus' wounding (*Il.* 6.86–101), Helenus advises Hector to exhort their mother to gather the aged Trojan wives at the temple of Athena. It is an opportunity for Hector to take the advice of his brother, Troy's best seer, and dart back into the city where Queen Hecuba can organize a special women's appeal to the goddess whom Homer calls Athena. Whether Athena is worshipped at Troy, ancient peoples often borrowed each other's gods. It was not unusual in Anatolia to offer a prayer to a god or goddess for military success, and indeed it is not unusual even today.[54] There she should place upon Athena's knees the best and dearest of her robes and vow to her that she will sacrifice in her temple twelve sleek and unyoked heifers, if only Athena will take compassion on the city, the Trojan wives, and their little children. Hector goes, repeating the message to his mother, with the necessary adjustments from the third person of the verb to the second (6.264–285). Hector's mother in turn repeats the request to Athena's priestess, Theano, who addressed the goddess with the same words that Helenus, Hector, and Hecuba used (303–310).

In the heat of the battle that ensues (*Il.* 7.44–53, 77–85), Athena and Apollo supporting the opposite sides contrive a respite between the combatants. At the same time, Hector's brother Helenus, having overheard the conversation of the two gods, conveyed their words to Hector, asking him at the same time to act as a messenger to the Greeks. Hector, accompanied by the herald Idaeus, stands between the two armies once again, proposing a duel between him and the individual the Achaeans would choose to fight against him. In view of what has transpired in the duel between Alexander

---

[54] The Hittite King Tudhaliyas IV (1237–1209 BC), for example, prayed to the Sun-Goddess of Arinna for victory against an unnamed enemy, possibly the Assyrians, Itamar Singer, "Tudhaliyas' Prayer to the Sun-Goddess of Arinna for Military Success (*CTH* 385.9) in *Hittite Prayers*, 108.

and Menelaus, the Achaeans are at first hesitant but eventually decide to draw lots for the selection of Hector's adversary. The lot falling on Aias Telemonius, the deal is clinched. Hector's proposal entails that the victor will strip the defeated of his armor as part of his spoils, but that he will give up the body for proper burial. Unlike the earlier duel between Paris and Menelaus, whose purpose was the termination of the war, there is no termination clause here. This duel is simply intended to provide an interesting interval for both sides.

Two important facts emerge from this duel agreement. The first is that the heralds, one from each side, are to be assigned to referee the duel; the second that neither of the duelists manages to knock the other out by the end of the day. Since it begins to get dark, the heralds, Talthybius and Idaeus, Achaean and Trojan heralds respectively, take the initiative to stop the fight before an untoward accident happens. As Hector is the challenger, Aias does not wish to agree before Hector does. As soon as Hector gives his consent, the duel is amicably terminated. On this occasion, the heralds are described as messengers of gods and men and are characterized as "prudent" (*Il.* 7.276).[55] The emphasis on prudent (πεπνυμέν⊙) strongly adverts to their proverbial wisdom an example of which is their timely intervention before something unfortunate happens due to darkness. Is Idaeus' address to both of them as 'dear sons' a mere formality that indicates simply his older age or is it a reflection of his feelings about the war in general, revealed so unrestrainedly by a herald with the reputation of wisdom at 7.390–93? Although Idaeus' address is mystifying, one thing emerges clearly in this instance: the right of a messenger to exercise his initiative.

We observe the same right of initiative in the incident that follows soon after the duel ends. In this incident, the Trojans and their allies hold an assembly in the process of which the Trojan Antenor, feeling obviously guilty like many other Trojans over the ostensible cheating in the duel between Paris and Menelaus, proposes Helen's return along with her posses-

---

[55] πεπνυμένῳ ἄμφω, both prudent. The characterization is repeated at 9.689 and 3.148 for another pair of heralds. For the various use of the scepter see note on *Il.* 2.109, Kirk, *The Iliad* ad loc. who admits that the uses of the scepter were ancient and hallow, something that may imply Bronze Age origins. The scepter as a hallowed symbol was known and used by the messengers of primitive tribes as well, Sir Walter B. Spencer, *Wanderings in Wild Australia*, 1 (London, 1928 312–14; Regnar Numelin, *The Beginnings of Diplomacy* (London, 1950) 167.

sions in exchange for a peaceful resolution of the war. Paris strenuously objects to the return of Helen but is ready to return her possessions, even to add compensation to Menelaus from his own possessions (7.362–64). To break the impasse in the assembly, Priam submits his own motion as a compromise between the above two proposals. He suggests that the next morning the Trojans dispatch Idaeus to the Achaean camp to relay Paris' proposal and to add that the Trojans stand ready to make a truce that allows both parties to burn their dead (7.372–78). Priam's motion is accepted, and Idaeus leaves the following morning for the Achaean camp.

Idaeus lays before the Achaean assembly Priam's proposal along with Paris' refusal to return Helen. There is no evidence in the epic that Idaeus is authorized to divulge Paris' refusal. Consequently, Idaeus, distinguished though he is for his wisdom and caution, goes surprisingly beyond the bounds of the authority invested in him as messenger since, in addition to the unauthorized statement, he further intimates that Antenor's proposal has received wide acclamation in the assembly, and that he personally wishes that Paris were dead. No doubt Idaeus is here signaling Paris' general unpopularity in Troy (*Il.* 3.453), but whether as negotiator for the Trojan side it is wise on his part to do so at this critical juncture is very doubtful. In the end, at the urging of Diomedes, the Achaeans reject the Trojan proposal about Helen's possessions and Paris' inadequate compensation, agreeing only to a truce for the burning of the dead (*Il.* 7.400–404).

Idaeus' attitude is puzzling. As a Trojan messenger, he has the obligation to promote the official Trojan proposal for the purpose of making peace. Instead, he divulges what transpired in the Trojan assembly, something that is bound to anger the Achaeans and wreck all possibilities for peace. Idaeus' action might have been artistically required for the epic plot, but from the practical standpoint it shows the exercise of poor judgment on the part of an envoy distinguished for his wisdom, and it is no wonder that the Achaean response is quick and immediate. Except for the conclusion of the truce for the burial of the dead, Idaeus' mission proves a failure.

DIVINE MESSENGERS

Beyond the human messengers we find in the Homeric literature, we also encounter deities serving in the role of messengers. Thetis and Iris repeatedly serve in that capacity, the first on behalf of Zeus and Achilles, the second on Zeus' behalf. From the evidential standpoint, the use of gods or goddesses as messengers may seem absurd; nevertheless the ancient Greeks imagined the world of the gods in many respects like their own, and taken from that perspective, the use of and references to divine messengers may help us in the examination of human messenger practices. One might gainsay that the gods are carriers of messages and not diplomats; yet to the degree that they carry messages for others, play the role of mediator, as Iris does, and exercise their initiative or judgment in the presentation of the message, they fulfill duties similar to those of the human messengers. Thetis' service as Zeus' messenger for her son reveals valuable insights about messenger activities in the ancient world. After all, divine messengers are not portrayed much differently in general from the humans, except in the supernatural qualities they allegedly possess, such as their extraordinary speed, immunity to danger in traveling, invisibility where needed, and so on. Such supernatural qualities, therefore, will not be taken into consideration in the investigation of messenger practices.

In Book One (397 ff.), Thetis goes to Zeus as her son's messenger, asking him to return the favor Thetis earlier bestowed on the father of gods and men. Having found Zeus on Olympus, she places her left hand on his knees, while with the right hand she clasps him below the chin, the traditional position of suppliants. She then proceeds quickly to a relatively full statement of her son's request and the circumstances that triggered it. She could reinforce her petition by setting out her earlier benefaction to Zeus, an act that would have strengthened her claim to a counter-benefit from Zeus (*Il.* 1.396–406) but she does not; instead, she opts to be more discreet by explaining how much Zeus would despise her, if he refused to accede to her petition. Thetis connects her appeal to the heroic theme of *timê*. She intentionally avoids reminding Zeus of the humiliation from which she saved him, because it would have been a tactless reminder of an experience he would rather forget (514–16). Though fearful that Hera would react negatively to Thetis' petition, Zeus' answer to Thetis is in the affirmative.

Subsequently, Zeus orders Dream to go to Agamemnon to relay Zeus' message. In this instance, Dream assumes the form of old man Nestor, a figure universally respected by the Greeks and delivers Zeus' message during Agamemnon's sleep. He is told to unleash an attack upon the Trojans now when all the gods are unanimous in their support of the Greeks (*Il.* 2.8–15). Having delivered the message, Dream departs immediately (*Il.* 2.50–52). Bronze Age people took dreams seriously as messages from gods, as did their descendants in the Iron Age. Agamemnon is so excited that he calls a council of the other kings to pass on the news. They agree to get the men into their armor and on the field. But Agamemnon suggests a slight delay. He will call the men into an assembly first to test their morale (*Il.* 16.211–18). In the end, the test Agamemnon suggests turns into a fiasco to the point that the leaders have a hard time trying to restrain the troops from boarding the ships to return home. Thanks to Hera's intervention and Odysseus' use of a mixture of persuasion and force, the Greeks are prevented from sailing off for Greece (*Il*. 2.186–190).

The second instance in which Athena undertakes the role of messenger (p.132) is after the duel between Paris and Menelaus. In this episode Hera prods Zeus to contrive a way whereby the prevailing stalemate between Greeks and Trojans will come to an end. Unable to bear his wife's constant nagging, Zeus sends Athena to the troops to reignite hostilities (4.69–72).[56] The manner in which Zeus' command is to be executed seems to be left to Athena's initiative. Following the execution of this task, Athena is again sent as a messenger to Achilles, upon the death of Patroclus. Traumatized by Patroclus' death, Achilles vows not to taste food or drink before burying Patroclus. Concerned over Achilles' abstinence and its deleterious effects on his health, Zeus dispatches Athena to soothe his hunger by shedding into his breast nectar and pleasant ambrosia (*Il*. 19.341–48). Athena needs no prodding; she dashes off immediately to execute Zeus' command. She has to comply with Zeus' order, but again the manner whereby his order is executed seems to have been left to her initiative.

Still another god who serves as divine messenger in the Trojan War is Apollo. Unlike Iris, who is dispatched on all sorts of missions, Apollo is used by Zeus for a single mission to the Trojans. Apollo is a most appropriate choice for that mission since he is pro-Trojan and also possesses healing powers required for Hector's therapy. In this case as in other Near Eastern and Homeric cases, we see the use of the right man (or god) for the appropriate mission. Apollo has to shake his aegis over the Achaean warriors for the purpose of inspiring terror among them, and once he accomplishes that task to arouse strength in Hector's chest and protect him until the Achaeans take to flight. With the speed of a hawk, Apollo darts down to the Trojan

---

[56] *Il*. 4.69; Kirk, *The Iliad* ad loc.; Zeus at 4.72 gives concise instructions to Athena using Hera's exact words by adjusting *Il*. 4.65 and repeating 4.66 ff. For Agamemnon's dream there are plenty of parallels in the Ancient world and the Bible as well. King Naramsin of the Sumerian epic (c. 2000 BC), for example, saw the ruin of his city in a dream, J. S. Cooper, *The Curse of Agade* (John Hopkins University Press, 1983) 1.86, p. 55; a thousand years later King Hattusilis III (c. 1267–1237 BC) had a dream in which goddess Ishtar promised success in a dangerous court case, Hoffner, Jr., "Apology of Hattusilis III" in Hallo, ed., *Context of Scripture*, vol. 1, 200 and Pharaoh Merneptah (c. 1213–1203) received the word of victory from god Ptah in a dream; Scaplinger, *War in Ancient Egypt: The New Kingdom* (Oxford, Backwell, 2005); also Xerxes, Hdt. 7.12–19.

troops where Hector is recovering from a wound inflicted earlier upon him by Aias. He draws near Hector, identifies himself and speaks words of encouragement, telling him to be of good cheer because Zeus has sent him to succor him. It appears that it is left to the initiative of Apollo to instruct Hector as to how he can rout the Achaeans, promising him simultaneously help and protection.

In the *Iliad*, Dream, Athena, and Apollo serve as Zeus' emissaries, though his chief messenger is Iris. We have already seen Iris' role in the acquisition of Hector's corpse, but this is not her only activity as messenger in the *Iliad*. In Book Two (2.786), Iris goes to the assembled Achaeans to deliver a message from Zeus to their leaders.[57] On this occasion, we do not have the exact message given to her but from the context of what follows, we can safely surmise what the gist of the message must have been. Zeus' message seems to have told Iris to goad the Trojans and their allies to start the fighting against the Greeks. Assuming the voice and form of Polites, the son of Priam, Iris approaches Priam first and chides him for his love of words when action is necessary. Subsequently, she warns him that the Greeks have assembled and are readying for war. Turning then to Hector, the actual commander of the Trojan troops, she commands him to lead the Trojans against the Achaeans.

Like a perfect diplomat, Iris addresses Priam first, since he is the reigning king of Troy, turning to Hector only when she finishes with Priam. Zeus' message apparently consists of two parts, one for Priam and the other, the more significant, for Hector. Since both leaders are sitting side by side in the assembly, Zeus most probably includes an address to Priam, and Iris delivers it by following the protocol, hence her address first to Priam (*Il.* 2.796–801). If Iris' message is intended only for Hector, then prudent Iris uses her ambassadorial discretion by addressing the king first.

In *Il.* 8.399–408, Zeus sends another message, warning all the other gods not to intervene with his plans regarding the war since he has decided to aid the Trojans. What follows is an Achaean rout. Hera and Athena view the Achaean catastrophe with trepidation and being unable to bear it decide to ignore Zeus' orders and intervene. As they leave Olympus, Zeus spots

---

[57] Iris serves also as Hera's messenger in Greek mythology, see Robert Graves, *The Greek Myths*, 1, p. 270 and 2.230j. Poseidon used his own messengers one of them being appropriately Delphinus, Graves, 1, p. 59b; Apoll. 3.1.5; Heginus, *Poetic Astronomy*, 2.17; J. T. Killen, "Observations in the Thebes Sealilngs,' in *Mykenaika: Acts du IXe Collogue International sur les Textes Myceniens et Egéens, Athèenes, 2–6 Octobre, 1990*, BCH suppl. 25 (Paris, 1994) 67–84.

them from Mt. Ida and immediately dispatches Iris to warn them to cease and desist, unless they wish to see their horses crippled, their chariots smashed, and they themselves hurled out of their chariots and struck by his thunderbolt. Iris overtakes the goddesses as they exit the gate of Olympus. Before she delivers Zeus' message, however, she inquires why they sought to enrage Zeus with their disobedience. Following this cautionary warning, she proceeds with the delivery of Zeus' message, chiding Athena with caustic words like "bold bitch" (κῦον ἀδεές, *Il.* 8.423). Messengers from a king-lord to a vassal could sometimes use scurrilous language toward a vassal, but the reverse was not customary. In this case, for Iris, seemingly a minor deity in the divine hierarchy, to address a higher ranking goddess in such terms is, to say the least, piquing. Perhaps her empowerment by Zeus as his messenger and her perception that Athena is the major culprit in the contravention of Zeus' order emboldens Iris in her strong choice of language. Equally, her fear that the action of both goddesses might have deleterious results in the order of Olympus leads to the use of such words. Be that as it may, this is a fascinating scene of a "quasi" democratic divine society in which Iris feels free enough to chide a major goddess in the most scurrilous terms. The scene presents Zeus as angrier at Athena not simply because she has put her armor on as if she is going to war but also because she is Zeus' child and is expected to have greater respect for the paternal orders. At the end, Iris' intervention puts an immediate stop to the goddesses' plan for action and additional complications are avoided.

During another battle between the two hostile camps, Zeus sends Iris again to bear a message to Hector (*Il.* 11.186–94). The message warns Hector that as long as Agamemnon is raging amid the foremost fighters Hector should hold back from war, though he should continue to exhort the rest of the army to fight on. But as soon as Agamemnon is wounded and retires from the battlefront, Hector is to enter the fight and start slaying the enemy until he comes to the beached ships of the Achaeans. Iris comes to Hector, and once she delivers the message, she immediately departs (*Il.* 11.186–209).

Elsewhere in the *Iliad* Zeus uses Iris to send a message to his brother Poseidon. With this message, Zeus asks Poseidon to cease helping the Achaeans and retire to the sea. The message also contains a threat against Poseidon, if the latter shows reluctance to conform. Iris leaves immediately to relay the messages and upon finding Poseidon, she greets him tactfully with honorific titles, explaining the purpose of her errand. To disassociate herself from what is an obviously offensive message, she cleverly elucidates that she is not carrying an order, though in essence the verb *kelefse* (commanded) clearly denotes as much (*Il.* 15.174–76). Despite Iris' effort at "window dressing," Poseidon finds the message and its tone offensive. He does not deny that Zeus as the elder of the two deserves Poseidon's respect but resents Zeus' imperial tone, citing their natural equality as brothers. After all, he is not one of Zeus' children to be told what to do, especially since they share earth and Olympus, and Zeus has no exclusive authority over them.[58] Much like an independent Homeric hero, Poseidon finds Zeus' command offensive to his honor, as Iris is afraid he would, hence her preliminary efforts to soften its impact.

Poseidon is determined to resist Zeus' pretensions but prudent Iris intervenes. Is she to deliver that harsh and unyielding answer to Zeus, she asks Poseidon? She suggests that Poseidon change the tone of his answer by pointing out to him that only the hearts of fools remain unbent; the hearts of the wise are changeable (*Il.* 15.203). She also reminds him that the Erinyes followed Zeus as the first-born, a special reference to the sanctity of the family about to be disturbed if Poseidon persists in his attitude.[59] Poseidon compliments Iris for her wisdom, though he continues to denounce his brother's presumptuousness. In the end, he changes his answer, realizing that Zeus is going to allow the destruction of Troy anyway. Notwithstanding Poseidon's changed answer, Iris does not hasten to depart because even Poseidon's toned-down answer is not sufficiently satisfactory to her. She points out the weakness of Poseidon's argument and patiently waits for

---

[58] *Il.* 15.190 ff.; for details see Kirk, *The Iliad* ad loc. The cosmic division cited in this section of Homer has Babylonian parallel but it is not necessarily a borrowing from it, Burkert, *Die orientalisierende Epoch der griechischen Religion and Literatur, Sitzungsberichte der Bayerischen Akademie der Wissenschaften, Phil.—Hist. Klasse* (Stuttgard, 1984) abt.1. The gods had clasped hands, cast lots and divided the universe. Anu took the sky but gave the earth to his subjects, the Sea to Enki. See parallels in Apoll. 1.2.1 and *Orphica*, for proof that Homer drew this tale from the early story of Titanomachy, like other allusions in the deceptions of Zeus (14.153–353) see Kirk, *The Iliad* ad loc. In both texts the lottery follows the Titans' defeat, to which Zeus alludes at 224 ff. See further Pindar *Ol.* 7.55; Hesiod, *Theog.* 73 ff.; 881–85; Heracleitus, *Homeric Allegories* 41.5; *Od.* 14.208; Stesich., *Thebaid* 209 ff.; H. L. Levy, *TAPA* 89 (1956) 42.46. The division of the patrimony continues in modern times in Greece among the male heirs, since the girls are often given dowry, E. Fridl, *Vasilika* (New York, 1962) 60–64; I. J. F. de Jong, *Narrators and Focalizers: The Presentation of the Story in the Iliad* (Amsterdam, 1987) 180–92; On the negatives in 162 see P. Chatraine, *Grammaire Homérique*, 2 (Paris, 1963) 333–336; Kirk, *The Iliad* ad 176 claims that some ancient texts must have used κελεταί σε for σ' ἐκέλευσε.

[59] Zeus' threat is contained in the participle ἐπιόντα and the phrases that follow, *Il.* 15.164, 178–79.

an even milder response. Only when she receives a satisfactory answer does she leave. An unwise, indifferent, or inexperienced messenger might have hurried to relay to her sender an offensive answer, which could have had destructive consequences. Iris' prudence forestalls the worst, as Zeus explains to Apollo (*Il.* 15.224–27).

Although Iris appears in the *Iliad* as Zeus' messenger, her role does not preclude her from servicing others, namely Hera, who sends her as a messenger to Achilles, unbeknownst to Zeus (*Il.* 18.166 ff.). Although in this case we do not have Hera's message, we cannot be too far off target in presuming that the message is not much different from the message she delivers to Achilles. The message spurs Achilles to assist in the recovery of Patroclus' body, which the Trojans and Greeks are fighting over. The stakes are high in that if Hector seizes the body, he will decapitate it and impale the head, which he boasted he would do. His threat is ironic and incongruous in view of Hector's concern with his own body, as manifested in the earlier duel with Aias as well as in the agreement he seeks to strike with Achilles, just before their final, fateful encounter (*Il.* 7.76–81; 22.342–43).

Achilles complains to Iris that because his armor has been captured by Hector, his mother has explicitly forbidden him to get involved in the fighting until she returns with a new armor from Hephaestus. Iris acknowledges his situation but advises him to show himself at the trench, in the hope that his mere appearance will frighten and scatter the Trojans, thereby giving a respite to the war-weary Achaeans. We do not know whether Iris' admonition is anticipated in Hera's original message or simply that Iris exercises her initiative as a messenger. From the limited evidence at our disposal, the latter seems to be true (*Il.* 18.170.86).

All of the cases examined above have revolved around the messengers in the *Iliad* and the practices associated with them. The same procedure will be pursued in the discussion of the messengers in the *Odyssey* in order to establish their possible similarities to the Iliadic embassies and the extent to which their ambassadorial practices reflect the world of the pre-Homeric and Homeric world.

MESSENGERS IN THE ODYSSEY

The information in the *Odyssey* is not as plentiful as that in the *Iliad*, and the circumstances of messenger activities are somewhat different. There is also a slightly different perspective in the *Odyssey*, which describes interstate embassies that operate farther apart geographically than those in the *Iliad*. The term interstate denotes politically and geographically autonomous areas, predominantly homoethnic, though not always, headed by big men who cherish their independence and autonomy in their greater or smaller political units. The important feature in the interstate communications is their similarity to those of the Near East. In the *Iliad* as in the *Odyssey*, there are missions undertaken by "state" representatives as well as by divine messengers. The embassy of young Telemachus is one point in case. Before he can undertake an embassy, he has to acquire greater confidence in himself. He seems to have the potential, but he needs encouragement, which he receives through divine intervention. Goddess Athena goads him and distills the required confidence into him.

Telemachus undergoes this change in the beginning of the *Odyssey* (1–10). There the poet speaks about the present and the future of *Odyssey*'s hero (11–21), the subject of discussion in the divine assembly of Olympus, in the absence of Poseidon. In a proposal submitted by Athena (81–95), the gods decide that Hermes should go to the island of Calypso to notify her of the gods' decision, to wit that she must release Odysseus so that he can return to his island. On the other hand, Athena herself is to go to Ithaca to motivate the son of the hero to embark on a voyage in search of information about his father.

Telemachus welcomes Athena in the form of Mentis and entertains her in his father's palace (113–143). After dinner, a dialogue begins between the two (156–318) which ends with a loaded statement, namely that if her interlocutor is really the son of Odysseus, this relation binds him to certain obligations. She endeavors to build Telemachus' morale in order to direct to him the second deliberate question (222–229), but Telemachus' answer is not direct (231–251). Athena makes a reference to Odysseus again, urging Telemachus to surpass the intermediate stage between young adulthood and maturity by suggesting that he should grasp the bull by the horns and immediately demand the withdrawal of the suitors from the palace. Next, he should undertake a trip to Pylos and Sparta and, depending on the information he collects, should determine the future of the suitors' relation to his mother. To kindle his interest, the goddess cites to him the case of Orestes (3.250–305).

In the midst of their discussion, Penelope makes an unexpected visit to them. What impresses us in the scene that follows is the sudden change of attitude by the ostensibly "shy" Telemachus and his address to his mother (349–359). He disputes the reason for his mother's coming down from the upper rooms and leaves her dumbfounded by asking her to return to her quarters; from here on, he says, she should recognize the role he intends to play in the palace. Then he displays a second example of his bravado, this time toward the suitors (368–419). He speaks boldly to them while he further decides to call an assembly in Ithaca for the next day and announces its agenda. Stunned, the suitors want to know if the gods are teaching him to be a man (*Od.* 1.381–82, 400–411). Telemachus gives straightforward and bold answers to the suitors (389–98, 413–19) by which it becomes clear that Telemachus has undergone some "miraculous" change that has brought a sudden maturation. He has been freed from his mother's overprotection and domination and is not afraid to face the suitors, at least not as much as before.

Despite Athena's prodding, Telemachus relapses to hesitancy when Athena suggests an exploratory trip regarding his father's whereabouts. He claims that his "youth" and his "inexperience" make him hesitant to query older persons such as Nestor who possess wisdom and experience.[60] His inexperience and youth notwithstanding, Athena continues to encourage him to undertake the trip, assuring him that he will do well despite his initial trepidation. Having mastered his fears, Telemachus leaves for Pylos, after shrewdly escaping the careful guard of the ever-plotting suitors. Athena sets sail with him, serving as his mentor, escort, and guide.

By some strange coincidence, Odysseus in his youth had also gone on an embassy to Messene, sent by his father and the elders of Ithaca to collect a debt for the three hundred sheep and their shepherds some Messenians had ostensibly stolen from Ithaca. The *Odyssey* describes Odysseus as a very young man and the trip as long. Nothing is said about Odysseus' "diplomatic" experience. The epic's silence on this matter may point to Odysseus' precocious and charismatic nature in contrast to Telemachus' timidity, of which the greater extent is undoubtedly due to the lack of paternal guidance and his traumatic experiences with the suitors. Homer does not cite the specific place to which Odysseus went beyond the general reference to Messenia. Had he journeyed to Pylos, Homer would have surely mentioned Odysseus' landing in Nestor's region. The story of Odysseus' embassy is of significance because it demonstrates that, like the Near Eastern kings, the Homeric kings do not shy away from sending their young sons on diplomatic missions to represent them and their community when the occasion requires it (*Od.* 21.11–21). Obviously, sending an heir on an ambassadorial

---

[60] *Od.* 3.21–24 and Heubeck, *A Commentary* ad loc.

mission is not merely a Homeric or Dark Age myth, if we are to judge from Near Eastern history, but a well-known Bronze Age practice.[61]

When Telemachus' ship reaches Pylos, Nestor and his people are celebrating Poseidon's feast near the beach. Recent finds of archaeological evidence suggest that these sorts of communal feastings were typical of the Mycenaean culture, in which the anax (*wanax*) was involved.[62] A fragment of a tablet from Blegen's dump unearthed in 1995 has been associated with several fragmentary tablets of the Un series, all previously known. The resulting joints of the tablet, while still incomplete, point to a list of commodities, including wheat and barely, an ox, honey, unguent and figs. It is hard to see here anything but another list of banquet supplies. In Mycenaean times, such meals were a mechanism whereby the chief man could assert and enhance his authority by rewarding his dependents and friends. It would be safe to say that such occasions had a ritualistic dimension, even though it is not always possible to distinguish purely religious feasts from those that served political purposes. The same is also true about similar banquets in the Dark and later ages in Greek history.

As soon as Nestor's people spot Telemachus' company, they come forward to meet the unexpected guests, asking them to join in the celebration of Poseidon. Following the libations and prayers in honor of the guests' arrival, dinner is served, and only when the guests finish eating does Nestor ask Telemachus about their origins and the purpose of their coming. One could easily surmise from recent archaeological findings that libations and prayers associated with Poseidon's feast were regular customs in Mycenaean times, their origins buried deeply in the Bronze Age. A bolster-shaped altar in front of a bench unearthed in Mycenae belongs to a Tsountas House shrine. The altar has a hollow extension on the western side,

---

[61] Moran, AL, *EA* 137.36–51; 138.71–80; 198.24–31. The parable of the Vineyard in the New Testament may be an echo of the above practice, Mk. 12.6–9; Matt. 21.33–46; Lk. 20.9–19.

[62] E. F. French, "Cultic Places at Mycenaea," in R. Hägg and N. Marinattos eds., in *Sanctuaries and Cults in the Aegean Bronze Age* (Stockholm, 1981) 41–48; K. Kilian, "Zeugnisse mykenische Kultausübung in Tiryns," in Hägg and Marinatos, eds., *Sanctuaries and Cults* (1981) 49–58; (1981); Robin Hägg, "The Role of Libations in Mycenaean Ceremony and Cult," in R. Hägg and Gullög E. Norquist, *Celebrations of Death and Divinity in the Bronze Age Argolid, Proceedings of the Sixth International Symposium at the Swedish Institute at Athens, 11–13 June, 1988*, pp. 177–184; R. Hägg, "Official and Popular Cults in Mycenaean Greece," in *Sanctuaries and Cults*, 35–39; Kilian "Zeugnisse mykenischer Kultausübung in Tiryns," in *Sancutaries and Cults*, 49.58.

while a runnel leads from it to a jar in the floor, suggesting that it was used for libations.[63] Similar examples of ritualistic vessels have been found in other places as well. In House G in Asine, a deliberately broken jug was fixed upside down at the east end of a bench, suggesting that libations were offered there. A broken jar-neck at Ayios Konstantinos in Methana may have served as a receptacle for libations as well.[64]

Nestor is overjoyed to meet Odysseus' son but is unable to enlighten him about Odysseus' whereabouts. He suggests that Telemachus go on to Sparta in the hope that Menelaus might know more. He offers to expedite his trip by providing a chariot, horses, and his son Peisistratus as a guide and escort (*Od.* 3.480). Eager for any news, Telemachus seizes Nestor's suggestion, departing the next morning for Sparta, accompanied by Peisistratus. Before Telemachus' departure, hosts and guests pray, the prayers undoubtedly being accompanied by the pouring of libations to Athena for a safe and successful trip and crowning them by a meal. When the meal is over, Nestor's wife loads the chariot with all sorts of provisions and dainties for the trip as the hosts see the guests off.

Menelaus is extremely pleased to see the two youths in Sparta. He sets a rich table for them and their companions, and after the hearty meal he asks about their identity and the purpose of their trip to Sparta. Though no mention of libations and prayers is made before the dinner, the washing of the hands certainly implies some such activity. Menelaus suggests that Telemachus stay at his palace for at least eleven or twelve days. Telemachus counters by begging Menelaus to understand that, despite his willingness to remain in Sparta, personal and family business dictate his quick return (*Od.* 4.747). Telemachus' explanation points to his recognition that the guest's departure depends largely on the host's consent and that the best Telemachus can do without being rude is to beg his host for his understanding (*Od.* 4.598–99).

Telemachus' desire for a speedy departure is further intensified by Athena who appears in his sleep and advises him to speed up his return to Ithaca. Consequently, Telemachus wakes up in the middle of the night urging Peisistratus to yoke the horses and prepare himself for immediate depar-

---

[63] Hägg, "The Role of Libations in Mycenaean Ceremony and Cult," in *Celebrations of Death and Divinity in the Bronze Age Argolid*, 178.

[64] Å. Åkerström, "Cultic Installations in Mycenaean Rooms and Tombs," in French and Wardle, eds., *Documents in Mycenaean Greek*, 2nd ed. (Bristol, 1988) 201–202.

ture. Peisistratus objects for two reasons: first, because traveling during the night is dangerous, and secondly because it is not customary for the guest to depart without the host's approval or consent (*Od.* 15.45–55). Acknowledging the validity of these objections, Telemachus decides to postpone his departure until dawn. In the morning, Telemachus divulges to his host his desire to depart and Menelaus consents only on the understanding that he will be allowed to serve them a meal and place on their wagon some gifts. Menelaus has no wish to hold Telemachus back without his consent (vs.66–68), voicing his disagreement with the practice of holding back a guest longer than the guest desires. "Due measure in all things is better," he said, pointing out that it is equally wrong to hasten the departure of a guest who is loath to go (*Od.* 15.72–74).[65] Menelaus' response demonstrates the rational Greek approach which likely regulated the principle of hospitality and other prevailing customs. Subsequently, libations are poured and the customary farewell banquet takes place, at the end of which Menelaus presents a beautiful chariot with its horses as a present to his guest. Telemachus thanks him for the expensive gifts but asks him if it would be possible to exchange it with something more suitable to the terrain of Ithaca (*Od.* 4. 590 ff.).[66] When this is done, the guests leave for their return trip to Pylos.

---

[65] *Od.* 15.72–74; Heubeck, *A Commentary* ad loc. and *Od.*1.315

[66] Another potential analogy with the Near Eastern practices might be reflected in the number of horses Menelaus was giving Telemachus, three horses for the chariot, the two regular and one as a spare. A similar occasion we find in *Il.* 16.152. Achilles kept as a spare the horse Pedasus which he had taken when he captured Éetion's city, a mortal horse next to the immortals Xanthus and Balion. Chariots usually have two horses in Homer, one has three, *Od.* 4.590. Chariots with three horses and soon four were "invented" in the Levant during the ninth century and reached Greece and Etruria by the eighth century according to P. A. L. Greenhallgh, *Early Warfare* (Cambridge University Press, 1973) 27–29; *Il.* 15.679–84 and note in Kirk, *The Iliad* ad loc. The extra horse before the ninth century was not yoked but was invariably controlled by traces (περηορίαι) harnessed along side through a ring in the yoke. Kirk, *The Iliad II.* 15.75 where Kirk does not consider Pedasus as a spare as Pedasus is the mortal steed among immortals, see E. Cassin, J. Bottéro, and J. Vercourtter, eds. *Die altorientalischen Reiche, II, Das Ende des 2. Jartausends, in the series Fischer Weltgeschichte*, vol. 3 (Fischer Bücherei, 1966) 54. There is a related reference to Solomon's stables in the *Fischer Weltgeschichte* that they consisted of fourteen hundred chariots with four thousand horses, almost three horses per chariot, vol. 4, p. 155; *CAH*, vol. 2, part 2, p. 589; W. G. Albright, *Archaeology and the Religion of Israel*, 3rd ed. (Baltimore, 1953) 135 ff. We also learn that in a rebellion that broke out in the thirty fifth year of Tuthmosis III's reign Tuthmosis marched

Before they reach Pylos, they stop in Pherae to spend the night at the house of Diocles, as they had done on their way to Sparta.[67]

Once the company comes within a safe distance of Pylos, Telemachus suggests to Peisistratus that they part company before their approach at Nestor's house. This request stems from Telemachus' certitude that Nestor will keep him at his palace for some time before he lets him return to Ithaca. Since he feels that it would be contrary to custom to refuse Nestor's hospitality, Telemachus prefers to leave directly for Ithaca without another stop. Peisistratus complies reluctantly, aware that his compliance contravenes the prevailing etiquette regarding hospitality and that his father will rebuke him. Both instances exemplify the powerful influence the old aristocratic traditions exercise on Bronze Age social relations.[68]

---

to deal with it, encountering the Mitanni at a place called Arana, northwest of Aleppo, and sending them fleeing headlong. In spite of the chronicler's insistence on the great size of the Mitanni chariot force, only ten prisoners were taken, the chief prize supposedly being 60 chariots and 180 horses, a team and a spare for each chariot, *CAH*, vol. 2, part 1, 3rd ed. P. 458. The stables for horses and chariots in Megiddo have been excavated together with the remains of the interior of the building. The stables were fit to accommodate about a hundred and fifty chariots and around four hundred and fifty horses, W. F. Albright, *From the Stone Age to Christianity*, 2nd ed. (Baltimore, 1946) 123; Albright, *Archaeology*, 66, 135; *CAH* vol. 2, part 2, p. 589.

[67] *Od.* 21.16–21; Russo, *A Commentary*, ad loc. Odysseus had stayed at Ortilochus' house when he visited Messene as envoy for his father and the Ithacan elders in order to collect the compensation for the robbery some Messenians had committed. The Ortilochus referred to here is the father of Diocles in whose house Telemachus stayed on his way to Sparta and on his return from Sparta. That Odysseus and Telemachus opted to stay at Ortilochus' house may indicate the existence of some kind of guestship between the two houses. W. A. McDonald, "Overland Communications in Greece during LH III," in *Mycenaean Studies* (Madison, Wisc., 1964) 224–34.

[68] Achilles had ended the meeting with the two Achaean envoys dispatched by Agamemnon and the council with the abrupt remark "go inform the Achaeans of my decision," a remark that seems to have infuriated Aias, *Il.* 9.649. He squashed equally rudely Priam's attempt to depart immediately after getting Hector's corpse. Achilles' attitude is a reminder to Priam that the host makes the decision regarding the guest's departure, and that Priam, his pain notwithstanding, should not forget it. In the instance of Telemachus' stay in Sparta, Peisistratus had to remind him of the etiquette of guest departure, and as a result Telemachus had to ask Menelaus's permission to depart earlier than Menelaus wanted him to go, *Od.* 4.594–599.

HERMES VISITS CALYPSO

As noted earlier, the *Odyssey* begins with Odysseus' sojourn at goddess Calypso's island. In a fascinating scene, Homer portrays Hermes' speeding to the island to deliver Zeus' message (5. 43–46). Prior to his arrival at Calypso's palace, Hermes' only stop was at her island in order to look at its marvelous scenery. Once he reaches Calypso's house there is no need for introductions because Calypso knows him. She is nonetheless inquisitive about the purpose of his visit as visits by Hermes are very infrequent (*Od.* 5.89–90). She poses the question which Hermes, not so oddly, fails to answer; nor does the nymph wait for his answer. Instead, as if embarrassed by the question, she rushes into her palace to set the dinner table. Only when Hermes satisfies his hunger and thirst does he volunteer to answer her question (*Od.* 5. 91.100).

In the conversation between the two divinities, we observe some interesting features bearing on our topic. As in the cases of human messengers, Hermes admits that he dislikes going on long embassies which he finds fatiguing. In addition, he complains, that fatigue is compounded by the drabness of the journey's terrain since there are no aesthetic attractions, such as cities of mortals to add color to it. Clearly, Hermes' complaints are similar to those aspects that often make the messengers' tasks unpleasant. Humans too are overawed by long distances, dreary places, and the long stretches of deserted areas, where dangers lurk in the form of marauders, bandits, or wild animals, not to mention the many serious perils in the early days of seafaring.

Calypso's reaction to Zeus' message is petulant. She characterizes the gods as cruel and envious; yet she has to comply with the message and promises that she will provide Odysseus with the necessary supplies and the proper advice for his voyage to Ithaca. Odysseus, however, has to make the trip to Ithaca alone since she has no ships at hand to send him along with an escort-convoy (*Od.* 5.140–41).

CYCLOPES, LAESTRYGONIANS, LOTUS-EATERS, AND AEOLUS.

The other three instances in the *Odyssey* in which messengers were involved are, first, Odysseus' beaching in the land of the Lotus-eaters (*Od.* 9.88). Odysseus selects two of his men accompanied by a herald to go forth and scout the land. The herald's presence is intended to provide the envoys with sancrosanctity. The natives simulate a welcome for the newcomers by giving them lotus to eat, but the lotus causes them to forget the purpose of their mission and their waiting comrades. At the end, Odysseus has to retrieve them forcefully and sail off immediately. Soon after, his ships put anchor at the land of the Cyclopes (*Od.* 9.195). Leading an embassy of twelve, Odysseus goes to Cyclops' cave expecting the traditional hospitality due to envoys and guests. Cyclops' response is barbaric. Battering six of Odysseus' envoys, he eats them for supper. Homer characterizes Cyclops' conduct as lawless (*Od.* 9.106, *athemiston*), underlining the fact that disregard for messenger conventions and council assemblies place the Cyclopes at the status of savages. They live in caves, Homer says, each for himself, lacking regard for communal life which Homer views as a humanized agent. To top it all, they know no "awe" (*aedos*) and have no respect for the gods.[69] As Hoekstra remarks, the implications are clear: the poet paints a picture of a people on the lowest cultural level, devoid of all that gives human life its distinctive quality. Ignorance and lack of respect for universally accepted human conventions demonstrate their lack of civility. No wonder that Homer portrays the Cyclopes as the embodiment of inhumanity capable of acts of extreme barbarity.

Something similar transpires in the third case, Odysseus' arrival in the land of Laestrygonians. When two messengers and a herald are sent to them (*Od.* 10.102), the king's daughter shows them the way to the palace, where the enormous queen calls her husband from the assembly. Instead of extending the conventional hospitality to the emissaries, the king slaughters one of them and devours him for dinner (*Od.* 10.116); the other two save themselves by fleeing to the ships. Following them, the Laestrygonians kill several of Odysseus' comrades before the rest can sail away to security. Amazingly, although the Laestrygonians know the use of assemblies (*agorai*), they do not seem to differ much in savagery from the previous two people in their disrespect of human conventions. If they are a step up from the Cyclopes state in their use of assemblies, they still remain in a savage state.

The behavior of the Lotus-eaters and the Laestygonians stands in complete contrast to that of Aeolus. When Odysseus dispatches two of his men and a herald to scout Aeolus' dominion, the latter invites the men to his palace and extends them ample hospitality, without inquiring about their identity and provenance until he entertains them with food and drink. Prior to their departure, he supplies them with provisions for their trip and binds the adverse winds in bags, allowing only the Zephyr to speed their sails home (*Od.* 10.25). If he refuses to welcome them the second time, when

---

[69] *Il.* 9.106–15; *Temi/themis*, are divinely appointed ordinances for human assemblies. The irony in the expression is intentional: the Cyclopes do not recognize any divine ordinances, see also Heubeck, *A Commentary Od.* 9.106.

they are blown back to his island, he does so because they showed themselves unworthy of Aeolus' kind treatment and gratitude by allowing their base desires to lead them into misfortune. They have only themselves to blame for whatever befalls them because they invite the anger of the gods upon themselves.

SUMMATION

In sum, almost all of the above incidents in the Homeric poetry describe situations in which messengers are involved in interpersonal or "interstate" relations. The proximity of the Aegean culture to the Near Eastern cultures points to the possibility of common origins for their diplomatic rules. History may begin in Sumer or the Old Egyptian Kingdom but many customs and practices in the Near East and the Aegean basin are so old that no one can pinpoint the exact location of their origins. Once these practices were formulated, to be sure, they became the common possession of the entire area. What we also know is that these practices were not the products of some international convention, like the Geneva Conventions, formulated at a datable point in history, but that they had evolved *mutatis mutandis* over a long period of time. By the middle of the third millennium BC, they were definitely in practice among the Near Eastern States. We also surmise, judging by our modern sources, that similar practices if not so well formalized or in the same form, were applied by the so-called primitive peoples in underdeveloped parts of the world whose residents possessed some sense of morality.

If a story or practice is found among people whose civilization is considered more "ancient" than the civilization of a "later" people, we assume that the latter copied it from the former. Such an assumption appears logical, though it lacks corroboration. Consequently, the divergent view that similar practices in neighboring areas may have a common root cannot be excluded inasmuch as there is no proof to the contrary. The same is true of areas geographically far apart from each other. If we do not know of contacts that might have led to inter-borrowings, we can speak of amazing similarities owing to a higher degree of moral sense among them, but we possess no evidence of an exchange of ideas. The mythologists who have found surprising similarities among myths and stories of diverse places ascribe them to two reasons: either these myths (or stories) traveled from one place to another, or they have been devised independently. This last explanation is not difficult to accept if we consider that many different peoples who reach a certain level of civilization begin often to think and feel in a similar way, though the fine-tuning of their practices and the institutionalization of their ideas may depend on the level of civilization they have attained and other factors such as climate or temperament. Comparative mythologists have managed to prove the diverse origins of many stories in the *Odyssey* wherein the popular stories are in abundance even though their details may often differ.

One could argue that the history of the diplomatic principles obtained in the Homeric epics do not precede the times of Homer nor do they reflect the times of the Greek Dark Age or even that of Homer. On the other hand, it is equally legitimate to accept that Homer found these conventions and that their origins go at least as far back as the Bronze Age, if not much further. The close similarities of the diplomatic customs in the area of the Aegean and the Ancient Near East argue in favor of some common origins. This is the view that this study supports.

5 HOMERIC AND NEAR EASTERN ANALOGIES

Around the twelfth century BC, the Near East and the Aegean experience some sort of an upheaval, the details of which are not fully known to us, except in a general outline. The limited literacy of the Linear B appears to have disappeared in certain areas of Greece along with the collapse of the palace system. Alphabetic literacy most probably introduced from the Levant, gradually but steadily replaces the Linear B script beginning with the Dark Age. The memory of the past is not, however, totally lost. Ancient cultures rely on old customs and on their memory for certain facts, events, and rules, while speech itself can be patterned to assist memory. "Poeticized speech" is a device contrived to perpetuate what Havelock describes as the oral documentation of a non-literate culture, a serious instrument, the only one available in storing, preserving, and transmitting the sort of information which was felt to be important to require separation from the insignificant and commonplace.[1]

Fundamental to orality is dependence on the spoken word, although, as it has been said, even in literate societies encoding of information does not by any means exclude retention of information from the past. In oral societies, sound cannot be captured without the aid of written means and, as a consequence, recall is aided by several means, namely, fixed formulas of speech often adapted to a rhythmic meter, focused on the concrete, monumental events meriting memory, and others. The common denominator of the stories is that the narrative be intelligible and interesting to narrators and listeners. With these essential facts in mind, I would like to risk the danger of tautology by summarizing what has been said so far regarding the ideas pertaining to Homeric international rules and practices by comparing

---

[1] Eric A. Havelock, "The Transcription of the Code of a Non-literate Culture," in *The Literate Revolution in Greece and Its Cultural Consequences* (Princeton University Press, 1982) 116–17; Jan Vansina, *Oral Tradition as History* (University of Wisconsin Press, 1985) 170–71; Carol Thomas, *Finding People in Early Greece* (University of Missouri Press, 2005) 70–71.

them quickly to those of the Near East for the purpose of further supporting this essay.

The Homeric epics contain basically oral material which has its roots back in the Bronze Age and is characterized by the feature of oral tradition as mentioned above. In the Homeric world, we encounter messengers, carrying messages between the Achaean and Trojan camps or other close destinations. In the examples of messengers dealing with interstate (king to king or chief to chief), high officials are utilized to perform ambassadorial tasks.[2] These men are chosen because of their expertise, prudence, intelligence, and speaking ability, in short because they hold a position of trust in the administration and are familiar with the issues. When the affair(s) concern(s) all the allied leaders of the Achaean world, the council in the *Iliad* chose two persons as envoys, one of whom is the main spokesman of the mission, charged with conducting the business with the interlocutor(s), while the other discharges a complementary role, like Aias. In the charming encounter between Athena and Telemachus, the latter hesitates to assume the role of envoy to Nestor because of his inexperience in diplomatic exchanges and speech and his awkwardness to query an older person (*Od.* 3.21–24).

INSTRUCTIONS

Messengers in the Homeric and the Near Eastern world receive special instructions, relating to their handling of the negotiable subject at the court of their host. In the embassy to Achilles, we see Nestor instructing the envoys as to what to say and how to deliver the message he gives them. Homer suggests that most of these glances are directed at Odysseus who, as leader of the embassy, has the major responsibility for crafting the arguments intended to change Achilles' mind. Nestor's glances and his hand and body movements are intended to impress the envoy's interlocutor (*Il.* 9.179–181).

Instructions to the envoys notwithstanding, generally the process of argumentation allows the envoy(s) considerable leeway in handling questions that might come up in connection with their negotiations. There are several such occasions in the Near East and Homer. In the discussion of

---

[2] Agamemnon sent the heralds Talthybius and Eurybates. Talthybius was Agamemnon's man but the status of Eurybates is not certain. Talthybius has been described by Homer as "prudent" and a member of the king's staff. Similar qualifications prevail among primitive tribes in the choice of their messengers, H. A. Junod, *The Life of an African Tribe* (London, 1927) 394, 421, 423–25.

the Homeric evidence, we have perceived that messengers imparted the message they received as faithfully as possible. When it came to a vibrant discussion wherein questions and objections were raised, messengers exercised their initiative to intimate to respondents that better crafted responses might be more expedient under the circumstances. If a harsh answer from a lord to a vassal would not have mattered much, an impolitic answer to a king enjoying equality was bound to produce ill will and possibly diplomatic unpleasantness.

On the occasion of Idaeus who serves as the carrier of a Trojan proposal to the Achaeans, his unauthorized revelation contributes to the failure of the peace agreement he is dispatched to conclude (*Il.* 7.372–78). Iris uses her judgment repeatedly, refusing to accept her respondent's answer until he is persuaded to tone it down. In doing so, she spares both sides incalculable consequences. Prudently, Poseidon comes around to her way of thinking, complimenting her for her wisdom and her prudence.

LIBATIONS AND PRAYERS

Prior to the departure of messengers, it is customary in the Ancient Near Eastern and Homeric world that libations be poured and prayers be addressed to the divine, asking for protection of the messengers and success for their mission. Upon the messengers' departure, sender and messengers fill bowls with wine and pour libations to all the gods, praying for a safe and successful trip (*Od.* 2.431). The same is repeated when the messengers return from the trip (*Od.* 15.147–49). The mention of hand-washing before dinner for a guest or envoy often entails the pouring of libations and prayers as part of their welcome and stay. The same is repeated upon the departure of envoys. Prayers and libations are offered for a safe trip back home even when their mission has proven unsuccessful (*Il.* 9.657). We find something analogous to the practice of libations and prayers in the Near East, for the same purpose, i.e., the safety and success of the embassy. Needless to add, prayers and libations are customary among human messengers. Divine messengers simply receive their instructions and immediately depart for their destination.

Associated with the practice of libations, prayers, and sacrifice is the custom of asking for favorable omens. Upon the conclusion of the sacrifice to gods, signs are examined to reveal the propitiousness of omens. If the signs are good, the envoys depart; otherwise the trip is postponed for a more auspicious time when the new omens will be favorable.

Envoys' Departure

It is worth repeating that the envoys depart with the blessings of those who sent them. The same happens at the other end, as the visiting messengers take off for their return trip. Socio-political conventions require that the messengers take their leave with the approval of their host. At the end of their conversations with Achilles, Odysseus and Aias are told to leave in order to report to the Achaean council the outcome of their deliberations (*Il.* 9.659). When Priam expresses the desire to forego Achilles' hospitality and depart immediately upon receiving Hector's body, Achilles becomes infuriated (*Il.* 9.560–64).[3] Fearing the worst, Priam postpones his departure for the next morning although, in the end, his departure is changed by divine intervention.

Repeated complaints are voiced by the messengers' lords in the Near East against hosts who detain messengers unnecessarily long; these complaints are prominent and, unless the explanations proffered are adequate they are likely to produce ill-will between kings. The force of this tradition compels Peisistratus to advise the inexperienced Telemachus not to depart from Menelaus' house without his host's approval and knowledge. Telemachus acknowledges without demur the wisdom of Peisistratus' advice (*Od.* 15.51–53). In contrast, Menelaus condemns the prevailing practice of keeping guests and messengers beyond their will, thereby advocating flexibility in the application of this traditional custom. But political interests were served in divergent ways in the course of ancient diplomacy and the same may be true of Bronze and Dark Age diplomacy in the Aegean area. Telemachus' departure from Pylos without Nestor's permission is a violation of established principles for which Telemachus solicits Peisistratus' help by asking him to justify his violation to Nestor (*Od.* 15.199–201).

Hospitality, Identification, Purpose

The above discussion brings us to another facet of ancient international relations. Guests and envoys were not supposed to be asked about their origins and purpose of coming until they enjoyed the host's hospitality first. Exceptions to this rule obtained on certain occasions, as in the case of Agamemnon's heralds who came for a sinister purpose known to Achilles in advance. But even in that case, the host is not expected to take his dis-

---

[3] Achilles had ended the meeting with the two Achaean envoys dispatched by Agamemnon and the council with the abrupt remark "go inform the Achaeans of my decision," a remark that seems to have infuriated Aias, *Il.* 9.649.

pleasure out on the envoys much though he might be angry with the sender. The envoys are to be respected since they enjoy sancrosanctity. This protection might not have been extended in all cases but exceptions do not nullify the validity of the principle. The rule of hospitality includes the gods as well, as we have seen in various instances where gods are involved either as messengers, hosts, or both. Questions regarding messenger identification follow a similar line, when gods are disguised as humans.

On the island of Phaeacia, two different identification questions are submitted to Odysseus at different times: the first is by queen Arete, moved by her curiosity following the dinner, asking Odysseus about the provenance of his clothes. Either for dramatic purposes or because it is customary for the lord of the house to ask the personal questions, Homer does not reveal Odysseus' full identity at this point; he has Odysseus simply respond to the question of the provenance of the clothes. Satisfied by her guest's answer, Arete does not press further with questions about Odysseus' origins. It is two days after Odysseus' arrival in Phaeacia that Alcinous asks his guest details about his identity. The most convincing identity of Odysseus in Phaeacia, however, occurs when he breaks down and weeps during Demodocus' narration. Irrespective of the intended dramatic effects by the poet, Alcinous' inquiry conforms to the traditional format which requires that questions about the guest's identity and purpose of coming be asked after he has been entertained. Obviously, the welcome of messengers is governed by a traditional protocol the roots of which are to be found deep in history, as the Near Eastern practices amply show. How binding this custom is becomes evident from the fact that Odysseus and Aias raise no objections to a dinner, notwithstanding the fact that they have already enjoyed a sumptuous dinner at Agamemnon's quarters prior to the departure of their embassy for Achilles' quarters, which could not have been far off (*Il.* 9.90). Fear that they might displease their host could have been the reason for their compliance.

CREDENTIALS

Closely associated to messenger dispatch in the Near East is the need for his possession of proper credentials. It seems self-evident that a messenger unknown to his host would have to produce some convincing evidence of his identity and purpose. In the Near East, messenger's usually carried with them papers which proved the carrier's identity and his authority to negotiate. If such papers were missing, the host was justified in his doubts about the messengers authorization to negotiate. This is not always true of most of the Iliadic messengers, chiefly because everybody knows each other and credentials are superfluous. In the world of the *Odyssey*, it would be appropriate for the host to expect some sign or type of credentials to be shown by the guest. Otherwise, in the less structured Homeric system, liars and cheats could easily produce plausible stories to fool their hosts.

Though Telemachus is not known to Menelaus, Helen and Menelaus recognize a close physical similarity to his father, Odysseus. When Peisistratus corroborates that Telemachus is indeed Odysseus' son, they accept the corroboration without much ado. Something similar happens to Odysseus in Phaeacia. Several prominent Phaeacians are not convinced about Odysseus identity until he breaks down and weeps during Demodocus' narration. And additional confirmation of his real identity occurs by Odysseus' athletic achievement during the contest in his honor (*Od.* 8.83 ff, 186 ff, 395 ff.) On more serious occasions, a true Aristotelian recognition clinches the question of identity. The recognition of Odysseus by Eurycleia from his boar wound and Odysseus' revelation of the secret stories known only to them prove to establish the indisputable evidence of his identity.

In the instances of divine messengers unknown to the recipients, the messenger's affirmation of his identification seems to suffice, perhaps because the messenger's appearance denotes some awesomeness. Iris announces herself to the trembling Priam and tries her best to dispel his fear of her. Skeptical Hecuba needs more information regarding the genuineness of Iris' mission and urges Priam to test it by a prayer to Zeus. He does, and the message of Zeus is confirmed by the aquiline appearance (*Il.* 24.292–95). Hecuba's insistence implies that, in more serious situations, the Greek recipients of messages expect some serious corroboratory evidence.

SACROSANCTITY, DANGERS, ESCORTS, PROVISIONS

Messengers in Homer and the Near East are as a rule protected by the traditional principle of sacrosanctity. Chryses travels to the Achaean camp holding his credentials, fillets on a staff of gold, obviously claiming double sacrosanctity as a messenger and as Apollo's priest. In contrast, Achilles might fume against Agamemnon but does not fail to greet his heralds politely. Two heralds accompany Odysseus and Aias in their embassy to Achilles, thereby sanctifying the messengers' mission with their presence and also serving as witnesses whose testimony Odysseus invokes upon the envoys' return for the truth of his report. Idaeus (*Il.* 7.372), Talthybius, Eurybates (*Il.*1.320 ff.; 334), Odysseus, Menelaus (*Il.*10. 254 ff.), and Hector (*Il.*7.55 ff.) are not molested when they go to their respective rivals' places carrying messages on behalf of their people because they are protected by the prevailing principle of sacrosanctity. On occasion, there occur violations of this principle but these violations do not necessarily negate the existence and importance of the principle itself. An egregious example of sacrosanctity violation is that of the Persian envoys killed by the tradition conscious Spartans. This brutal act weighs so heavily on the Spartans' conscience that they decide to pay for it by sending two of their most prominent members to be killed by Xerxes in expiation of this crime.[4] This example shows that the greater the sophistication of the age, the greater the chance that the traditional principle may be violated.

As with the Near Eastern messengers, Homeric messengers are as a rule escorted by a squadron of troops. Priam is escorted only by the elderly herald Idaeus who serves also as his mule-driver because Hermes assumes the duty escort for both since their mission requires more significant protection than the mere presence of a few strong men. That messengers are subject to all sorts of dangers has already been adverted to. Besides the dangers on the road, the hosts themselves can prove dangerous if the carriers bring unpleasant news to them.

The fury Agamemnon unleashes toward the seer Calchas for giving him bad news is a classic example of royal wrath against carriers of bad news. King Oedipus in Sophocles' homonymous tragedy acts similarly against the bearer of bad news, and so does King Pentheus in Euripides' *Bacchae*. King Priam, aware of Achilles' temper, is scared out of his wits at the thought of going to Achilles' quarters, despite the divine assurances. No wonder that his wife refuses to let him go, since she can imagine countless dangers lurking everywhere for her husband. Any strange apparition, movement, or noise in the dusk or darkness can provoke fear, as in Hermes' sudden appearance before the elderly duo. It causes Priam's hair to stand up and his limbs to be paralyzed (*Il*.24.354–57).[5]

---

[4] Hdt. 5.17; 7.134–37; *IG* II² 116, 141; Mosley, *Envoys and Diplomacy*, 79. When the Greek embassy made up of Menelaus, Odysseus, and Palamedes arrived in Troy from Tenedos, the Trojans not only refused to entertain the Greek proposals but some of them appeared ready to murder the envoys and might have done so had not Antenor, in whose house the envoys were lodged, intervened to stop the shameful act, *Il*. 3.307; Apoll. *Epitome*, 3.28–29; *Dictys Cretensis*, 1.4; Numelin, *Beginnings of Diplomacy*, 16.

[5] Fascinatingly, Hermes sooths Priam's fear by posing as Achilles' *therapon*, a Myrmidon nobleman's son, ready to help the trebling old duo. To pacify the trebling old men Hermes even claimed to have traveled to Troy on the same ship with Achilles, Greenhalgh, "The Homeric *Therapon* and *Opaon* in their Historical Implications," *BICS* (1982) 83. n. 48. One of the possible implications connected with the

Dusk seems to be the most perilous part of the day for travelers, merchants, and messengers, when flight is most difficult and the marauders, who might have followed their victims during the daylight hours, choose to strike when their intended victims begin to think of the best way and place to bivouac before complete darkness envelopes them. That the fear of the elderly twosome is entirely justified becomes evident by the pertinent question of the young man (Hermes), who justifiably asks why they are driving their wagon during the night when other mortals are asleep, and whether they are not afraid of the Achaeans who sojourn nearby. If the Achaeans notice the trove they are carrying, Hermes continues, they will certainly kill or rob them. Like Priam, Bellerophon is also escorted by anonymous gods to Lycia (*Il.* 6.172), while Telemachus enjoys the company of Athena who serves him as guide and councilor.[6] Her role seems to have been taken up

---

role of *Therapon*, which the author of the article does not mention, is that Hermes serves as an escort envoy, for the two elderly envoys in a similar role that envoys from the host countries served in antiquity, as we have already seen.

[6] *Il.* 11.771–81 and Kirk, *The Iliad* ad loc. Θεῶν πομπῇ, the connection between Greece and Lycia in the pre-homeric times constitutes a theme repeatedly cited in Homer as well as in several myths. It is possible that all the references to Lycia may allude to some real relation between the two areas. The stories of Proteus and Acrisius and the flight of Proetus to Iobates, king of Lycia, whose daughter Sthenenboea or Anetia he married are very prominent. In a mythical version, Proetus, the king of Tirynth, had invited from Lycia three, in another seven, Cyclopes (both numbers are emblematic of their sanctity even today in agricultural communities) to construct the wall of his city, Apollod. 1.155; Har. Koutelakis, "Κύκλωπες και Μεγαλιθικά Μνημεία," *Corpus* 68 (2005) 41, 43. Proetus returned at the head of the Lycian army to support his claim of succession to the Argive throne, Apoll. 2,21; 2.4.7; scholiast on Eur. *Orestes*, 965; Servius on Vergil's *Aeneid* 3, 286; the Bellerophon story is chronologically set a generation after these Lycian references, Homer, *Il.* 6.155; 16.328 ff.; Apoll. 1.9.3; 2.3.1. The story of Bellerophon's entertainment by Diomedes' grandfather Oineus in Calydon is an additional informational morsel that may strengthen the Mycenaean interconnections of these Lycian references. This type of story appears for the first time in literature in an Egyptian myth before 1200 BC., which describes the wife of Anubes falling in love with her brother-in-law Bata. But even prior to Anubis' story the wife of the Egyptian Petefres is said to have fallen in love with Joseph, καὶ ἦν Ἰωσὴφ καλὸς τῷ εἴδει καὶ ὡραῖος τῇ ὄψει σφόδρα, like Bellerofontes who was also endowed with κάλλος by the gods (*Il.* 6.156–57), Kakrides, *Homeric Themes*, 31. Even in the classical times the dangers to travelers and messengers were not absent. Mosley, *Envoys and Diplomacy*, 83. This is the single instance in Homer of a written

by Peisistratus for the Pylos-Sparta-Pylos section of the trip (3.29–30; 325). Bandits always suspect that messengers carry presents for their hosts, and it is one of the reasons that Peisistratus advises inexperienced Telemachus not to leave Sparta until daylight. It is not accidental that the young people opt to spend the nights at Diocles' house both on their way to and from Sparta in view of the oncoming darkness (*Od.* 3.488; 15.186).[7]

Besides the security escorts, messengers in the Near East are often accompanied by a colleague from the host country together with escort troops. While on the return trip, the colleague-envoy serves as an escort, and upon arrival at his host's court, he frequently serves as witness for the envoy's veracity (*Il.* 9.689). Phoenix' role in the embassy to Achilles seems to bear some such similarity to the host messengers' role. It is possible that the poet contrives Phoenix' unexplainable presence in Agamemnon's quarters to use him as a trustworthy witness of Agamemnon's repentance.

Messengers are well provisioned before they leave home or the place of their hosts for their return trips, especially if those trips are to be long. The morning Telemachus leaves Pylos, Nestor's wife places bread, wine, and a variety of other dainties in the chariot (*Od.* 3.479). Helen and the maids do the same upon Telemachus' departure from Sparta. Calypso clothes Odysseus and supplies him with provisions for the trip, sending a fair wind behind him to make his voyage safe, if the rest of the gods will it (*Od.* 5.165–70; 263–67). Aeolus certainly does as much the first time Odysseus stops at his island, even stuffing and tying the winds in bags to make Odysseus' trip uneventful (*Od.* 10.17–18; 40–45). Lastly, the Phaeacians exceed themselves in generosity of provisions. They send Odysseus off on a ship equipped with escorts, abundant presents, and ample provisions for the trip.[8]

---

message. It indicates that Homer might have been an oral poet but not an illiterate one.

[7] Between the double name of Ortilochus and Orsilochus scholars seem to prefer the former, Heubeck, *A Commenatry* ad loc.; *Od.* 21.16–21; Russo, *A Commentary*, ad loc. Odysseus had stayed at Ortilochus' house, the father of Diocles, when he visited Messene as the Ithacan envoy to negotiate the compensation for the robbery some Messenians had committed in Ithaca. See also W. A. McDonald, "Overland Communications in Greece during LH III," in *Mycenaean Studies* (Madison, Wisc., 1964) 224–34.

[8] Before leaving Aulis for Troy, the Achaeans had received ample supplies of corn, wine, and other provisions given to them by Anius of Delos, Graves, *Greek*

Gifts

An essential feature of the ancient messenger's responsibility is the transport of gifts that help his master establish new friendships, retain old ones, or use them in exchange for some favor. In the process, messengers often receive gifts for themselves. Interestingly, Linear B tablets occasionally refer to textiles (Knossos) and perfumed oil (Pylos) as *ke-se-nu-wi-ja/xenwia*. The root suggests a connection with the Greek word guest, host, stranger (*xenos*), which is associated with the word hospitality and formal gift exchange. The early existence of the term in the Mycenaean times indicates that the custom of gift-giving and exchanging, precedes by some centuries the Homeric times. Gift exchanges thus serve many purposes in the Ancient Near East and the Aegean world. In a culture wherein a man's image depends to a great extent on the opinion of others, it is natural that the exchange of gifts plays a major role in social relations. Gifts are used to befriend or remunerate others or to compensate them for the commission of social indiscretions.[9] Apologies and expensive gifts are the only antidotes for the restoration of the damaged honor of the insulted party. It is often the best that an offender can do, even though that is not at times enough. In the feud between Achilles and Agamemnon, the latter universally acknowledges that lavish liberality is not sufficient to cure the deep wound his opprobrious language and his outrageous acts caused. The purpose of Agamemnon's extensive enumeration and detailed description of the gifts with which he intends to restore Achilles' damaged honor corresponds to the frequent enumeration of gifts by the Near Eastern kings who exhibit their generosity and the esteem in which they hold others, particularly the recipients of the gifts.[10]

The old adage, "never look a gift-horse in the mouth," is not quite true in the Ancient Near East. Horses and other gifts are always meticulously

---

Mythology, vol. 2, p. 283t. Beyond supplies, Odysseus received many rich gifts from the Phaeacians which Homer enumerates after the Near Eastern fashion.

[9] Shelmerdine, "Review of the Aegean Prehistory VI," 562. Interstingly, a number of ethnics in the tablets reflect associations with other lands. Sometimes these ethnics appear to belong to men's names: Mistraios (Knossos), Egyptian, Memphite, Alasios (Cypriot) and so on, which may mean not only stranger, or guest, but also trader, or merchant. See also n. 157.

[10] Moran, AL, *EA* 7.63–72; 9.6–18; 14 passim; In *EA* 24 the following paragraphs speak of gifts 9.11.13.14.24.25 and so on. Marcel Mauss, tr. by Ian Cunisson, *The Gifts, Forms and Functions of Exchange in Archaic Societies* (Norton Library, 1976) 15–30.

inspected and evaluated by both the sender and recipient. The general attitude of donors is to emphasize the quality and quantity of the gift items dispatched, while the recipient reserves for himself the right to disagree. If the gifts are not appropriate to the seriousness of the occasion or the expectations of the receiver, he complains vehemently to the giver for having sent presents unbefitting the status of the receiver or the occasion. Similarly, when in their proposal of peace and alliance to the Achaeans, the Trojans fail to promise sufficient remuneration to Menelaus for dishonoring him, Agamemnon inserts a remuneration clause as a necessary complement to Menelaus' restoration of honor (*Il.* 3.386, 459). A significant addendum to the generous gifts Agamemnon bestows upon Achilles is the proposal of a marriage alliance between the two royal houses. Similar activities occur in the Near Eastern cultures, though in the height of Egyptian power it is mostly the Near Eastern kings who grant a bride to the Egyptian King, not the other way around. Nestor loads Telemachus with valuable gifts, as do Menelaus and Helen, the latter two conferring them as an expression of their gratitude and the high honor in which they hold his father and his family for all that Odysseus did in Troy on their behalf (*Od.* 15.114 ff; 125 ff). An echo of the "gift-horse" attitude is to be found in the Glaucus-Diomedes encounter where Glaucus receives a gift of unequal value in comparison to the gift he gives.[11]

Glaucus does not complain about the unequal gift, but Homer, defending the traditional practice of gift equality, points out that Zeus must have deprived Glaucus of his wits to have accepted a gift of less than one tenth of the value of the gift he gave. If the gift offered by a donor happens to be impractical, it is not considered offensive for the donée to ask for a more suitable exchange. When Menelaus offers Telemachus a very expensive gift consisting of three beautiful horses and a costly chariot, the gift befitting the high esteem he has for Odysseus and his family, Telemachus wisely rejects it as unsuitable to the terrain of rocky Ithaca. Menelaus promptly exchanges this gift with an equally valuable but practical gift (*Od.* 4.590–91).

---

[11] Donlan, "Duelling with Gifts in the Iliad: As the Audience Saw it," *Colby Quarterly* 29 (1993) 155–72. In his "Unequal Exchange between Glaucus and Diomedes in Light of the Homeric Gift-economy," Phoenix 43 (1989) 1–15, Donlan states (p. 2) that Agamemnon's gifts (δῶρα) are intended not only to compensate for his outrage but, by their abundance, to elevate his own prestige and to put Achilles under severe obligation.

The principle of give and take lies deep in human nature and is found in primitive societies as well. For primitive man, it is not strange to exchange gifts, and such gifts can either spring from pure goodwill or simply from an expression of gratitude and sympathy. Soon the practice of giving presents develops into an institutionalized practice, that is, it becomes a question of giving rather than exchanging and in others more of an exchanging rather than giving. Sometimes the donée states what he wishes for in exchange; in this instance, the gift is not an expression of goodwill but rather a formal reminder that something is desired in return. In other cases, the gift can also be a bribe, compensation for injuries, or connected with religious conceptions. What is exchanged represents a whole system of courtesies, rites, feasts, military service—all of which Mauss groups under the rubric of *prestations totales*.[12]

RELATIONSHIPS AND GIFT EXCHANGES

In the Homeric world, there is the guest-friendship or ritualized friendship relationship—something equivalent to the brotherhood relationship of the Near Eastern kings even when no blood or marriage relationship is involved. *Xenia* (guest-friendship) in Homer is a specialized and institutionalized relationship, following a pattern of balanced exchanges. Guest-friends (*xenoi*) can be expected to provide hospitality for guest-friends just as Nestor or Menelaus does for Telemachus or to look after the welfare of their guest-friends in a wider sense by providing political or military support. As with other kinds of friendship, the assumption underpinning the relationship is equality. The relationship exists between individuals of equal social rank, and an equal or better return for any gift or service is expected (*Il.* 6.213–31). The exchanged gifts are the tangible representation of the relationship that is created. People seal their established friendship by exchanging gifts which show the good will to the man from whom one receives a gift. In some cases, the guest-friendship encourages the request or refusal of some gifts considered unsuitable. In the Amarna Letters, the quality and amount or number of the items received are often disputed, especially Egyptian shipments of gold or gold items (*EA* 3.13; 7.69–720). In other cases, it becomes evident that a strictly commercial evaluation inter-

---

[12] *Il.* 6.234–36; Donlan,"The Unequal Exchange," *Phoenix*, 1–15; Donlan, "Reciprocity on Homer," *CW* 75 (1981–82) 137–75; Mauss, *The Gift*, 15–30; R. Seaford, *Reciprocity and Ritual, Homer and Tragedy in the Developing City-States* (Oxford University Press, 1994), 199.

feres with a gift-exchange, as alluded to in the case of the Diomedes-Glaucus. In order to determine the non-equivalence of gifts, an economic value is attached to them since both confirm the inherited relation of guest-friendship and are evaluated against a common measure. Gifts can also take the form of favors inasmuch as favors produce gratitude in the recipient and induce a favor in return, so that favors can be the things given or done for someone in return for a favor.

It is said that a king or a wealthy man in society takes care to pay his own debts and to give a gift in return that is of greater value than the gifts he receives, thus putting the giver in a state of debt to the king or a wealthy person (Hdt. 3.139–41). While Greek reciprocity is stabilized by a rough equality of exchange, which according to Aristotle constitutes equality (*isotês*), the basic ingredient of friendship (*philia*, Nic. Eth. 8. 1158b27–28), the Persian King's exchanges are marked by inequality.[13] The King gives more than he receives and by so doing he hopes to keep the recipient in his debt, thereby creating a state of imbalance in the relationship. Beyond that, the royal king is supposed to remind the recipient that the king is the supreme archon of the land, and no one can match his power and wealth. This is not unique to the Persians; Solomon had earlier followed the same practice (2 Chron.9.9–12). It is part of the aristocratic ideology which is seen as individual and competitive with an emphasis on personal virtue. The values associated with the traditional aristocratic values continue to persist during the time that the polis was still ruled by aristocrats. Though popularly elected and conforming to the corporate and cooperative objectives of the *polis*, the aristocratic leaders continue to transfer and transform the pre-city aristocratic values in the exercise of domestic and foreign policy. It is in this context that Thucydides' Pericles talks about a similar kind of "unbalanced relationship," when Athens, by her purported generosity, supposedly keeps the allied states in her debt (Thuc.2.40.4). Like the kings, Athens hopes to remain the dominant partner and direct the leadership of the

---

[13] Such was perhaps the case for the Egyptian Pharaohs in the Amarna period of the Persian King in the time of the Persian Empire, and of Pericles during the time of the Athenian Empire, since Pericles openly admitted that he sought to place the recipients under obligation to them, and to elevate the donor's (Athenian) honor. Donlan above (see n. 11) believes that the offer of Agamemnon, had it been accepted, would have made Agamemnon the "winner" in honor. Whether, however, it would have placed Achilles under severe obligation, as Donlan asserts, is a debatable point.

Athenian Empire. In such instances, the gift-giving ideology supersedes the financial value framework and is based on pride or renown.

One recognizes that such a relationship or friendship is frequently characterized by a higher degree of expediency or utility when compared to the pre-polis aristocratic friendship. Individual *xenia* might often be guided by a strong dose of expediency, but overall it seems to be characterized by stronger, affective personal elements. Nevertheless, because expediency is in many instances an element of friendship (*philia*), in his great work on friendship Aristotle does not fail to discuss its utilitarian type.[14] This type of friendship is contracted for the benefit that may accrue to both of the friends (*Nic. Eth.*1156a14–29). In most cases, when the motive for which such friendship was established changes, friendship ceases to exist (*Nic. Eth.*8.1156a19–24). The fundamental factor in this sort of relationship is that it is based on an implicit understanding. So Aristotle warns that since the affective element is not the bond of friendship, the terms of this association should always be kept in mind if one is to avoid future misunderstandings (*Nic. Eth.* 8.1163a18).

BRIDE-PRICE

Agamemnon's formerly mentioned marriage proposal to Achilles leads us to another of the many tasks messengers performed in the Near Eastern world. A significant part of messenger missions entails carrying marriage proposals, inspecting a prospective bride for their lord, bringing a bride-price from the prospective groom to the father of the bride, and carrying the bride's dowry-gifts and the new bride to her new country.[15] The com-

---

[14] *Nic. Eth.* 8.1156a-30; *Eud. Eth.* 7.1236a33–34; Lynette G. Mitchell, *Greeks Bearing Gifts, The Public Use of Private Relationships* (Cambridge University press, 1997) 7–8.

[15] *Od.* 8.274, 318–20; for ἕδνα–ἔεδνα see *Il.* 16.178.190; 22.472; *Od.* 6.159; 8.318; 11.117; 13.282; 15.8; 16.161, 529; A. M. Snodgrass, "An Historical Homeric Society," *JHS* 95 (1974) 114–25; M. I. Finley, "Marriage, Sale and Gift in the Homeric World," *Revue Internationale des Droits d l" Antiquité* 2 (1955) 167–94. In an interesting article about the ongoing war in Western Sudan in *The New York Times* (Dec. 5, 2005) A5, Marc Lacey touched upon the value of the camel in the life of the local people, mentioning how a peasant by the name of Alshaib had given the family of his fiancée a bride-price of six camels and one cow. See also the similar story in connection with Tegla Loroupe, the Kenyan runner, *New York Times*, Nov. 18 (2006) A4. The stories point to the persistence of certain customs from the ancient times and their widely spread practice even among the lower classes.

mon practice of bride-price we find in the Homeric world has its roots in the Bronze Age since we find it commonly practiced in the Near East. The bride-price seems to have been at least as important, if not more important, than the dowry. In a Homeric story, Idomeneus refers to Othryoneus as offering no wooing gifts to Priam for the hand of his daughter Cassandra; he has promised instead to perform some extraordinary deed of valor for the Trojans. Sadly, he perishes before he is able to fulfill his vow, something for which Idomeneus taunts him (*Il.* 13.3374–84). Agamemnon, in addition to the many gifts he promises to Achilles, is ready to give him any of his three daughters Achilles wants to marry without the traditional bride-price (*Il.* 9.146).

Homer also narrates that Borus, the son of Perieres, marries Polydora, the daughter of Peleus, giving gifts of marriage past counting (*Il.* 16.177–78). He also cites the similar story of Polymele and Echecles (*Il.* 16.190) and explains that Neleus offered countless bride-gifts for beautiful Chloris (*Od.* 11.282) and how Penelope is literally bombarded with offers of bridal gifts by her suitors in their effort to bend Penelope's resistance. He further adverts to the exhortations of Penelope's father and brothers to marry Eurymachus (*Od.* 15.17–18) because he surpasses the other suitors in his offer of bride-price and his willingness to increase further the bride-price if what he has offered is not satisfactory (*Od.* 15.1–18). Odysseus is grateful for Nausicaa's help, expressing his gratitude in an indirect way by considering blessed in heart he who would prevail with his gifts of wooing to lead her to his home (*Il.* 6.158–59). Lastly, the gods themselves are not above such human practices, particularly for a much-desired bride. Shamed by the infidelity of his wife Aphrodite, Hephaestus demands from her father the return of the expensive bride-price he has paid for her (*Od.* 8.318).

SALUTATION AND POSTURE

Similarities are also to be found in the manner of salutations of the Near Eastern and Homeric kings, although there are some radical discrepancies here which mirror the social and political differences among the two locations but which call for a quick comparison. In contrast to the long-winded salutations used by the Near Eastern kings, salutations in the Homeric epics are short, simple, and direct. When Chryses makes his pleas for his daughter, he addresses Agamemnon, Menelaus, and the other Achaean leaders in simple terms, such as "Sons of Atreus and you the other well-greaved Achaeans," (*Il.* 1.17). He then simply adds the wish that they may achieve their goal and return safely to their homes. Similarly, when Odysseus goes to Chryses, he simply addresses him with the vocative of his name (*Il.*

1.402). Equally simple is the address of Thetis to Zeus as 'Father Zeus' (*Il.* 1.503), whereas the address of Athena to Odysseus is more flattering than majestic, "Son of Laertes, sprung of Zeus, Odysseus of many wiles" (*Il.* 2.1.173). In Athena's case, of course, one cannot expect the use of a grandiose address from a goddess to a mortal, but her greeting to him is no different than that coming from a mortal. Likewise, when Idaeus addresses the Achaean kings, he uses the rather simple form, "Son of Atreus and you the other princes of the Panachaean army" (*Il.* 7.385). In contrast, the names and epithets the kings exchange at their wrathful moments are much more "colorful" to the modern readers as they must have been to the assembled Achaeans in front of whom they are hurled. These few examples point to a simplified and direct salutation form in contradistinction to the elaborate and longwinded address used by the oriental kings toward one another.

Somewhat related to the above topic is the positioning of the messengers when delivering their message. Perhaps their positioning has something to do with what we describe as "body language" nowadays; if so, body language techniques are almost as old as human history itself. In connection with this subject, it is notable that the positioning of the messengers often differed, depending on certain factors. Divine messengers commonly stand near the person to whom they are to deliver the message. Athena stands near (ἀγχοῦ) Achilles (*Il.* 2.172) as does Iris (*Il.* 2.790; 15.173; 24.169) when she delivers her messages to the recipients, perhaps because these messages are strictly personal. Human messengers do something similar when they deliver a message which other people present should not hear (*Od.* 4.25). On the occasions they address a group, messengers usually stand in the middle of their audience. In a way, they have to because of the need to be heard by both sides, as Hector does when he sets forward his peace proposals (*Il.* 3.77–78; 7.66). The two envoys to Troy, Menelaus and Odysseus, deliver their speeches in front of the assembled crowd of Trojans and most probably answer questions or deliver counter arguments to the arguments of the Trojan speakers. The body language in the epics then, as in the Near East, seems to be a feature of considerable significance. In this instance, Homer equally stresses the differences between the two speakers. Menelaus is pictured as speaking fluently and clearly, with an economy of words, whereas Homer's description of Odysseus' speech is indicative of Odysseus' unique body language technique. His remarks are delivered with a characteristic skill—his unique trademark. At first, he softens up his audience by simulating the ignorant by doing nothing more than holding his scepter and looking at the ground. But then, when his turn comes, Odysseus' words flow out on the assembly like a snowstorm. He stands as he speaks and looks down with eyes fixed upon the ground, not moving his staff backwards or forwards but holding it stiffly. His position gives the impression of a foolish man, if not for the artful manner of his speech that attracts the admiration of his listeners (*Il.* 3.205–224).[16]

Despite Odysseus' admirable oratory, the Trojans do not give the Greek envoys what they want. Perhaps public opinion in Troy is against giving back Helen at this point because by doing so would be admitting that it was a mistake to accept her in the city in the first place (*Il.* 3.73–74). It is also possible that the assembly fears that returning Helen would be an act of appeasement. Antimachus even suggests that the Trojans kill the envoys then and there. This might be a smart move but also a disgraceful outrage contrary to their traditions regarding the treatment of envoys. Antenor proposes the return of Helen and her treasures. After the day's bloodshed, he has plenty of supporters. He reminds them that they have already broken an oath (128) by shooting Menelaus after having sworn to resolve the war through a duel. Pandarus puts the Trojans in the wrong. No good could come out of this violation.

The incident points to two different styles of artful speaking: one, the traditional aristocratic style followed by Menelaus as he moves his staff to and fro to emphasize certain points, making eye contact with his listeners; the other, Odysseus' personal style that no doubt adds to his reputation for cunningness which, combined with his charming eloquence, make him a very effective speaker. That speakers stand holding staffs passed on to them by a herald when addressing an assembly becomes evident from the Trojan assembly meeting wherein Antenor submits his motion and sits down as soon as he finishes (*Il.* 7.354). The same procedure is followed by Paris and King Priam when they also propose a motion in the assembly (*Il.* 7.365 ff.).

VERBATIM DELIVERY

Messages and messengers are inextricably tied to the manner in which messages are delivered. The use of cuneiform tablets in the Near East tends to free the carrier from memorizing the message. Yet, even in the literate world of the Near East, there are instances in which messages are to be delivered orally. In these cases, messengers are expected to have strong mem-

---

[16] For the body-language technique when delivering messages among primitive people see W. J. Sollas, *Ancient Hunters* (London, 1924) 33–39; J. E. Lips in Fr. Boas, *General Anthropology* (New York, 1938) 504–12; N. W. Thomas, *Natives of Australia* (London, 106) 31.

ory and deliver their message as verbatim as possible. In Homer, the process is reversed, with almost all of the messages being oral, except in one instance (*Il.* 168–169). This single instance adverts to Bellerophon, who is wrongly accused by the wife of the Argive King Proteus, a "modern" Mrs. Robinson named Antheia, as having made advances. Unlike the cinematic "Graduate," Bellerophon refuses to succumb to her mischievous sexual appetite and suffers the consequences. He is sent to Proteus' father-in-law in Lycia like a typical messenger, carrying a secret written message ordering his own execution.

When Zeus dispatches Dream to Agamemnon, he orders him to relay the message as close to the language given to him as possible. Dream does so (*Il.* 2.11–15) with the understandable changes in the person of the enclitic and the required changes in the person of the verb. Hera's message to Athena is also delivered to Odysseus (*Il.* 2.179–81) with one minor change in v.179, where Athena replaces Hera's adjective "brazen-coated" with her own exhortation to Odysseus not to tarry, which is in line with Hera's message.[17] The main part of Paris' message given to Hector for delivery to the

---

[17] For some minor problems with the text *Il.* 2.178–179, see Kirk, *The Iliad* ad loc. There was an earlier world of extensive oral communication long before written law was introduced. The very early Greek communities had run on "oral" or customary law, that is, generally accepted norms of behavior whose transgression would tend to be judged and punished by the elders of the community (*Il.* 18.479–508); Michael Gagarin, *Early Greek Law* (University of California Press, 1986) 26–33; Rosalind Thomas, *Literacy and Orality in Ancient Greece*, (Cambridge University Press, 1992) 68–73 says that even when laws began to be written down, oral law continued and there can have been no abrupt transition into written law. In other areas we have also similar conditions, that is, our written evidence, which is anyway scanty for the early times, stands for just a fraction of what was actually transacted in antiquity. In another sense even the written word was for a long time subordinate to the spoken, something like a mnemonic aid for the recollection of what was to be communicated orally rather than a text to be read in its own right, R. Finnegan, *Oral Poetry, Its Nature, Significance and Social Content* (Cambridge University Press, 1977) ch. 3 and 8; André Lardinois, "The Wisdom and Wit of Many: The Orality of Greek Proverbial Expressions." in *Speaking Volumes, Orality and Literacy in the Greek and Roman World, Mnemosyne Suppl.* 218 (Leiden, 1001) 95. Orality played an important role in the early life of the Roman Republic and even the empire, and it would be reasonable to see verbal or oral pronouncements as primary and their written manifestation as secondary. For more details, see Fergus Millar, "Government and Diplomacy in the Empire during the first Three Centuries," *The International History Review* 10 (1988) 358.

Achaeans is so close to the original that one gets the impression it is almost verbatim, a poetic device of course which may not be unrelated to the message delivery requirements of the ancient world. Hector's message to the Achaeans omits the part dealing with the return of the Achaeans, since that part is self-evident. The message Hector delivers to his mother on behalf of his brother Helenus is similar to the one he received, except for minor alterations in some of the verses. Otherwise, the message keeps to the original language. Only at the end which describes Hector's violent outburst is the message different, but that part is unrelated to Helenus' message.[18] The same verbatim character underlines the message of Zeus to Iris for Hera and Athena as well as the message given to Athena by Iris, since the main source of Zeus' anger is Athena and only secondarily Hera (*Il.* 8.350–56, 381–395). Priam's compromise motion that Idaeus carries to the assembled Achaeans contains the nucleus of Paris' proposal together with Priam's addendum which herald Idaeus delivered almost verbatim, with the necessary adjustments, of course. For purposes unknown, on this occasion Idaeus digresses from his messenger obligation by adding his own parenthetical comments related to the transactions of the Trojan assembly and the mood that prevailed in it, something unusual for a messenger with an established reputation for prudence. Finally, Iris' rendition of Zeus' message to Poseidon is almost verbatim to Zeus's message. Verses *Il.* 15.160–67 in the *Iliad* are repeated to Poseidon with adjustments for the second person at 176–83, save for the rephrasing of 163 ff. and 179 ff. Otherwise, the message is almost verbatim, a format most probably expected to be followed by messengers in the Homeric times, and no doubt in the times preceding Homer's age. Being a skilful diplomat, Iris greets Poseidon tactfully with honorific titles and mindful of his sensitivity to his honor calls her errand a message rather than an order.

The use of repetitive formulaic phrases by Homer is a known fact and needs no elaboration; homerists and philologists are aware of Homeric formulas since, at least, Parry's time in the early twentieth century. In addition, Kakrides has pointed out that Homer repeats key words for the sake of emphasis and that the same is done by modern Greek demotic poets

---

[18] *Il.* 6.86–98, 269–280. Hector's instructions to Hecuba generally accord to Helenus' recommendations, except for some details. The most obvious addition is the introduction of Theano as priestess of Athena, and her performing the important actions of opening the temple and offering the prayer, Walter Burkert, *Greek Religion*, 96.

who might not have been as familiar with Homer' poetic techniques. He perceives in this use a long tradition that supersedes Homer who, he thinks, borrowed the technique from his forerunners.[19] The theory, consequently, prevails that the almost identical delivery between the received and relayed messages is due to the formulaic format of epic poetry. But after this investigation in the history of Near Eastern messages and messengers, one wonders whether this writer might be stretching the subject too far by hypothesizing that the quasi-verbatim repetitions in the format of the relayed messages might also be due to Homeric poetry's effort to depict prevailing practices. Is it also very possible that the Homeric practice of formulaic repetition in the delivery of messages, constituted an imitation of the prevailing custom in the Bronze Age, which dictated that messages be delivered as faithfully close to their original format as possible? If the dictum again that art "imitates life" is true, this possibility cannot be totally excluded. One thing is definitely clear: even the quasi-verbatim delivery of messages does not prevent messengers in the Near East and Homer from elucidating points connected with the messages, if elucidation is needed.

SONS OF KINGS AS ENVOYS

Another analogy which also traces its seeds to the remote past is the dispatch of princes (sons of kings) as messengers. We have seen such examples in the Ancient Near East and in the *Odyssey*, where Odysseus as a very young man is sent to Messene to negotiate a compensation treaty for the

---

[19] Homer's repeated formulaic expressions need no amplification. Kakrides, *Homeric Themes*, pp. 58 and 60. He points out that Homer repeated certain words as an emphasis technique, a technique which is also used by modern Greek demotic poets, who most probably were not familiar with Homer's poetry. Examples, *Il*.13.22–26:

χρὺσεα, χρυσέῃσιν,
χρυσόν, χρυσείην,

Βλέπω τὸ Χάρο κι' ἔρχεται στοὺς κάμπους καβαλάρης ·
Μαῦρος εἶναι, μαῦρα φορεῖ, μαῦρο ' ν ' καὶ τ' ἄλογό του
Μαῦρο ' ν ' καὶ τὸ ζαγάρι του ποὺ ἔρχεται κοντά του.

Where the epithet "black" is repeated four times in the last two lines, (underlining mine).

Messenian theft of Ithacan sheep and shepherds. In most Australian tribes, when young boys are chosen to act as messengers, it is because they are held in high honor. There is no doubt that something similar happened here among the Ithacans, otherwise they would not have sent young Odysseus on such a sensitive mission.[20] The Ithacans must have prized young Odysseus' precociousness and his ability to articulate his thoughts clearly and succinctly, since they trusted him with such a sensitive undertaking. The same appreciation of Odysseus' negotiating ability becomes repeatedly manifest in the *Iliad* in as much as Odysseus is the envoy of the Greeks in most of their diplomatic dispatches. In a way, Odysseus becomes the analogue of the Egyptian messengers Haamašši and Mane,[21] the Mitanni Keliya, Pirissi, and Tulubri,[22] and other messengers in the Near East who, prized for their negotiating talents by masters and interlocutor kings, find themselves constantly on the move, conveying messages back and forth.

ARCHIVES

It is well known, that Near Eastern treaties contain a clause concerning their deposition and regular recitation. The agreement between Suppiluliumas and Mattiwaza, the King of the Mitanni, contains a clause according to which a copy of the tablet must be deposited in the temple of the famous Babylonian Sun god Shamash, the special protector of the Hittite King and queen, while another copy is to be placed before Tešub, the lord of Kurinnu in Kahat.[23] This is a customary practice in the Near East and needs not be belabored here.

The Minoan writing A and the Mycenaean Linear B writings point to the maintenance of chancellories in these cultures, but whether or not official documents such as treaties were kept there is unclear, since no Mycenaean treaty documents touching upon Mycenaean diplomatic practices have survived. What we know is that in the early archaic Greek period, very close

---

[20] Primitive tribes occasionally choose young boys held in high esteem to act as messengers, Parker, *The Euahlayi Tribe*, 64.9.

[21] Moran, AL, *EA* 11.9–15, 16–22; *EA* 27.37–40, 55–58; *EA* 19. 17–24; 20.8-13, 14–17, 18–22, 23–27, 64–70; 21.24–32; 24.§5–§7, §10, §11 and passim; 26.7–18; 27.7–8, 13–18, 69–73, 93–98.

[22] Moran, *EA* 19.25-29, 39–42, 71–79; 20.18–22, 23–27; 24.§9–10, §27–28; *EA* 27.89–92, 93–98, 99–103; 28.12–19; *EA* 27.60 (see n.13) and 89–92; 28.12–19.

[23] Perhaps a sanctuary, Weidner, *Politische Dokumente*, 28 n. 1. For similar practices see also Dennis J. McCarthy, *Treaty and Covenant: A Study in Form in the Ancient Oriental Documents and in the Old Testament* (Rome, 1963). 183–84.

chronologically to the writing of the Homeric epics, copies of interstate treaties were already deposited in the archives of temples of the Greek cities, while still other copies were usually set up at such famous Panhellenic religious centers as Olympia and Delphi. In some cases, because of the worn-out condition of the stelae, the stipulation regarding the setting up of the inscription at the sanctuary cannot be traced, but the presence of the stele itself in places like Olympia and Delphi, considerably distant from the geographic location of the signatory cities, leaves little doubt that copies of Greek interstate treaties were customarily deposited there. In harmony with this practice, we have a record of a treaty document in Olympia, though the copy deposited in the archives of the signatory city has been lost.[24] Even if Olympia was not under the control of Elis, the presence of a slab describing a treaty underlines the resolve of the two allies to deposit a copy at Olympia. In a similar manner, the Greek cities of the Anaetoi and Metapioi as well as the cities of Sybaris and the Serdaeans, far from Olympia and Greece, deposited copies of their treaties (dated between 550–525 BC) in Olympia where the mutilated texts have been discovered. Copies of the signatory cities must have been correspondingly deposited at some temples of these cities but unfortunately they have not been found.[25]

Significantly, the custom of placing copies of documents at the temples of gods is not limited to treaties. Appropriately, a stone on which the text of the constitution of the Cretan city of Dreros had been inscribed (ca. 650–600) has been located on the wall of the temple of Apollo Delphinius in Dreros. Its location confirms that temples served as repositories of important state and interstate documents.[26] Needless to say, the practice of entrusting treaties to the temples of gods went on unabatedly into the Classical and Hellenistic times. The invocation of gods as witnesses, the curses, blessings, and other features contained in these documents are similar to the

---

[24] W. Wittenberger and Karl Purgold, *Die Inschriften von Olympia*, no. 2 and R. Meiggs and D. Lewis (M/L), *A Selection of Greek Historical Inscriptions to the End of the Fifth Century B.C.* (Oxford Clarendon Press, 1969) n. 17; Georg Busolt, IGI² (Berlin, 1983) 64, n. 4. 706; L. I. Highby, *The Erythrae Degree*, Klio Beiheft 36 (1936) 63–64; Christian Callmer, *Studien zur Geschichte Arkadiens: bis zur Gründung des Arkadischen Bundes* (Lund, 1943) 80.

[25] Hermann Bengtson, *Die Staatsverträge des Altertums*, nos. 110; 111; 120. The treaties have been found in Olympia, the panhellenic sanctuary where they were deposited. No doubt copies must have been deposited also in the local sanctuaries of the cities involved, which have been lost. For bibliography see Bengtson ad loc.

[26] Meiggs and Lewis, (M/L) eds., *A Selection*, no. 2.

Near Eastern practices, suggesting that the practice of temple or palace-temple deposition must have been in existence among the Homeric Greeks and that it survived the Mycenaean collapse, despite the absence of hard evidence. Oddly, a similar practice is found among the primitive tribes of Hawaii and elsewhere. In these areas, when the terms of a document were agreed upon, the parties repaired to the temple. In the absence of literacy, a wreath of *Maori*, a sweet-scented plant, was then woven by the leading chiefs of both parties and deposited in the temple. In both cases, the deposition of the document at the temple and the wreath of *Maori* meant the sanctification of the agreement by the gods, who thus became the protectors of the agreement and the punishers of the violators.[27]

This investigation of the Homeric texts relating to messengers and their messages evinces that except for minor alterations stemming from local cultural, social, political, and geographic factors, Homeric diplomatic rules adhered in the main to the pattern common in the Near Eastern world. In the present study of diplomatic rules, there is no clear evidence of Near Eastern diplomatic forces exercising an influence in the shaping of the diplomatic practices mirrored in epic poetry. On the contrary, the only certain picture emerging from the discussion of these practices is that messengerial practices in the Near East and the Eastern Mediterranean are similar and so old that their history gets lost in the "hazy" pre-historical times. The only fairly reliable conclusion one can, therefore, draw from the analysis of the Near Eastern and the Aegean basin study is the commonality of traditional rules which guided the conduct and exchange of envoys in their communities. The theory that Homeric epic poetry reproduced only the ideas of the Dark or the Homeric Age cannot be sustained. Homeric poetry may understandably reflect ideas of the Homeric Age, but it also does something more than that; it portrays diplomatic practices which are very similar, if not identical, to the Bronze Age practices of the Near East whose roots hail deeply in the Bronze Age. The logical question in a reader's mind is whether these practices were copied by the Homeric Greeks from the Near East or whether they preexisted in the Aegean basin culture, used by the people who lived their. There is no absolute answer to this question. But inasmuch as Homer, first, ascribes some of the events and concomitant practices he describes to pre-Dark Age times and, secondly, scholars assure

---

[27] W. Ellis, *Narrative of a Tour through Hawaii, or Ownyhee* (London, 1826) 32; R. W. Williamson, *The Social and Political Systems of Central Polynesia* 2 (Cambridge University Press, 1924) 176 and vol. 3, 195–99.

us that Homer has extensively borrowed epic material from his predecessors which he molded into his own suitable form. Homer used this material in the composition of his epics, and it is almost certain that these practices antedated the Dark Age, going back at least to the Mycenaean world. Perhaps future scientific discoveries may enable scientists to elucidate definitively the relationships between the pre-Dark Age and post-Dark Age inhabitants of Greece in many cultural areas. Already an attempt has been made in *Archaeology Meets Science*, which deals with revolutionary discoveries in the area of food and drink in the Minoan and Mycenaean times.[28] Future research tools and methods may force us to revise drastically our present conclusions about the Bronze Age period. Until that time, a better explanation than the mere theory of influence of one civilization upon the other may be that the peoples of the Near East and the Eastern Mediterranean area shared certain unwritten customs (*themistes*) and traditions, with roots so deep in history that they traditionally ascribed their origin to the gods.

---

[28] Tzedakis and Martlew, eds., *Archaeology Meets Science*, 18, 36, 44.

6 Concluding Remarks

In the preceding five chapters of this essay, we sailed quickly through the wine dark sea of the Aegean in an eastward direction. Our voyage took us to the coasts and highlands of Anatolia and beyond. We visited western Asia all the way to the banks of the famous Tigris and Euphrates rivers. We traveled the southeastern littoral of Mediterranean to the banks of the Nile and ventured into the interior of Egypt, winding past the pyramids and the ancient Egyptian temples. The aim of this voyage was to trace the complex network of the ancient roads and paths followed by the ever kinetic messengers of the Near Eastern states and empires as they carried their masters' messages in pursuit of their diplomatic tasks. We witnessed the complex network of ancient trade routes which once connected the lands of Egypt, Syria, Mesopotamia, and Anatolia during the height of the Near Eastern empires and facilitated the movement of the diplomatic agents of those empires. Ocean routes also connected the eastern Mediterranean with the islands of the Aegean Sea for much of the second millennium BC. We have seen numerous messengers and traders traveling to and fro from the heart of Nubia to the end of Mesopotamia and beyond, day and night, in the cold of the winter and the blazing sun of the summer, exposing themselves to innumerable dangers on behalf of their kings and their countries. Kings and their messengers operated largely within certain parameters and were expected to respect basic principles that had crystallized as a result of long traditional practices and the requirements of the messengers' profession. Occasional violations did not *ipso facto* negate the validity of these principles. On the contrary, in the absence of a court of last resort, punishment for violations was left to the gods, the ultimate arbiters of the universe and the keepers of world order. Although the space wherein the world of the Homeric epics moved was very narrow, the same basic principles seemed to have prevailed even on those occasions when the narrow space of the epics was superceded. Consequently, the emerging picture of the Homeric diplomatic practices shows strong similarities to the oriental diplomatic rules.

Perhaps one way to describe this magnificent panorama of large and small states in the second millennium and the subsequent first part of the first millennium would be to paint it as a world in an active state of continuous gestation which resulted in a complex network of contacts and exchanges of ideas and cultural innovations. In recent years, the former historical theories that relied on invasions and colonization to explain the whirl of cultural dynamism and the changes that occurred in the area of Greece and the Aegean seem to have lost plausibility as they depended on scanty archaeological data and scholarly hypotheses of dubious validity. In this new context, it becomes difficult to identify the real causes of change that operated in these human cultures. The notion, for example, of earthquakes as the cause of ostensibly profound and permanent changes is being viewed today with suspicion.

What we observe instead is a tenacious and persistent adaptation of ideas, traditions, and customs in sundry human practices which were preserved and passed on from one period to another, though often physical buildings were lost or much of what remained of them underwent considerable adjustment. In this sense, the Dark Age that follows the disturbances of so-called Sea People presents a fair degree of coherence in the sequence of its developments by which society inherited a great deal from its very early predecessors and transmitted much of it in turn to the succeeding ages. It was from such a fermentation that the Archaic Greek culture emerged. Despite the collapse of the Mycenaean civilization which seems to have coincided with the coming of the Sea People and the upheaval which it might have generated, many diplomatic practices of the preceding times seemed to have survived in the culture that emerged out of its fall. We can safely conclude, therefore, that the Homeric epics that appeared at the beginning of the Archaic Age contain several elements of the Bronze period along with material of the Dark Age. Inevitable changes that came along with the passage of time and the movement of the Dorian people during the Dark Age depended largely on the numbers and the character of the newcomers, the level of their civilization as compared to the indigenous population, the position they acquired in the new society, and the number of women they brought with them.

Usually the complete conquest of an earlier culture depended on the size of the invading group compared to that of the native population. The stamping out of the conquered culture seldom happened on a large scale in ancient history. On the contrary, the opposite is often true, unless the newcomers were of entirely different origin and arrived in exceedingly superior numbers to the point that they irretrievably overwhelmed the local element.

If they did, then a regression was very likely to result.[1] Such a process seems doubtful to have materialized in Greece when the Mycenaean and the Dorians came to the Greek mainland. Both groups were allegedly inferior in culture to the natives and most probably in numbers as well. The only exception one can think to this rule in terms of numbers *may* be the Dorian element of Sparta. The mixture of the two cultures and peoples, if we can speak of two decidedly distinct cultures and peoples, gave rise to a civilization that retained many of its old characteristics, as the similarities in the social traditions that we encounter between the Near East and the Homeric culture tend to suggest, unless we accept that these similarities were borrowed by the inhabitants of Greece from the Near Easterners during the latter part of the second millennium BC. But such an assumption might be dangerous and perhaps false.

It is true that the Mycenaean civilization, partly contemporaneous with the Late Bronze Age culture, left us no mass of contemporary documentation from which the outlines of its history can be reconstructed as it happened with the Eastern world. Although it might be true that contacts with the East have been plentiful, it does not necessarily follow that massive absorption of Eastern traditions became part of the inheritance and history of the populations of Greece. The alternative solution to this dilemma would be to accept the view that the inhabitants of Greece possessed several traditions (social, political, religious) which were quite similar to those of the peoples of the Near East, and it is very possible that these traditions survived the fall of the Mycenaean civilization. Such a theory has no incontrovertible foundation since, as it was emphasized earlier, there is no contemporary Late Bronze Age evidence to underpin it. To strengthen the argument of continuity presented in this essay, we had to resort to the assistance of the abundant Near Eastern material, to anthropological evidence from primitive tribes, and the analysis of the earliest Greek evidence that can be gathered from the Homeric epics.

A number of identifiable cultural points which bear similarities to the Near Eastern practices have been analyzed in the preceding chapters which point to the excellent possibilities of further research on cultural, political, social, and religious affinities. The universal predominance of these practices in the areas of Greece and the Near East adverts to the commonality of practices among the peoples who lived in these areas. For the international relations scholar, the comparative analysis of the Near Eastern mate-

---

[1] Dickinson, *The Aegean Bronze Age*, 24.

rial presents a fascinating challenge. Although this material is incomplete, it nevertheless contains sufficient evidence to permit a concerted study in reasonable depth which adumbrates the appearance of an early system of international relations that constitutes the progenitor of modern international relations. It is in the second millennium that we observe an increased rhythm of interactions among the Great Powers of the Near East, from the Mediterranean to the Persian Gulf, in the form of regular dynastic, commercial, and strategic considerations. The by-product of the political management of this interconnected set of relationships is a diplomatic system consisting of rules, conventions, procedures and institutional customs that governed the communications and negotiations between great and smaller states. For whatever it is worth, some further comparisons between the Near Eastern, Aegean, and Byzantine practices were made here, mainly because the Byzantine Empire, having survived as the Eastern portion of the Roman Empire was made up by Greeks and Easterners. They also had to deal with Eastern states that occupied the areas of the ancient territories or neighboring places.[2]

Seen from the standpoint of the Near Eastern states, this study of the system of international relations has achieved two complementary objectives: theoretical understanding of the abiding nature of relations across sovereign states of the Near East, and greater insight into the contemporaneous inter-nascent affairs represented by the districts over which the Homeric chieftains ruled. The study of these relations enables us to investigate the validity or explanatory utility of controversial modern assumptions and theories regarding the early Greek culture from a novel angle. One may remonstrate that inferences about these early international relations are of a rather tenuous nature since they rely on somewhat primitive political socie-

---

[2] Sometime after I had written the above comment on the Byzantine Empire, I noticed Evangelos Chrysos' pertinent statement in his article "Byzantine Diplomacy, A.D. 300–800: Means and Ends," in Jonathan Shepard and Simon Franklin, *Byzantine Diplomacy*, 30 which was brought to my attention by a young friend Demetrios Karademas, a brilliant graduate student in Byzantine History at the University of Athens. Chrysos explains that "Byzantine diplomacy does not simply continue the Roman tradition but traces its forms to the international community of the eastern Mediterranean world in the distant past. Some of these forms were actually in use in the early second millennium B.C." (as the reader of this essay will have noticed, they go even farther, at least as far as the third millennium) "as we know from the archives of the Mari kings in western Asia and the Pharaohs of the El-Amarna period."

ties of social rather than a properly political texture. It is true, nevertheless, that a careful analysis of the institutions of these early societies can shed ample light on the understanding of international relations, if one takes into account sociopolitical and anthropological analyses along with the historical approach.

For instance, it is immediately evident even from a cursory reading of the Near Eastern evidence on interstate relations that such relations were shaped on the model of interpersonal relations. External relations in the evidential material of the Near East and Homer are presented in the form of hospitality, intermarriage, personal honor, exchange of services and goods much as the procedures of relationships in daily life were used in a slightly modified form. The family metaphor is immediately evident in the pervasive use of the terms employed in the Near East, such as my "brother" or my "father," the latter metaphor reserved for more senior partners. Although this terminology is not "officially" employed in the Homeric epics, nonetheless the personal character of the relations among the Homeric kings is even more obvious. And if the "nuclear family" model is not always the most suitable to explain the type of relations that existed, the "clan" or "small community" model definitely is.

Even in the most demanding exchanges of the inter-dynastic Near Eastern relations, the interpersonal level is the only one in use and the same is true of the Homeric relations. Yet in both areas, behind the apparently "childish" interpersonal quarrels and petty complaints, there is the dominant question of personal and state pride. The protest by the Babylonian King Kadašman-Enlil at not having been invited to a feast in the Egyptian residency at Amarna (*EA* 3) is analogous to some of the complaints made by the Homeric kings about each other. As Liverani has appropriately suggested, these types of complaints allude often to the failure of reciprocity, politeness, and lack of regard which may be a constant problem in a small-scale society but seem odd when transferred to relations between courts.[3]

The address form of the letters underscores the personal character of their correspondence, though admittedly there are differences from state to state. Each letter is separable into two unequal segments. The first consists of the heading, address, and salutation. The heading of the vassal's letter contains a "prostration formula" and some ritual-like characteristics which are formalistic, relatively unvarying, and highly predictable. In the body of the letter lies the utilitarian part of the message. This part is the specific re-

---

[3] Liverani, "The Great Powers Club," in *Amarna Diplomacy*, 19.

quest, the proposal, démarche, complaint, arrangement for the political or commercial transaction, the very stuff of political exchange which led Cohen to argue that in the Amarna Letters we see irrefutable evidence in the development of a fully-fledged diplomatic system that reflected many features present in the classic European diplomacy of more than three millennia later.[4]

It should be stated at this point that the reference above about the salutation segment of the oriental epistolography was also part of the Greek exchanges. The form of salutation, from what little evidence we gather from Homer, was plain, befitting the less structured form of the Greek society so early in history. Brotherhood existed among the Homeric kings but without the gradations that appear in the Amarna Letters and the Asiatic world. If Agamemnon appears to be more elevated than the other kings, he was so because of the elevated regard for his kingdom as well as because the other kings had chosen him as their commander-in-chief, a position that entailed universal respect. However, when Agamemnon blundered, the other kings did not hesitate to make it known to him.

Most of the international negotiations were conducted through representatives or agents who were authorized to represent their principals and assumed symbolic significance. The way these agents were treated reflected the status of the relations between the states as well as the status of their masters. In his eagerness to forge friendly relations with the king of Egypt, Tušratta reminded the Egyptian King that he had treated his messengers with great respect by bestowing upon them very high honors. If one king's envoy was not treated as well as the envoys of other kings, then that king complained about his own status vis-à-vis the addressee. The complaint externalized the fact that there were disparities among the "brothers" and that not all "brothers" were equal, if they were not treated as such. During the Amarna Letters period, the understanding was that all of the "brothers" were equal, but several of them approached the Pharaoh with deference, while the Pharaoh conducted himself with an air of superiority.

Some of the sensitivity of the complaining parties was often misplaced. A messenger had to assure his apparently petulant and ignorant Babylonian King, who behaved as if Egypt were down the street from his kingdom, that it was really a distant country miles away, and that it took days and

---

[4] Kevin Avruch, "Reciprocity, Equality, and Status-Anxiety in the *Amarna Letters*," in *Amarna Diplomacy* 157; Cohen, "On Diplomacy," in *Diplomacy and Statecraft*, vol. 7 (1996) 266.

months to send news and receive answers. The petulance and bickering that unfolded in the *Iliad* stemmed from disparate causes, but even in the *Iliad* the quarreling among the Achaean leaders produced the impressions of pettiness. Yet in both places the personal ego, wrapped around the question of honor, was the dominant issue.

The rules of hospitality that protected the messenger during his stay abroad prevented him also from leaving without the host's permission (*EA* 28.2). The same principle obtained in the Homeric epics: the messenger had to have the approval of his host, although a greater degree of rationality prevailed in the exercise of this permission. There might have been occasions, however, in the Dark and the Mycenaean Ages in which messengers were detained for a long time for whatever reasons, if we are to judge from Menelaus' remarks to Telemachus, but the data are missing. Odysseus had to stay in Phaeacia until his host was ready to dispatch him to his land, while Calypso might have kept her guest for a much longer time, if not forever, had not the gods ordered her to release him. True, Odysseus was not an envoy to Phaeacia and at Calypso's court but a guest; yet similar rules seemed to have prevailed in the cases of messengers and guests. Inordinate retention of an envoy might lead to protests, but as it was beyond the power of the envoy to do otherwise, reciprocation was the only alternative left to the envoy's master. The unfairness of detention was recognized by Homer who voiced through Menelaus the formulation of a more rational guideline regarding the departure of guests (*Od.* 15.68–74). The Romans had a reputation for keeping envoys of federated or subservient states for a long time in Rome, while in the Byzantine period it was customary for envoys to receive permission from their host in order to depart.[5] As in the Near Eastern cases, the envoy always ran the risk of being used as a hostage by the host ruler.[6] Under normal circumstances, the host was considered responsible for the envoy's safety while at his host's place and for the arrangements of his safe return. The ruler's guards in places the envoy crossed would normally protect him and place themselves kindly at his services even though guards at times could be frightening.

On the other hand, the modern doctrine of diplomatic immunity, whereby a diplomat is not liable in the courts of the host country for his

---

[5] R. Guilland, *La Correspondence de Nicephore Grégoras* (Paris, 1927) 39.

[6] Guilland, *La Correspondence* 47; O. Lampsides, *Andreou Libadênou. Bios kai Erga* (Athens, 1975) 49; N. Oikonomides, "Byzantine Diplomacy, A.D. 1204–1453: Means and Ends," in Shepard and Franklin, eds., *Byzantine Diplomacy*, 86.

illegal acts, is not attested in ancient Near Eastern records nor in the custom practices of the epics; yet, on one prominent occasion in the Amarna Letters, the strong contemporary suggestion is made that at the very least, the host country could demand that the offending diplomat be tried and punished by his own king (*EA* 29.173–82). Under less friendly circumstances between the two countries or kings, however, the envoys could have been made to suffer contempt or even punishment for theirs or their master's sins. Moreover, unjustified and unprovoked attaint to the person or the dignity of an envoy by the host country would be regarded as an attack on the envoy's country, and hence a *casus belli*.[7]

Great kings were generally able to reaffirm their higher authority by granting the messengers a protection that was the practical outcome of their superior power. But while escorts or letters of warning may be the customary tools for preventing problems with the local chiefs or vassals, the same was not true of brigands and malefactors. Even the local kings were not always in full control of their respective territories. Remote villages, pastoral tribes and bands of outcasts were not infrequently responsible for robberies, perhaps even murders of messengers passing through their shifting hideouts in the Near East and Greek worlds. These people knew that messengers often carried gifts and other valuables.

The fundamental norms of hospitality in the Near East and Homer were gifts, which could not be asked for, ought to be given, accepted, and appreciated, and reciprocated in an increased amount whenever possible. Yet in Mesopotamia, gifts were often requested, and kings would complain if the gift was not proportionate to the request or if it were not given on time for the requested purpose. In Homer and the Near East, the gift-giving ideology was not framed so much in terms of financial value, though this also transpired occasionally, as much as in the form of personal pride and renown as well as the suitability of the gift. Within the category of luxury goods transferred from one court to another, special mention should be made of expert personnel, principally among them physicians and specialists in disease diagnoses and exorcisms. The Amarna Letters and the Mari correspondence attest to a request by the king of Hatti for a physician for the sister of the Hittite king who was suffering from sterility. The king of Ugarit also asked for a physician and an expert in vulture augury from the

---

[7] In a Biblical account we read of the shameful treatment of King David's envoys whose half beards were shaved off and their clothes cut off at the middle. David responded to this offense with an armed expedition, 2. Sam. 2.1–14.

king of Cyprus (*EA* 35.25). The same is true in the Mari texts and elsewhere in the Near East where demands were made for architects, masons, and skilled workers in general.[8] The premise behind allowing qualified experts to travel to foreign courts was that they would be sent home as soon as their professional task was completed, a prerequisite that was very seldom satisfied.[9] Beyond the compelling evidence of the Boğhazköy Letter, which fully confirms the renowned prestige of Egyptian physicians, who were closely followed by Babylonian physicians and exorcists in healing reputation, more poignant is the information in Tušratta's letter (*EA* 23) in which he announces the dispatch of a statue of Shaushka (the Hurrian equivalent of the Akkadian Ishtar) of Nineveh, probably to heal the old and suffering Amenophis III.[10]

Closely associated with the international marriages was the custom of the bridal gift, a quasi-universal practice in the Near East and Homeric world. Like many other gifts, the quality and the value of the bridal gift reflected the importance of the sender and the reputation of the person and the family of the receiver. The gifts of Agamemnon to Achilles were many as well as rich because his intent was to compensate Achilles for the damage done to his honor. As the great king of Mycenae and commander–in–chief of the Achaean troops, Agamemnon wanted to impress all of the Achaeans with his overgenerous gifts. Like Agamemnon, the early Assyrian King Shamshi-Adad, who wished to have his son Jasma-Adad marry the daughter of King Qatanum, urged his son to impress the family of the bride by increasing the bridal gifts.[11]

---

[8] Lanfranchi and Parpola, *SAA*, vol. 2, p. 81, No. 95.

[9] Zaccagnini, "The Interdependence of the Great Powers," in *Amarna Diplomacy*, 146.

[10] Zaccagnini, "The Interdependence of the Great Powers," in *Amarna Diplomacy*, 147. How strong and deeply embedded these beliefs still are in the area is attested to by the dispatch of the famous 'miraculous' icon of Panagia from the island of Tenos to the dying King Paul of Greece, in the early sixties, in the hope that it might cure him of his serious sickness.

[11] The practice of giving bridal gifts was obviously very widespread in the ancient Near East and Greece. In the fascinating scene of the Old Testament in which Abraham sent his trusted servant to Mesopotamia to find a bride for the young Isaac, we also learn that he loaded the servant with bridal gifts, gold, silver, raiments, Gen. 24.33–25. Several of the customs examined in this paper show how widespread these customs were. Laban requested at first that the servant's entourage remain with his family for at least ten days. Abraham's servant, on the other

When the consignment of Egyptian gold sent by the Pharaoh to Tušratta as part of the bridal gift turned out to be debased, the recipient was dismayed. Fortunately, the Egyptian delegation headed by the prudent Mane reacted correctly; its members showed a similar dismay, which pleased Tušratta. Then, with his eloquent rhetoric, Mane defended the good intentions of his lord, as a prudent envoy should, and Tušratta accepted Mane's explanation, expressing his complete satisfaction. The effective intervention of Mane demonstrates likewise the leeway envoys enjoyed in the exercise of their duties. Like Iris in the Homeric epics, oriental messengers had the freedom to elaborate on their mission or message and to provide elucidations whenever the occasion required it. From this standpoint, Cohen was right when he perceived in the Near Eastern system of envoys the origins of western diplomacy.[12]

Contrary to the dictum "never look a gift-horse in the mouth," horses and all other gifts exchanged were often subject to an examination. Almost always gift items were meticulously inspected and evaluated by both the sender and the recipient, especially the latter. If we are to judge from the reaction of Homer to the gift Glaucus received from Diomedes, gifts were submitted to a vigorous evaluation in the Homeric times, a custom that must have had earlier roots. Since gifts were a sign of social and political prestige whenever they were intertwined with foreign relations, they were

---

hand, asked that he be released from this obligation because he was in a hurry to return to Palestine. Lodging and food were offered to the entire entourage. The hosts had not inquired into the identity and purpose of the servant's trip, exactly as it happened elsewhere in the Near East and the Homeric world, but in this case the servant refused to accept his host's hospitality before he had explained the purpose of his coming. On his way to Mesopotamia, the servant was given provisions and an escort, and like Priam, he was purportedly accompanied by an angel to guard him during his trip (Gen. 24.7; 40). There is no mention, of course, of libations before the servant's departure; only an oath is mentioned in the name of the God of Heaven and Earth which clearly denotes that, as in the Near Eastern and Homeric instances, prayers were said before the servant's departure from Palestine to Mesopotamia and from Mesopotamia to Palestine (Gen. 24.52). The reference to the God of Heaven and Earth seems to correspond to the swearing formula of the Near East and Homer where the Helios (sun) and the sun-god Shamash were mentioned because, like the God of Abraham, they saw all and could not be deceived. Burkert has pointed out the oriental and late Greek parallels for the conjunction in oath of invocations to the sun, earth, rivers, and underworld (Walter Burkert, *Greek Religion*, 175).

[12] Cohen, "On Diplomacy," in *Diplomacy and Statecraft*, 266.

carefully scrutinized and their recipients, unlike Glaucus, did not hesitate to express their displeasure at a gift's inadequacy. Beyond their "financial" value, whatever that value may have been, the suitability of the gift to the donée as well as the history behind the gift's origin greatly enhanced the value in the eyes of the recipient and his friends. A regular chain of exchanges provided the basis for positive international relationships, while a constant rhythm of comings and goings by envoys not only reassured the various kings about their friendly relations with their colleagues but also implied the dispatch and arrival of material goods.[13]

Where an international society exists, relations among its members are generally governed by common political conventions as well as by agreed rules of law which may or may not be incorporated into written legal codes. In the ancient Near East, the conventions that made up international law had an old and venerable tradition and were attested virtually from the beginnings of written records, which obviously antedated their written form. The same is true of Greek customary law, which was appealed to in diplomatic protests and negotiations. The system of customary law was under the jurisdiction of the community gods who constituted the highest court. Enforcement was by the gods or legitimate self-help, when possible. Unlike us, the ancients did not draw a clear separation between juridical and divine law. Everyone believed in the gods, and even the agnostics and skeptics had to tailor their religious ideas to the requirements of their community. People perceived the gods as part of the real world just as they perceived the earth as being flat. The divine legal system governed human behavior no less that human courts and their sanctions did. Natural calamities such as plagues, droughts, floods, and defeats in war were attributed to divine justice, and steps were taken to make legal reparation in light of them. The gods judged every one, be he a king, commoner, or slave, and every individual within a state could seek recourse to divine justice through prayer. The gods were the ultimate court of appeal where human courts could not or would not provide justice. Since there were no international tribunals to act as the final adjudicators of inter-communal or international disputes, states also appealed to the gods to punish the culprits, and the subjects of these states believed that eventually the gods would not allow an injustice to prevail. Divine judgment became the court of first instance. Thus Achilles appealed to his goddess mother as Chryses did to Apollo, while the Greeks

---

[13] Zaccagni, "The Interdependence of the Great Powers," in *Amarna Diplomacy*, 148.

turned to the gods when Paris violated the oaths of the duel that had been agreed between the Achaeans and Trojans. The international law was based on customary law which was dominant in the area. The idea that god is the ultimate adjudicator of all unjust acts, so prominent in the ancient world, continued to prevail in the Christian world as well. Oral agreements or the ceremony of treaty signing required religious oaths to be uttered because the Christian world was fully aware that promises and oath violations were a frequent occurrence. They believed that God would be the ultimate court of appeal in such cases.

The distances Near Eastern messengers had to cover were frequently great and since writing was in common use from the beginning of the third millennium BC, the messages were mostly written.[14] The written nature of

---

[14] The overwhelming number of messages in the Homeric world is oral. Memorization continued in other fields of interest in the Greek world. In Athens public speakers and orators cultivated the habit of delivering their disputations orally. Even those who prepared speeches by writing them down learned them by heart before they delivered them in front of an audience. Oral delivery was thought of not just as commendable but necessary. Learning poetry and prose texts by heart for oral delivery seems to have been part of the pedagogical program of the teaching schools and sophists. This is shown by a famous passage in Aristotle's *Sophistical Refutations* (183b) where the model texts were handed out for memorization by the schools of Gorgias, Plat. *Phaedr.* 228, and the method of Hippias, who is reputed to have developed an effective system of mnemonotechnics. In addition, we have few passages that suggest that the preparation of a speech was inseparably connected with its memorization (*Arist. Knights* 347–490). The written text was rehearsed all night long for delivery the day after. In a passage of Aeschines (*On the Embassy* 2.43), the phrase *deinos eipein kai mnemonikos* is employed. In the *Clouds* the first question Socrates (483) asks of Strepsiades was whether he had a good memory (*ei mnemonikos ei*). One of the arguments that Gorgias' pupil Alcidamas employed in his criticism of the written speeches was that memorization of a speech was troublesome and forgetting parts of it during delivery was extremely embarrassing (*Sophist* 18–21). In an orally delivered speech one is forced to remember the exact wording of it during its delivery or at least the *akribeian* of what is in the speech. This advice reminds us of Homer verse (*Il.* 15.159) and of Thucydides' claim that he stuck to the *akribeian* of what was said by the speakers (1.22). Johan Schoemann, *Entertainment and Democratic Distrust*, in *Epea and Grammata, Orality and Literacy in Ancient Greece* vol. 4, *Mnemosyne Supplements*, 230 (Brill, 2002); S Usher, "Lysias and his Clients," *GRBS* 17 (1976) 36. In antiquity, public speaking was also seen as a form of entertainment with the audience expecting a clever argumentation and an aesthetically fulfilling form of presentation. Sources from the fifth century confirm that the de-

the message did not preclude knowledge of its contents by its carrier, except on rare occasions. The messengers were as a rule confidants of the kings and were also instructed how to answer questions that could be raised in connection with the message. In the Homeric epics, we observe that the carriers were high officials of the king when the message was either personal or concerned a king's state; if the message concerned the entire Achaean community, persons of common trust and extraordinary ability would be selected from the leaders of the Achaeans. As in the Near East, the messenger did not go alone but was accompanied by a substantial retinue. On his return trip, very frequently the messenger would be accompanied by a messenger of the host king who was entrusted with the business of his king and also served as a guide and security as they crossed the host king's or allies' land, or the borders of satellite countries. Once the embassy reached its destination the host king's messenger would serve as a witness to the truthfulness of the envoy he accompanied. The task of the accompanying messenger was not considered complete until he returned to his king with whatever information he carried for his master.

Messengers and envoys continued to be busy in the East from time immemorial, executing diplomatic missions according to well-established customs. Missions were sent and received for the notification of the accessions to the throne of new sovereigns and the reaffirmation of the status quo of existing relations with foreign rulers linked to their states by treaties in the Near East. If similar activities occurred in states like Mycenae, it is not easy to know; although it cannot altogether be excluded since the absence of records predicates neither of the two possibilities, Near Eastern customs, the Homeric epics, and primitive tribal customs suggest that they most probably did. Embassies were received or sent off to announce decisive victories or important events as royal marriages, births of children in the royal purple, constructions of new palaces and other similar events. Occasionally, when this cycle of comings and goings was temporarily disrupted for whatever reason, kings affected by this discontinuity did not hesitate to notify or complain to their counterpart (s), as the Easterners did.

There were also other factors that impressed envoys in their visits of various places. The impression made upon envoys by the seats of governments they visited, the palaces, the gardens, the culture in general, was a potent propaganda factor in the dealings among states from antiquity to

---

mocratic audiences expected the speaker to deliver a convincing and pleasant show (Thuc. 3.47–50).

Byzantium. The aura of the mighty Egyptian Empire was not simply due to its magnitude and size but also to the cultural accomplishments of Egypt. The young Telemachus, a country bumpkin from Ithaca, was dazzled by the magnificence of Menelaus' palace in Sparta. So were the many visitors and envoys who visited Athens in the latter part of the fifth century and after. The empire had disappeared but droves of people went to Athens to see the city and admire the marvelous monuments constructed during the time of the empire.

Mention has been made above of host envoys attached to the visiting embassy on its return trip. Did a similar diplomatic practice exist in the Homeric world? The lack of evidence does not help us, but there is a paradoxical circumstance associated with the embassy to Achilles that may allude to this practice. Besides the heralds who accompanied the embassy, Phoenix, the third person who traveled with Odysseus and Aias, was supposed to champion the cause of the Achaeans, within the limitations of his position. He led the way of the embassy, nonetheless, like the host messengers in the Near East, and like them at the arrival of the embassy to Achilles' headquarters, he served as a spokesman in support of the envoys' arguments and the sincerity of Agamemnon's repentance. Why and how was Phoenix, Achilles' man (*therapon*), unexpectedly at Agamemnon's headquarters and among the council of the Achaean kings, at a time of deep enmity between Achilles and Agamemnon? Homer does not explain, but is it possible that Phoenix' role may reflect a custom similar to the Near Eastern envoy practices? If this is true, why did not Homer contrive some reason to explain Phoenix' presence in the Achaean council? Inasmuch as Homer remains silent about Phoenix' mysterious presence in Agamemnon's headquarters, we shall never be certain about the reason of his presence in the Achaean council. Be that as it may, we do know that Nestor's son Peisistratus served as Telemachus' guide and escort to his trip from Pylos to Sparta and back.

This summary comparison of the practices relating to messengers in the Near East and in Homer has hopefully demonstrated some of the existing similarities between the two civilizations. It is the opinion of this writer that these traditional diplomatic practices in the Greek world cannot have emerged in the post-Mycenaean period, despite the fact that Homeric poetry has been synthesized in the post-Mycenaean times. Admittedly, there is no air-tight evidence to prove how far back these customs trace their origins. But their early existence in the diplomatic practices of the ancient Near Eastern states, and their close similarity to the Homeric world practices, suggest that it would have been very odd if the missing link, that is, the Mycenaean envoy practices differed greatly from the practices presented here.

The upshot of this investigation therefore is that the Aegean and Near Eastern envoy practices had common roots. As Dickinson has remarked, although the responses of these cultures to various geographical and geopolitical settings and social developments may have varied, their responses to several of their problems were very similar, and these similarities are mirrored in the commonality of their diplomatic practices.[15] These cultures had their roots in a common well whose waters spread all over the area of the Near East and Greece. Irrespective of the date of the final synthesis of the Homeric epics, many of the customs and traditions depicted in them definitely trace their roots much deeper in history.

---

[15] O. Dickinson, *The Aegean Bronze Age*, 258.

AFTERWORD

THE DIACHRONIC ENDURANCE OF MESSENGER PRACTICES

A fundamental theme implicitly associated with the discussion of the Amarna Letters is "primitivism" or "modernism," that is, the extent to which we can interpret some of the practices of the remote past as contemporary, or at least quasi-contemporary, by meaningfully comparing ancient with modern diplomacy. The champions of the primitivist approach caution against anachronism, warning that the Amarna Letters and the phenomena they describe can only be understood within the context of the times and cultures of the people that created them. The reader is warned against reading the logic of modern thought and practices backward into remote periods. For the primitivists the ancient Near Eastern material is to be understood in terms of the small community, whether the family, the neighborhood, or the village and they wonder whether the ancient material is relevant to the study of modern international relations at all. The virtues of this approach notwithstanding, one has to bear in mind that the ancient political practices discussed thus far found application in a fairly wide area over a long period of time, much longer than the development of modern international practices, and that these practices often dealt with human problems similar to ours, irrespective of the models used by their ancient framers. Furthermore, like the ancient practices, several modern practices also have their origin in religious beliefs which have had their genesis in the areas of the Near East and have greatly influenced them and, by extension, us. All these issues plus others have led some scholars to claim that the international rules of diplomacy discussed above provide evidence of a "full-fledged" diplomatic system.

Geoffrey Berridge, a diplomatic historian, is skeptical of the above description of ancient diplomatic rules as a sophisticated and full-fledged system. He is particularly critical of any attempts by modern scholars to identify such ancient practices as the incipient tendency to diplomatic immunity, the faint indications of resident ambassadorial practice, the hazy existence of a diplomatic corps and other such ostensible practices as bespeaking the existence of a full-fledged international diplomatic model in the making. His advice is rather than measuring ancient diplomatic rules with the yardstick of modern diplomatic standards to evaluate instead its effectiveness in the light of contemporary requirements. From this standpoint, he concludes that ancient diplomacy, though simplistic, was adequate to the needs of the time.

The truth seems to stand somewhere in-between. Political scientists and historians incline more toward a "modernist" approach, namely by recognizing many modern diplomatic phenomena as the developed continuation and expansion of ancient customs. While accepting the prevalence of household and familial metaphors in the ancient and Homeric world, political scientists and historians apply present-day concepts to discover evidence for an international society in the making, underpinned by rules and state interests. They detect in the ancient system clear signs of working techniques of communication and negotiation, commitment and credibility that are characteristics, in effect, if not in intention, of a functional international system of interstate relations governed by Realpolitik and the maintenance of a balance of power.[1] They acknowledge that at first sight the relevance of the ancient Near Eastern material is not obvious to the contemporary student of modern diplomacy mainly because language and contents of the material clearly reflect a remote age. Most of the great powers' correspondence particularly in the Amarna Letters and in the Near Eastern literature deals with such exotic issues as betrothals of royal princesses, the exchange of precious gifts, arrangements for golden or gilded statues, the treatment of messengers, addresses, delays of emissaries, dowries, all of which may provoke indignation over issues that are considered unimportant to our contemporary world.[2] On a deeper level, however, the student of diplomacy finds a lot which is interesting and contemporary. Behind many seemingly frivolous details, the real issues at stake are fascinatingly modern: personal and state prestige in the international sphere, spheres of influence, deter-

---

[1] Cohen and Westbrook, *Amarna Diplomacy*, 227–28.

[2] Cohen, "On Diplomacy," in *Diplomacy and Statecraft*, 246. Although both Cohen and Berridge focus their attention and draw their conclusions mainly from the Amarna Letters, they frequently refer to other Ancient Near Eastern evidence. Their references point to the incontestable fact about the existence of a diplomatic mechanism for the management of interstate relations, dating from at least one thousand years before the Amarna correspondence. This is much earlier than western historians have hitherto realized, and their allusions in passing to a "rudimentary" diplomatic system beginning with the latter half of the second millennium may not be entirely felicitous, Martin Wight, *System of States* (Leicester University Press, 1977) passim.

rence, alliance formations, trade issues, the rise and decline of great powers. Such issues reveal business-like diplomatic exchanges far removed from "abstract, philosophical," categories thus helping the reader understand the prerequisites for a working diplomacy. In sum, the reader can perceive that, starting with the third millennium BC to the times of the Homeric poems, there were forces at work which contributed to the emergence of continuous international contacts based on permanent institutions and ordered structures, both "features of true diplomacy."[3]

These features reveal essential features about the conduct of diplomacy, its instruments and goals. Thus the material in the Near Eastern archives and that of the Homeric poems permits us to observe in some detail the constitutive phase in the development of the essentially central features of Western Civilization. The diplomatic forms and modalities that appear here, having evolved over centuries, presage the structures of the modern practices in the diplomatic world. Not only does the material reflect key mechanisms that we have come to take for granted, such as good faith in negotiations, written and oral communications, protocol, protests, claims for reparations and so on, but also to be found are principles that underpin present-day diplomatic exchanges such as the need for truth and accuracy, credibility, the sanctity of agreements, diplomatic inviolability and immunity, the importance of unhindered communications and reciprocity. For instance, the embassy of Odysseus and Menelaus was received by the Trojan assembly, prior to the outbreak of hostilities, to demand the return of Helen and her possessions as a *sine qua non* for the prevention of war. The Trojans, however, not only rejected this peace proposal, but at the suggestion of Antimachus who was in the pay of Paris, they urged the assembly to violate the diplomatic immunity of the envoys, something that went contrary to the standing principles regarding envoys at that time but also something so basic that has become a fundamental principle of the Geneva Convention today.[4]

---

[3] Cohen, "On Diplomacy," in *Diplomacy and Statecraft*, 246–52.

[4] *Il.* 11.123–42; Harold Nicolson, *The Evolution of Diplomatic Method* (New York, 1954) 3. In the above paragraph we see that the Achaean Assembly before Troy received ambassadors and heard their peace proposals. The practice continued among the democratic cities of Greece and Sparta. In contrast, whatever the function of the assembly of the Roman People (Populus Romanus) the conduct of foreign relations was not one of them. Even in the Republican times, it has been one of the features distinguishing the city-state of Rome that ambassadors from foreign powers never came before the assemblies of the people. In the Republican times

There are three essential items in this story that are relevant to our theme: Firstly, in the Homeric world foreign embassies were generally received by the assembly as a whole, a harbinger of the democratic assemblies of the Greek city-states; secondly, Homeric embassies were often composed of two ambassadors, a feature that we also find in the beginnings of the modern era diplomacy; finally, Antimachus' proposal about the violation of the envoys' diplomatic immunity was evidently profoundly shocking to contemporary opinion, as it would be in modern times. When on a subsequent occasion Antimachus' two sons found themselves at Agamemnon's mercy, he refused to listen to their pleas for mercy; instead, he cut off their heads in retribution for their father's outrageous suggestions. No doubt, many among the Trojans perceived Agamemnon's action as the punishment of the ultimate court, that is, divine justice. Obviously, the diplomatic machinery of the Ancient Near Eastern times was more elaborate than is sometimes assumed.

---

the Senate had also performed the diplomatic function of sending embassies from within its own ranks to negotiate with foreign powers. Yet the Senate had no separate office dealing with foreign affairs. The function was embedded in the more general exercise of public political role and it had no core of specialist diplomats. Like the Senate, the emperor also had no specific agency for the bureaucratic or professional management of foreign relations, or the preparation of missives to foreign powers. All diplomatic transactions were conducted ad hoc either by the emperor, a member of his family, or the person delegated by the emperor. This became a common practice in the third century AD, and increasingly so in the fourth, M. L. Chaumont, "Un Document Méconnu Concernant l' Envoi d'un ambassadeur Parth ver Septime Sévêre" (P. Drua 60B), "*Historia* 36 (1987) 422–47. Two officials bearing the title *ab epistolis Latinis* and *ab epistolis Graecis* dealt with western and eastern affairs but whether they constituted a Foreign Office Department may be doubtful. Their titles indicate, however, that the primary languages used for correspondence in the East was Greek and for the West Latin, Fergus Millar, "Government and Diplomacy in the Roman Empire during the First three Centuries," in *International History Review*, 10 (1988) 373. In other cases an interpreter was probably used. The people had once voted on declarations of war and the making of treaties, but that function too disappeared in the later Republic. The subject is handled by J. W. Rich, in his *Declaring War in the Roman Republic in the Period of Transmarine Expansion* (Brussels, 1976). Millar, "Government and Diplomacy," 348. The early emperors of Rome kept up the pretence of sharing powers with the Senate by presenting to the Senate the foreign embassies. The custom was discontinued after the beginnings of the third century AD, Millar, "Government and Diplomacy," 349; 366–67.

The belief in the existence of religious sanctions, mitigating the unrestrained barbarism of war was analogous to our Geneva Convention, which have been set up for the protection of combatants and non-combatants, making the atrocities of war less abhorrent. Like the Geneva Conventions so ancient civility rules were often transgressed, even though such violations did not invalidate the significance of the existing norms. Indeed, there are admirable occasions in the face of brutality that exhibit respect for the standing conventions. Homer again tells us that when Ilus snubbed Odysseus because the latter asked him for poison in which to dip his arrows, Ilus turned the request down because of fear of the gods. Thus in antiquity as today, there did exist conventions the violation of which was regarded with abhorrence (*Od.* 1.259–65). Weinfeld had already demonstrated that Greek and Roman convenantal agreements closely followed those that crystallized in Mesopotamia and Anatolia in the second millennium BC and perhaps earlier.[5] The existence of early links between the Eastern littoral of the Mediterranean and the Aegean through such commercial centers like Ugarit was also well known.

According to Cohen a number of conditions has been conducive to the rise of the system of diplomacy in the general area of the Near East: imminent danger among the existing states there; the recognition that no single power could remain forever safe; the interconnected series of needs calling for coexistence and cooperation. These needs had to be handled in a legal framework, in peace as in war.[6] The situation among the Near Eastern states, suggests that the powers there had considerable business to conduct, dynastic, strategic, commercial, and that they were continuously affected by constantly fluid developments beyond their frontier areas. This explains King Tušratta's proposal of a treaty of mutual assistance and cooperation with Egypt, which is not so very different from Article V of the North Atlantic Treaty of 1949.

---

[5] M. Weinfield, "Covenant Terminology in the Ancient Near East and Its Influence on the West," *JAOS* 93 (1973) 190–99. Again similarity does not necessarily imply copying or borrowing.

[6] Cohen, "On Diplomacy" in *Diplomacy and Statecraft*, 249–50; Cohen, "on Diplomacy" in *Diplomacy and Statecraft*, 249; Artzi, "The Rise of the Middle Assyrian Kingdom," 34–34; P. Artzi and Malamat, "The Great King. A Preeminent Royal Title in Cuneiform Sources and the Bible," in Mark E. Cohen, Daniel C. Snell, and David B. Weisberg, eds., *The Tablet and the Scroll: Near Eastern Studies in Honor of William W. Hallo* (Bethesda, Maryland, 1993) 33; Garrett Mattingly, *Renaissance Diplomacy* (Penguin, 1973) Chs 6–9; Adam Watson, *Diplomacy* (Routlege, 1991) ch. 1.

And in our lands *peace prevails*. If only an enemy of my brother did not exist! But should in the future an enemy *invade* my brother's land, (then) my brother writes to me, and the Hurrian land, armor, arms, ...and everything concerning the enemy of my brother will be at his disposition. But should, on the other hand there be for me an enem[y] – if only he did not exist! – I will write to my brother, and my brother will dispatch to the land of Egypt, (sic) armor, arms, ... and everything concerning my! enemy.[7]

The dearth of Mycenaean documents makes it harder for us to express ourselves with the same certitude about the prevailing conditions in that world, but some occurrences like the oath that supposedly bound Helen's suitors, all of them chieftains representing principalities, prior to her engagement to Menelaus, led them to the grand alliance that carried on the Trojan War.

A recurrent theme in the archives is the exchange of presents. These include: opulent dowries and marriage gifts, routine greeting gifts, symbols of normal peaceful relations; other supplementary greeting gifts including sometimes vast consignments of luxury items, such as sacks of gold, fine clothing, furniture, jewelry, timber, horses, expensive tools of war, chariots. As many scholars note gifts serve as the medium of non-verbal communication, conveying political points about state relationships as well as the standing of the parties. They are the equivalent of today's subsidies, foreign aid, expression of prestige and influence by the giver, as well as tools of cementing relations.[8]

The flow of foreign aid and trade along the major routes presupposed formal or informal agreement among the countries or the leaders affected. The financial benefits attached to these agreements must have conceded significant gains to the participants as they do today for states with similar agreements.[9] We find similar gift exchanges in the Homeric world, for instance from Agamemnon to Achilles, the Phaeacians to Odysseus, Menelaus to Telemachus, and so on. As observed above, the exchange of gifts was an indispensable feature of the Bronze Age society, serving a variety of purposes.

Balance through necessity was another "modern" feature that served as a prerequisite of the ancient balance system. Egypt, the main hegemonic power in the second half of the second millennium BC learned its physical

---

[7] *EA* 24, prg. 26.109–118.

[8] Cohen, "On Diplomacy" in *Diplomacy and Statecraft*, 250; Liverani, "Elements in the Amarna Trade," in *Three Amarna Essays*, (Malibum, 1979) 27; *EA* 7.63–72.

[9] *CAH* 3rd ed., 2, part 1.513–14.

limitations under Tuthmoses III. Unremitting warfare brought the Egyptian army to the banks of the Euphrates, but also to the realization that the Egyptian resources could not sustain for long a continuous imperialistic drive. Finally, c. 1300 Egyptians and Hittites, after a protracted and costly period of sparring both found themselves at a standstill at the battle of Kadesh that confirmed the limits of their power and ambitions.

Appearances were as important in antiquity as they are today. Kadasman-Enlil of Babylonia asked for the hand of an Egyptian princess in marriage as a symbol of his equal standing to the Egyptian King, who had earlier done the same for Kadashman's daughter. Told that "no daughter of the king of Egypt is given to any one from time immemorial," Kadašman devised what Cohen describes as a Potemkin-like trick. He asked for some Egyptian official's daughter, a beautiful girl in her stead, "for who is to know that she was not the king's daughter?" She was to be presented as the king's daughter and Kadašman's desire for prestige would be satisfied. In similar circumstances Agamemnon offered to give Achilles one of his daughters as part of the package of compensation to the latter's damaged prestige.[10]

Most international negotiations took place through agents who were authorized to represent their principals. As noted above, these agents—messengers in the ancient Near East and Homer, like diplomats in the modern world assumed symbolic significance. The way they were treated reflected the state of relations between the two states, and also that envoys were at the heart of the system of diplomacy. Many of the diplomats on the Near Eastern and Homeric circuit were senior envoys often received by the oriental kings as friends and peers as were the Homeric envoys.[11] In his eagerness to forge friendly relations with Egypt, Tušratta pointed out that he treated the Egyptian messengers "with distinction," showing them "very great honors," and exalting them "like gods" (*EA* 20.21). He also went out of his way to praise the Egyptian messengers: "I have never seen men with such an appearance" (*EA* 21.24–32). He especially praises Mane: "There does not exist a man like him in all the world" (*EA* 24 § 17. 95–102 ff). Mane and Keliya, the Egyptian and Mitanni envoys, figure in mission after mission, especially at times of approaching crises. Diplomats of this caliber

---

[10] *EA* 8.4–22; *Il.* 9.286–90; Cohen, "On Diplomacy," in *Diplomacy and Statecraft*, 254.

[11] *EA* 29.32–37; Aias and Odysseus in *Il.* 9 where Odysseus and Aias are senior members who serve as envoys of the Royal council to Achilles.

clearly enjoyed the complete confidence of their principals and of the principals on the opposite spectrum. The same is true of their counterparts in the Homeric poems. The same custom prevails even today, with individuals who have been employed in the capacity of trusted envoys, irrespective of party affiliation.[12] Unlike modern ambassadors almost all envoys in antiquity were visitors, not residents, though there are hints about the presence of resident envoys, as noted above. Thus, even this important feature of diplomacy which is thought to have originated in Renaissance Italy was not unknown in antiquity.

Judging from the extant material, scholars believe that the Near Eastern system performed four vital diplomatic functions: the negotiation of agreements as proposals of marriage; communication of initial proposals of cooperation or official protests and requests for redress; representation in ceremonials at life-cycle court and religious events; lastly, the collection and transmission of valuable information and the transport of gifts and commodities. Of these four categories the transport of gifts and commodities is not a strictly diplomatic function in modern times, though it was evidently an important function in the ancient times, since it is well-known from sources in the Near East going back to at least the third millennium BC. Commercial activities among nations are even more vital today and most embassies have on their staff economic and commercial specialists who deal with interstate trade. Homeric merchants seem to have been free agents, though we cannot certainly exclude Mycenaean merchants in the service of kings and noblemen.[13]

Customary international law held a ruler liable for compensation to friendly foreigners for their losses at the hands of thieves within his territory as modern international law does today. This is clearly referred to in *EA* 38 where the king of Alašiya (Cyprus) denies liability for the acts in

---

[12] A. Harriman, Cyrus Vance, M. Nimitz, Senator G. Mitchell, Richard Holbrook, to mention only a few.

[13] Fuad I. Khuri, "The Etiquette of Bargaining in the Middle East," *American Anthropologist* 70 (1968) 698–706; *EA* 35.10–34; *Od.* 8.161–64. Euryalus expressed his aristocratic contempt of the itinerant traders, *Od.* 15.415ff. Similar attitudes are widely quoted in literature, where often the attitude is easily disguised as moral condemnation of avarice, W. B. Stanford, *The Odyssey of Homer* ad loc. 2.319; 8.161; 24.300; Horace. *Serm.* 1.4.29; *Ep.* 1.1.45; *Properties* 3.7. This attitude changed by the seventh century, if we are to judge by the esteem in which Solon was held, see also Hdt. 4.152; *Cic. De Off.* 1.151 who has the same contempt for small merchants but not for the big merchants.

question, marshalling the argument that his people are not responsible for the banditry that occurred in his territory and that his own villages had been attacked and suffered from foreign pirates. Disclaiming all knowledge of the episode, he proposes either that the criminals be returned to Cyprus to be duly punished by him or that the Egyptian King do with the bandits as he sees fit. Similar episodes receive similar responses in the Homeric epics where in reference to the dispute between Agamemnon and Achilles the latter states that he has no personal reasons to fight against the Trojans since they never harried his kine or horses or destroyed his crops (*Il.* 1.152–57; *Od.* 21.16–19). A parallel story concerns the Ithacans who dispatched young Odysseus to Messene to collect damages for the three hundred ships that some residents of Messene had stolen from the Ithacans (*Od.* 21.16–19).

On another occasion pertaining to fidelity to treaty alliances Burra-Buriyaš, King of Babylon, protests to Amenophis IV (Akhenaten), about his reception of Assyrian envoys. Babylon had always turned down requests of Egyptian vassals for support or alliance, owing to her treaty of friendship with Egypt. On this principle, Burra-Buriyas asked the Pharaoh to reject approaches of his Assyrian vassal, particularly since the vassal had approached the Egyptian King without his lord's permission, advising the Egyptian King to send the impertinent vassal off empty-handed (*EA* 9.1–18). It was a futile request; Assyria had already broken away from Babylonian tutelage. Bowing to the realities of power, friendship and principle were overridden by the Egyptian court, though they had stood firm for two generations. This appeal of Burra-Buriyas is reminiscent of the appeal of the Corinthians to Athens prior to the outbreak of the Peloponnesian War, which was similarly overridden by the Athenians, most probably at the advice of Pericles, bowing to the necessity of Realpolitik (Thuc.1.37–43).

As it has already been mentioned several times above, in the absence of an International Court of Appeal or an international agency like the UN, people in antiquity going back to at least the Bronze Age regularly invoked the gods as the ultimate arbiters, in the making of agreements, wars and treaties. For that reason ceremonials were a central feature in the conclusion of agreements. Treaties were consecrated by the performance of elaborate rituals and animal sacrifices, solemn oaths were sworn in the name of the gods as witnesses evoked divine sanctions against infringement of their agreements. At the same time, the ancients were realistic enough to know that even these oaths might not be sufficient to prevent the parties from violating agreements as people today realize that fear of the existence of the International Court or the UN may not be able to prevent miscreant states from violating the International Convention, especially if they count on a victory.

Underpinning the whole ancient system was the assumption that kings were well informed about events that happened in and outside their kingdoms. Indeed, to a considerable degree a constantly updated basis of information must have been available to the authorities. In these circumstances the Near Eastern states, like modern states, must have required an apparatus of information gathering. Diplomats, residents or visiting merchants, and travelers must have fulfilled this need, alongside other sources of information, such as "intelligence" agents. Returning envoys would report on the outcome of their mission and the information they gathered en route from whatever sources. Dispatched missions are also reported for the express purpose of collecting information.[14]

Cohen concludes his essay with the statement that the Near Eastern evidence provides strong evidence towards a fully-fledged diplomatic system that was governed by a set of recognized conventions, established procedures and formal laws and a constitutive protocol. The Near Eastern states, he says, were recognizably members of a rather uniform civilization, joined together by all kinds of relationships, cultural, commercial, political, military, possessing complementary religious beliefs, their local differences notwithstanding. They shared similar government and structure of society as well as conceptions of law as regards contracts and ways of dealing with international criminals. The kings addressed one another as "brothers," whether they thought of themselves as such, but at the same time, they knew how to pursue selfish gains ruthlessly and unsentimentally. "As the Nicky-Willy relationship between the emperors of Russia and Germany before the outbreak of the First World War" demonstrates, when it came to a crunch, dynastic ties invariably gave way to geo-strategic considerations. For all the brotherly language, the Amarna club was not simply a community held together by bonds of friendly sentiment but also an association of

---

[14] *EA* 16 describes the case of Assur-uballit, king of Assyria, who was informed (or misinformed) by his sources that gold was like dirt in Egypt. On the other hand, the Egyptian King attacks the credibility of the Babylonian diplomatic reporting, which resulted in misunderstandings between the two "brother" kings, *EA* 1. Many diplomatic blunders throughout history confirm the significance of the absence of relevant information in the conduct of diplomacy and the immemorial tendency to blame the messenger for the sins of the rulers is a past custom. Blunders in the Iraqi War are presently attributed to poor intelligence information on the part of American intelligence.

independent sovereigns held together by negotiated agreements grounded in selfish calculations and the realities of power. The bonds that tied together the Homeric leaders appear to have been simpler politically, based chiefly on friendship and a spirit of camaraderie, which nevertheless could be easily strained for reasons either of prestige or personal interest.

Cohen's investigation leads him to the conclusion that Amarna diplomacy reflects many features present in the history of classic European diplomacy three thousand years after the end of the ancient Near Eastern world, chiefly, a law of nations, resident embassies, complex instruments and specializations and diplomatic immunity. These features are intrinsic, and "not historically or culturally contingent features of the diplomacy of developed international systems," without which the functions of diplomacy would not be performed in ordered international societies. With some hyperbole, he claims that western emphasis on the diminutive, intranational city-state systems of Greece and Renaissance Italy, has obscured this basic proposition. For him the Ancient Near East is a more authentic progenitor of modern diplomacy; in diplomacy, as in other human affairs, it turns out that "There is no new thing under the sun."[15] In his justified emphasis on the Near Eastern states he has, however, ignored the Aegean Bronze Age, the progenitor of the Greek Classical Age and its norms of diplomacy, which were passed on to the Classical Age, and upon which the Ancient Greeks improved and expanded to the point that even skeptical scholars like Berridge incline to consider the Greek diplomatic system as the progenitor of the modern system.

BERRIDGE'S VIEW

In his article contained in *Amarna Diplomacy*, Geoffrey Berridge strenuously disputes that Amarna diplomacy was a full-fledged diplomatic system, though he admits that a diplomacy of sorts was the feature of the relations among the prominent states of the Near Eastern world. In this system the kings communicated with each other on a regular or regulated basis in order to promote political and commercial relations. According to Berridge it is one thing, however, to accept this premise and another to maintain that the Amarna system, or to broaden the scope of the discussion, the Near Eastern state system "permits us 'to observe in detail a constitutive phase of development of a central feature [diplomacy] of Western civilization,'" or that the oriental system "provides uncontestable evidence of the existence

---

[15] Cohen, "On Diplomacy" in *Diplomacy and Statecraft*, 266.

of a sophisticated and effective mechanism for the management of international relations."[16]

Berridge criticizes Cohen's thesis arguing that from Berridge's own examination of the Near Eastern evidence Wight's characterization of the Amarna diplomatic system as "rudimentary" is more appropriate and accurate than Cohen's because the full conditions for a sophisticated and effective diplomacy were not intrinsic in the Near Eastern period. How adequate was the Near Eastern diplomatic mechanism to promote negotiations and the rest of the necessities that a sophisticated system requires? According to Berridge, a sophisticated system requires the following presuppositions: immunity of envoys, continuous contacts, well-qualified professional personnel, bureaucratic provisions for mediation, methods for "underpinning agreements, and flexibility of form and procedure. These prerequisites could not have existed before the introduction of the telegraph. To what extent did the features of a sophisticated telegraph-period obtain in the Ancient Near Eastern period?[17]

Analyzing briefly these features Berridge seeks to prove that Near Eastern diplomacy was rather primitive and those who speak of a sophisticated system commit an anachronism. Receiving governments, he maintains, have the obligation to safeguard envoys and the obligation to protect their dignity. These constitute the most fundamental features of diplomacy which should also extend to the envoy's entourage, his private residence, and his means of communication and transport, irrespective of the friendliness of the envoy's country. This is altogether vital if an ambassador is to discharge his duties efficiently. By virtue of his duty to gather information on local conditions and often deliver unwelcome messages, an envoy may provoke the ire of government to which he is accredited. Without the feature of immunity the embassy will not be able to perform its various duties properly.[18] A healthy diplomatic system can survive occasional lapses from this norm, but when these lapses become widespread the system is bound to suffer and may eventually collapse. How did the Near Eastern system measure up to the above requirements? Berridge disagrees radically with those who claim that in the Near East the person of the envoy was inviola-

---

[16] Berridge, "Amarna Diplomacy: A Full-fledged Diplomatic System?" in *Amarna Diplomacy*, 212–13; R. Cohen, *International Politics: The Rules of the Game* (London, 1981) 32.

[17] Berridge, "Amarna Diplomacy," in *Amarna Didplomacy*, 213.

[18] Berridge, "Amarna Diplomacy," 213; C. E. Wilson, *Diplomatic Privileges and Immunities* (University of Arizona Press, 1969) ch. 1.

ble.[19] A number of considerations make it difficult for him to accept the arguments of the proponents of ancient immunity who characterize that system as diplomatically developed. Among his strongest objections are the absence of residence and the serious implications that stem from it; also the fact that envoys were sent only by friendly or prospective friends, because an enemy's envoy might be offensive to the host country.[20] By extension, Berridge's criticism would apply to the diplomacy of the Homeric world wherein the same weaknesses seemed to have prevailed. Like the Eastern world the Aegean world provided the same traditional safeguards toward the protection of envoys. Chryses was threatened by Agamemnon when the former came asking for the return of his daughter and had to depart hastily before the exasperated king might resort to violence. Agamemnon's heralds dared not approach Achilles' headquarters from fear of his wrath. Priam was fully aware that he was taking his life in his hands when he decided to solicit Hector's body, while Menelaus and Odysseus ran the risk of death when they visited Troy to prevent the outbreak of the Trojan War by seeking a compromise. Yet in not one of these cases did harm come to any one mainly because the system, the traditional customs, that is, which obtained on such occasions functioned effectively.

His second important reason for rejecting Cohen's argument of a "full-fledged" Near Eastern system of diplomacy is that Near Eastern missions were limited in scope; consequently, embassy missions must have been small and not well-resourced, hence, if they enjoyed immunity it was only because they were intrinsically unthreatening to the receiving court. On these occasions, there was little incentive to subject the envoy to cruel treatment or take drastic measures to impair his functioning. Near Eastern diplomacy, in other words, was never submitted to the real test of a developed diplomatic system: the granting of immunity to envoys, especially resident envoys of hostile states, because they were limited in scope and

---

[19] Cohen, "On Diplomacy in *Diplomacy and Statecraft*," 257; A. B. Bozeman, *Politics and Culture in International Society: From the Ancient Near East to the Opening of the Modern Age*, 2nd ed. (Rutgers University Press, 1994) 30; Munn-Rankin, "Diplomacy in Western Asia," *Iraq* 18, 107–108.

[20] Berridge, "Amarna Diplomacy," in *Amarna Diplomacy*, 214; Meier, *The Messenger*, 30 (1988) 39; Artzi, "The Rise of the Middle Assyrian Kingdom according to El-Amarna Letters 15 and 16," in *Bar-Ilan Studies in History* (Bar-Ilan University, 1978) 25–42; *EA* 41 hints that Suppililiumas' letter to Egypt might have been sent at a time of cold war between the two countries, in which case Berridge's theory may not be air-tight.

time. It is true that envoys were subject to dangers in their passage through third countries or even by brigands in friendly countries, but the interesting aspect here is that all precautions were taken by both sides to secure the safety of envoys and efforts were exerted to encourage safe passage through third countries. He does, however, mention the detention of envoys by their host countries as proof of the lack of immunity, although even here it is not known if the host always acted out of malice toward the sender or the envoy.

CONTINUITY OF CONTACT.

In Berridge's view, a sophisticated system must feature continuous rather than sporadic contacts between parties, unless these parties are actually at war and preferably even then. Continuous contact makes information gathering more valuable and enables new initiatives to be taken, frequently without attracting undue attention that may harm negotiations.[21] In this context, he considers the mechanism of resident ambassadors as it developed since the Italian Renaissance city-states and beyond a clear sign of modernity, while he discounts the sparse references to resident ambassadors in the Near East. Nor does he mention the employment of consuls (πρόξενοι) by the Greek city-states as a possible progenitor of resident ambassadors. Similarly, he does not perceive the protracted detention of envoys as a quasi-permanent, albeit "negative" form of residence, inasmuch as it is not a permanent institutional feature that distinguished the tenure of envoys, if envoys were held contrary to their will, except where it might be explicitly mentioned as such. There must have been, however, frequent occasions on which envoys' tasks could not be completed in a short period and when practical considerations could cause them long delays. Delays of this nature could also be triggered by inauspicious omens—intentional or not—as well. Such delays may not fall under the category of ambassadorial

---

[21] Berridge, "Amarna Diplomacy," in *Amarna Diplomacy*, 2–5; D. E. Queller, *The Office of Ambassadors in the Middle Ages* (Princeton University Press, 1967) chs. 1–2. The Romans, unlike the Classical Greeks who used native residents of cities to represent their interests, maintained no resident ambassadors or legations either in "client" kingdom or among any other peoples with whom they had diplomatic or military contacts. The nearest to a Roman representative could be the officers of military units, found occasionally in allied kingdoms. But even this practice was not common, Millar, "Government and Diplomacy," 368. Despite this weakness, from Berridge's standpoint, the Roman State survived for a thousand years and so did the Byzantine Empire.

residency but they could fulfill the longer or shorter aims of the embassy which went beyond the limits of a single, concrete diplomatic target, lasting for many months. Berridge ignores this aspect since that too does not constitute part of a systemic process. Lastly, he seems to disregard Cohen's hypothesis that princesses married to foreign princes and their entourage might have served as informal agents, supplying their countries with valuable information to their country's envoys, perhaps for the same reason mentioned above, the lack of systemic organization.[22]

QUALIFICATIONS OF DIPLOMATIC PERSONNEL

Regarding the qualifications of envoys, Berridge concedes the presence of a considerable number of qualified envoys in the Near East, many of them mentioned by name. Evidently, many were professionals in the loose sense that diplomacy was either their regular calling or that a substantial part of their career was spent in diplomatic missions. There is also ample evidence that several envoys, Mane, Keliya, Odysseus in the *Iliad*, and so on, were almost indispensable in the conduct of diplomacy among certain states, because of their natural skill and their expertise as envoys, scribes, or linguists, though linguistic tasks were not an indispensable necessity in the Near East, since translators were readily available.[23] Since in the Near East and probably in the Bronze Age Aegean diplomacy was frequently linked with trade, diplomatic work was also carried out by people wise in the ways of foreign lands as a result of their constant journeys through or to these lands. At other times, merchants were the obvious choice to double as diplomats in the absence of regular diplomatic service, as they have been later on in the trading of cities of Venice, Florence, or countries like England. To this day prominent businessmen who have interests in foreign lands are frequently used to carry special messages to political personalities of those lands. Nicolson and others cite the custom in connection with Byzantine envoys, who were also expected to finance their missions.[24] It is understandable that

---

[22] Cohen, "On Diplomacy," in *Diplomacy and Statecraft*, 258; *EA* 1.52–62; Berridge, "Amarna Diplomacy," in *Amarna Diplomacy*, 216.

[23] Berridge, "Amarna Diplomacy," in *Amarna Diplomacy*, 218; Meier, *The Messenger*, 163–65.

[24] Nicolson, *Diplomatic Method*, 25 mentions bales of merchandize carried by the envoys to be sold for currency in the host's market. Nicolson is convinced that diplomacy was fostered by the pragmatism of the trader and the centrality of bargaining in the trader's work, *Diplomacy*, 3rd ed. (Oxford University Press, 1963) 50–55; 162.

missions of merchants, who traveled in caravans, might be slower than the regular diplomatic missions for urgent messages, and that it might be justifiably conjectured that if interrogated by the host authority on broader issues they would be at a disadvantage, especially if the questions were unrelated to the subject with which they were commissioned.[25] This shortcoming must have been taken into consideration by those who dispatched them. In view of the fact that trading was vital in the Near East, particularly for Egypt where trade was more centrally controlled, the conduct of diplomacy by merchants stood high in the hierarchy of the administration, and diplomacy by merchants could not have been a bad thing. Today, distinguished entrepreneurs who are also party donors are honored with ambassadorial positions.

BUREAUCRATIC DIRECTIONS

Did the ancient kings have specially trained persons who helped them maintain their foreign contacts and did they keep archives with records of correspondence and treaties? On the first question the record is not clear. What we know is that experienced personnel served as advisors to their kings, but the final decision resided with the sovereign who could readily issue personal instructions as it happens today. Kings could of course solicit the opinion of their council members as Agamemnon did in his capacity of *primus inter pares*, although admittedly the Near Eastern kings may have been in a much stronger position in this respect because of a better integrated system. Some of them, no doubt, relied on men who had become experts by cultivating their ability in the practice of foreign affairs, men like Manes, Keliya, Odysseus, or as in the *Iliad*, the king's personal heralds. Others, like Akhenaten, absorbed as he was in his religious revolution, must have left most of the vast business of state to the hands of their officials.[26]

There is no doubt that in the Ancient Near East palaces kept archives, preserved in special places in the palace, in temples, or both. We know

---

[25] Meier, *The Messenger*, 203. In Homer, merchants were valuable to their host as carriers of specific or general information. Eumaeus and Penelope regularly asked their guests, many of whom must have been merchants plowing the seas for a living, about news regarding Odysseus. Odysseus as Beggar in Eumaeus' hut (*Od.* 1.1–170–200) and in his own palace was questioned by both Eumaeus and Penelope and had to devise a plausible story regarding Odysseus' whereabouts.

[26] *CAH*, 3rd ed. 2.2. p. 52; Berridge, in "Amarna Diplomacy," in *Amarna Diplomacy*, p.219, n. 55.

from the archives found in the temples of archaic and later Greece that archives were deposited there by the Greek cities. The same is true about the practices of cities in Classical times. It is unfortunate that there are no similar records found in the Aegean Age communities. However, in view of the practices in the Near East and the survival of Linear B tablets with logistical material in the archives of Bronze Age palaces in Greece the odds are that the Mycenaeans palaces kept important diplomatic records somewhere, either in the palace or in the archival places of some temples, or both. As far as it is known, the first clear use of Linear B tablets for administrative purposes was on Crete. The first cache of tablets at Knossos is currently understood to date to LM II (c. 1400).[27] We know nothing comparable on the mainland until the end of LH IIIB (1340–1200 BC) in the Ug tablets and WuNoddles from Thebes, and the tablets from the Oil Merchant group of houses at Mycenae but it cannot be totally excluded.[28] It is generally believed that these tablets are concerned exclusively with palatial affairs and served as an aide-mémoire for the central administration. The great bulk of the Linear B tablets from the mainland come from Pylos but we have nothing to suggest that other kingdoms did not use them for the same purpose. Equally, the absence of tablets containing information on treaties or messengers does not preclude the use of tablets for these purposes. Furthermore, the treaties and agreements found in the Homeric writings and the oaths and rituals associated with them evince the type of treaties the Bronze Age produced, unless we adhere to the theory that Homeric practices do not reflect Bronze Age activities, a highly untenable theory, in view of the information analyzed above. A quick comparison of the Near Eastern and Homeric treaties, however, shows that many of them consist of a five-part structure, whose elements are (1) the Preamble, (2) the Recounting of Antecedent History, (3) the Stipulations, (4) the Blessings and Curses.[29] What is known with certainty is that in the Greek Archaic period and following it copies of treaties were regularly deposited in the archives of Greek city-

---

[27] J. Driessen, *An Early Destruction in the Mycenaean Palace at Knossos; A New Interpretation of the Excavations, Field-Notes of the South-East Area of the West Wing* (Monograph 2, Louvain, 1990) chs. 1 and 2.

[28] John Chadwick, "Linear B Tablets from Thebes," *Minos* 10 (197) 116 corrected by S. Symeonoglou, *The Topography of Thebes from the Bronze Age to Modern Times* (Princeton University Press, 1985) 40; V. Aravantinos, "Old and New Evidence for the Palatial Society of Mycenaean Thebes: An Outline," *Politeia*, vol. 2, 613–22, R. Laffineur and W.-D. Niemeier eds., Aegaeum 12, (Liège, 1995) 613–21.

[29] Karavites, *Promise-Giving*, 83.

temples, while other copies of those treaties were set up at such famous panhellenic religious centers as Olympia and Delphi.[30] Was that a novel custom or a continuation of Bronze Age practices? Precedent favors the latter version.

Mediation

Third-party intervention in a disagreement to promote peace is an essential feature of diplomatic settlements in our day. It is of great interest that there is evidence of its occurrence in the Ancient Near East, though one may argue in some of the existing cases in favor of mediation rather that arbitration.[31] Something similar is found in the Homeric epics, where the gods intervened to bring about a temporary lull in the war activities or effect reconciliation between parties. There are also third parties in the Trojan assembly who propose diplomatic efforts at reconciliation of the opposite sides. How extensive the practice was, especially among the great powers in the East, remains uncertain.

Methods for Underpinning Agreements

Diplomatic agreements are underpinned directly or indirectly by reciprocity. A sophisticated diplomatic system has mechanisms for reinforcing agreements. In this regard Near Eastern agreements score very highly. They are made impressive by embodiment in writing on stone, marble, bronze or silver tablets.[32] In addition, ceremonial rituals symbolized the nature of the arrangement concluded. A system of hostage-taking, all too well known in recent times, was practiced, and messengers were often detained. In the place of international bodies that presumably underpin agreements today, Near Eastern contractées resorted to oaths and the invocation of the gods as witnesses, offered sacrifices and enacted rituals in testimony to their promises, which implied the threat of divine retribution to be visited upon the oath-breakers. In view of the prevailing religious climate and the ease with which personal and natural disasters were attributed to the wrath of

---

[30] W. Dittenberger and K. Purgold, *Die Inschriften von Olympia*, no. 21; M/L n. 17; Hermann Bengtson and H. H. Schmitt, *Staatsverträge des Altertums*, 2 (Munich, 1969–75) no. 117; 120.

[31] George Roux, *Ancient Iraq* (Penguin Books, 1992) 140; Munn-Rankin, "Diplomacy in Western Asia," *Iraq*, 18; 76.

[32] Munn-Rankin, "Diplomacy in Western Asia," *Iraq*, 18, 91; Adda Bozeman, *Politics and Culture* (Princeton, 1960) 3.

gods, the threat of divine punishment was an effective method for securing agreements. Agreements between vassals could also be enforced, following the arbitration by their lord, like the Great Powers in earlier periods and the UN today.

FLEXIBILITY

Sophisticated diplomacy is flexible, incorporating varied malleable forms to cope with all foreseeable circumstances, provided there is a will to communicate. At this point, the ancient system did not fare badly, always bearing in mind distances, the means of transportation and communications, as well as the obstacles from sundry dangers.[33] Envoys were available for all sorts of missions. Messages could be committed to tablets or to memory whenever more practical. Even multilateral diplomacy was known. The dispatch of different envoys to different parties concerned with the same issue is adumbrated in the Homeric epics and there is no reason to believe that it was unknown or impractical in the Near East.

Berridge feels that it is misleading to characterize the Near Eastern personal diplomacy as a full-fledged diplomatic system, while on the other side he also admits that its personnel and services were in general adequate to the tasks at hand. He accepts that the system's methods for underpinning agreements were impressive and that there was an appropriate degree of flexibility of form and procedure, particularly in view of the availability of means in existence at that time.[34] He does not equate it with the modern sophisticated system simply because he perceives that it was marred by an incomplete and weakly held norm of immunity, or the absence of resident missions, other than those occasions during which envoys are detained for a short or longer period. The rest of the time diplomatic communications, especially among warring states, appear to be essentially nonexistent. He further describes the ancient Near Eastern system as "stunted and crippled," since special envoys were frequently detained, the bureaucratic ties supporting it were incomplete, and the almost nonexistent diplomatic communications between hostile states, "the real test of a developed diplomatic system."[35] All of the above defects ostensibly advocate against the categorization of ancient diplomacy as a full-fledged diplomatic system. Yet one could easily gainsay that the ancient system, despite its shortcomings,

---

[33] Berridge, "Amarna Diplomacy," in *Amarna Diplomacy*, 221.
[34] Berridge, "Amarna Diplomacy," in *Amarna Diplomacy*, 222.
[35] Berridge, "Amarna Diplomacy," in *Amarna Diplomacy*, 222.

was adequate to the tasks of the time, something that Berridge himself admits.

WEAK CONDITIONS

Berridge further underscores certain conditions of diplomacy that were either weak or nonexistent. These are: first, the plurality of states which are believed to be roughly equal in power; second, mutually impinging interest of an urgent kind; third, a minimal toleration of cultural, including religious and ideological differences; fourth, technically efficient international communications. He feels that with regard to the first and third conditions, the Ancient Near Eastern system was not wanting. In regard to the second there is room for considerable doubt, while with reference to the fourth, there is no room at all.

Since he has already accepted that in relation to the first and third points the ancient system was not wanting, there is no argument here. With regard to the second, one could easily argue that the exhaustive struggle between Egypt and Hatti, to give an example, c. 1300 BC, produced the mutually impinging interest for a peace which was at the end concluded between the two. It is possible also that the apparent danger in the horizon from the Sea People added to that mutual necessity. At any rate, condition three is of an obscure validity, since all the necessary details are not available to us for a safe conclusion. In the end, the system has to be judged by the standards of the time and its contemporaneous efficiency or not. That our age enjoys much superior diplomatic conditions which make the ancient "primitive" no one would deny.

The question of the qualifications of the translators in the system is also connected with the problem of flexibility. How accomplished the translators were in the language they supposedly possessed is an issue not easy for the modern man to determine, although for the Aegean world this might not have been a problem. Many translators must have been competent, if we judge from the two copies of the existing peace treaty between Egypt and Hatti. c. 1300, since the two templates of the aforementioned treaty that we possess, one from each language, corroborate the accuracy of their translation. This is an issue difficult to determine. But even this example may not, however, vouchsafe the accuracy of all translations, inasmuch as some linguists might have been more capable in handling the language of their object than others. This is an issue difficult to determine. Consequently, Berridge's statement that language misunderstandings are invariably corrosive in their effect on diplomacy may be unfortunately correct.[36]

Berridge concludes on a compromising note. Judged by modern standards, or even by the standards of ancient Greece, he finds the diplomacy of the Ancient Near East unsophisticated, slow, fitful, less than comprehensive in its coverage, incapable of maintaining a high level of clear and nuanced communication; yet, he also admits that looking at the topic from the circumstances of the times he finds this inability hardly surprising, admiring in a way the Bronze Age man for his ability to come up with a moderately sound system that facilitated his needs, despite the "primitive" conditions at his disposal. If Bronze Age diplomacy was on the one hand unsophisticated, on the other, it should not be overlooked that the system was able to achieve results. From this stand point, even Berridge admits that ancient diplomacy was adaptable to its needs and its environment, both of which it served adequately.

ANCIENT ROOTS

Like the rulers of the Ancient Near East and Byzantium, the Middle Ages and modern European rulers could not avoid the development of relations with one another. As a result, there grew a network of institutions through which modern states carried on these relations. The bases of these relations lie in the ambassadorial activities of the past from which grew the professionalism of diplomats and the idea of diplomacy as a career with distinct features and demands of its own. The centuries between the end of the Middle Ages and the Renaissance witnessed the rise of a body of gradually developing features that tended to strengthen the status of diplomats in the performance of their duties. While the status of diplomats slowly changed during these centuries as western society, its institutions and its needs gradually expanded, they also continued to show strong origins of early relations and adaptations to new ends. By the middle of the fifteenth century there clearly arose in Italy diplomatic approaches tried earlier but not firmly rooted in the way they appeared now, forming the basis of a "modern" system of interstate relations.

By the period of the late Middle Ages the *Res Publica Christiana* had formulated something like a common body of law, the area of the most

---

[36] Berridge, "Amarna Diplomacy," in *Amarna Diplomacy*, 223; M. Liverani, "Political Lexicon and Political Ideologies in Amarna Letters," *Berytus*, 31 (1983) 41–45.

nearly complete realization of this law being in the realm of what was known as traditional practices governing foreign relations, now called "International Law." Like most Medieval Law, this field of the law escaped systematic codification, deriving its force from formal practices, generally accepted principles and old-established customs, not from statutes or edicts or treaties. In this respect the prevailing international law resembled the ancient set of traditions which similarly derived their force from customs and traditions.

The most striking new characteristic of diplomats who were active in the fifteenth century was that they were gradually becoming resident envoys. In other words, many of them remained in their posts at the court of some foreign ruler for a considerable time, transacting business and transmitting information over a period of at least several months or even years. By the 1540's all the largest secular states of Italy—Venice, Florence, Milan, Naples—are reputed to have established permanent embassies in each other's capitals. Nicodemus of Pontremoli, who represented Milan in Florence in 1446, held his post in Florence for over twenty years and is reputed to be the first true permanent diplomatic agent, while the ambassador sent to Rome by the Duke of Savoy in 1460 has also been trumpeted as apparently the first to be officially and explicitly described as permanent *orator et ambaxiator continuus et procurator*.[37] In other words, the emerging system was something analogous to the system of proxenia (consuls) the Greek cities developed in the Classical times, wherein the proxenos (consul) was a citizen of the city where he resided and not necessarily of the city whose interests he represented. The reasons for this change are ascribed to the birth of new political needs in Italy and generally in Europe.

The duration of a permanent envoy's stay in his post varies. Furthermore, the position of a diplomat sent originally on some special and temporary mission could easily become extended and difficult to distinguish from that of a permanent representative. If conditions changed or new problems arose, he had to be sent new instructions which necessitated his prolonged stay. Even the status of some of these permanent ambassadors this early in history was in a state of flux. The first embassy accredited by Elizabeth I to a Catholic country, for example, was that to France in the 1580's, though

---

[37] L. Weckmann, "Les Origines des Missions Diplomatiques Permanentes," in *Revue Générale de Droit International Publique*, 3rd series 23 (1952) 170.

after 1859 the practice was discontinued for several years.[38] How long must a diplomat remain in any post for his mission to qualify as a permanent one? How different was the position of such an ambassador from the position of the Near Eastern envoys, who often remained in the courts or states of their host for a protracted length of time, well past their original intentions? Unfortunately, the majority of scholars dealing with modern ambassadors have ignored this protracted stay of Near Eastern envoys, nor do they reference the occasion of permanent ambassadors in the Near East, although several of Hammurabi's "permanent ambassadors" seemed to have stayed in that position for a number of months, perhaps years. The references in the Classical times to citizens of a city representing the interests of another city (πρόξενοι) maintained by the Greek city-states indicate that their position was permanent and many of these representatives came from the same family. This practice had a side benefit for the represented city in that it limited expenses for the city represented while it kept the represented city abreast about developments in that city.[39] One thing can be said about the "resident" ambassadors of the Bronze Age: even though permanent ambassadors were a rarity, the practice was not entirely unknown; hence one cannot be speaking of an entirely new practice among the Italian cities. In addition, when the system was introduced in the West the weaknesses of the system were inevitably reflected in the diplomatic machinery, since even the most successful and experienced diplomats seldom spent more than a part, usually a fairly small part of their working lives in diplomacy. In the early history of the institution the resident ambassadors were frequently replaced. What saved the continuity of the early residency emissaries at that time was that normally there were *two* envoys on duty at the same time, one of them often covering for the other.[40]

In contrasting the modern with the ancient system, Berridge emphasizes the lack of immunity in the ancient states as compared to the modern times. While it is true that an important characteristic of modern interna-

---

[38] M. S. Anderson, *The Rise of Modern Diplomacy, 1450–1919* (Longman, 1993) 11. In essence we cannot be speaking of a full-fledged diplomacy throughout most of the states as yet except in Western Europe and even there not in all the states, until the second half of the nineteenth century.

[39] Nicolson, *The Diplomatic Method*, 8. Foreigners were used on many occasions to represent the European kings down to the French Revolution without regard to their nationality; also Bertold Picard, *Das Gesandschaftswesen* (Graz, Wien, Köln, 1967) 16–17.

[40] Mattingly, *Renaissance Diplomacy*, 65.

tional relations is the freedom of the diplomat from legal action in both civil and criminal cases, this safety was patchy until practically the end of the eighteenth century, inasmuch as it could be argued that a diplomat accused of a "serious" crime was subject to the law and courts of the state in which he was serving. Nor was he, as in antiquity, always safe from an angry monarch. Even to date, though the embassies are supposedly guaranteed safety by international conventions, dangers against them and their personnel abound and the best example is the seizure of the American Embassy and its personnel in Iran in 1978.[41] For a long time in the modern era (after 1500) the immunity of the ambassador, like that of the Bronze Age envoys, was confined to the period from the day he took up his mission to the day he laid it down. Like them also a diplomat might be exposed to the full penalties of the law in the land where he was serving for a whole list of political crimes that gave him no immunity, such as espionage, conspiracy, treason, and the like. For these crimes he could be tried and sentenced by the prince to whom he was accredited, just as if he were that prince's subject. In some way, he was worse off than some of the ancient envoys who were sent back home to be tried by their own prince, unless their own prince gave permission to the prince to whom they were accredited to punish them for the alleged crimes.

It becomes evident that the law of immunity prevalent for a long time in the early modern era was designed to give the envoy privileges and immunities in the performance of his duties but not intended to protect him from punishment for abusing those privileges and immunities for other ends. Yet this notion of punishment for an envoy is alien to the contemporary notion of diplomatic immunity; for if his political acts are to be judged by the government to which he is accredited, how can we say that he enjoys any effective immunity?

Like the Near Eastern kings, kings and princes in the early modern times resorted to merchants who served frequently as their envoys. Lorenzo de Medici, the ruler of Florence and a banker and merchant, thought himself better served in diplomacy by Florentine merchants and bankers in the great commercial and financial center of Lyon, since they had closer con-

---

[41] It is unfortunate that religious and non-religious regimes in recent times have been encouraging violence against embassies, something that governments rarely did in the ancient times. The danger to modern embassies because of this attitude is obvious from the fact that embassy buildings are being converted into fortresses.

nections with the French court, than his ambassadors in France. Accordingly, Florentine merchants and bankers exercised a great deal of influence on foreign policy because of their contacts and knowledge of events and personalities abroad which they drew from their agents.[42] Even today the use of merchants as quasi-diplomatic agents, though not as frequent perhaps as before, is not an uncommon phenomenon. Their use utility lies often in the fact that they are shrouded by more secrecy since they are not watched as closely by news seekers, while they have often close friendships with politicians and leaders of foreign countries.

From the beginnings, ceremonials and rituals played a leading role in diplomacy as we have seen in the discussion of the Near Eastern and the Homeric material. The departure and return of envoys were associated with religious ceremonies intended to safeguard the safety and success of envoys' missions. Religious ceremonies were important as an ingredient not only in the Bronze Age but in Classical and Roman times and in the Middle Ages. Ambassadors ought to take their departure in a solemn and public manner so that their prestige and the solemnity of their expedition may increase, and the powers to whom they were sent may be more ready to receive them. The court to which they were dispatched should send a delegation to greet them and the greeting delegation should consist of persons of distinction and rank appropriate to the position of the ambassadors, the solemnity of the embassy, and the occasion. Envoy departure and reception was associated with prayers and the pouring of libations. Similarly, negotiations in the Middle Ages and early modern times were begun with prayers, while agreements were signed in a church or abbey and holy relics displayed to add greater gravity to the occasion. It also remained normal practice, once a treaty had been signed, for the participants to take a solemn and public oath in a church and to observe the signing of it on some particularly venerated relic, something analogous with the public oaths of the ancients and the invocation of curses upon the would-be violators of the signed treaties. Pomp and ceremony characterized also the departure of envoys.[43]

The list of similarities in practices surrounding embassies can be greatly expanded but such treatment would lengthen this chapter immeasurably. There are references to gifts in the period following the Renaissance,

---

[42] Maulde-la-Clavière, *Diplomatie*, 1.451; 3.152; Anderson, *The Rise of Modern Diplomacy*, 9–10; C. S. Gutkind, *Cosimo de Medici, Pater Patriae, 1389–1464* (Oxford University Press, 1938) 38.

[43] S. Anglo, *Spectacle, Pageantry and Early Tudor Method*, 38.

the gathering of information by envoys, fear of host states about spying in their midst, mention of hostage holding, references about the pay, feuds over protocol, the description of envoy qualifications and training, the setting up of archives for the preservation of records and official documents, and so on, the likes of which we read in the Near Eastern documents and Homer.

In sum, what general lessons can be learned from the diplomatic practices from antiquity to the modern times? The fundamental lesson is that from the beginning international relations were governed by certain universally accepted principles, even when occasionally the existence of these principles was violated. These principles evolved organically from the conscience of mankind independent of governments and institutions, and were most probably more ancient than the governments and institutions themselves. Westermarck has argued that the customs of primitive peoples were not merely the possession of a privileged circle of men but that they involved moral rules and expressed the moral ideas of the times during which they were established, and that they may suggest that the social organization of human communities is intrinsically connected with man's pursuit of decency. As Cicero said, "the customs of a people are precepts in themselves.[44] They proved very durable throughout because they derived from the rational in man and were by and large commonly accepted as natural universal law without which there would be nothing to prevent continuance of international anarchy.

The evolution of human civilizations brought about understandable changes in international relations. Some of the ancient customs in the process of time were metamorphosed and changed. We witness the practices of rulers or of their representatives formerly charged with religious symbolism, e.g. the signing of treaties, and the pronouncement of public religious oaths to have gradually disappeared and to have been replaced today by secular substitutes whose purpose, in their turn, is also to boost the solemnity of the transactions completed. This was inevitable as religion slowly yielded to secularism. With the rise of science and technology international relations became by and large increasingly more efficient; yet the basic ingredients of the practices discussed in this paper have not lost their validity. The introduction of the telegraph, the telephone and the plethora of electronic devices recently have made communications easier and instantaneous and the work of the envoys clearer but they have not dispelled the necessity of en-

---

[44] Cicero, *De Off.* 1.41; Westermarck, *Origin and Development of Moral Ideas*, 97.

voys, the collection of information by embassies, the need of protocol, or the need for personal contacts in the solution of interstate problems. Indeed, the accelerated speed with which communications are conducted in the modern time have not been always beneficial from the view point of diplomatic signaling.

Some modern scholars have noted that before the communication revolution, diplomacy owed its rise in part to the absence of speedy communications in a period when the governments of the territorial states maintained continuous political relations with each other. They have even argued that diplomacy owes its decline in part to the development of speedy regular communications.[45] Nor were all distances between states in antiquity so remote as to become a great hindrance to diplomatic communications. Although distances in the ancient Near East might have required several days or even months for messengers to reach their destination, scholars contend that the problems of communication were not insurmountable. On the contrary, the Neo-Assyrian Empire for example, was an empire of communications.

Indeed, it would have been impossible to rule a large multinational state without a smoothly and efficiently functioning system of communications. It was simply not enough to station troops at strategic points or to make sure that merchandize, tribute and other commodities flowed steadily to the heart of the empire. It was vital that the central administration would be constantly aware of what was happening within the empire and even beyond its borders in order to respond effectively and relocate its military and economic resources wherever and whenever necessary. A network of roads for the transfer of goods and the use of armies seems to have been in operation in Mesopotamia since the imperial times of the second millennium (or even earlier) by which the center kept tight control on the empire. A similar network of roads ostensibly existed in the Mycenaean world, serving the purposes of the Mycenaean world. For as long as the center could keep tight control on the empire, information, army, people, and goods, could move from one part of the Assyrian state to another through a network of roads to which the Assyrians attached great care to keep in good condition. At regular intervals there were stations serving as resting places for the royal army and as relay points for imperial messengers. Each station was to keep in readiness fresh horses plus chariots and drivers which the messenger passing through would exchange with his tired team, thus being

---

[45] Hans Morganthau, *Politics Among Nations*, 3rd ed. (New York, 1966) 546.

able to continue the journey at full speed without interruption. By this relay system, military and administration messages would be rushed from place to place to almost any part of the empire in a matter of few days.[46] This wonderful network of roads was later inherited by the Persian Empire which used it with equal efficiency. Later on in the history of the empire, however, when the unity of the Persian Empire weakened, the greatness of the distances and the scattered conditions of the forces of the empire caused serious problems (Xen. Anab.1.5.9).

The rise of modern super-national organizations has replaced the old religious and political leagues as arbiters and has provided a universal tribune for the airing of differences among nations, but like the ancient Greek Amphictyonic and political league formations, it has not yet succeeded in eliminating war, or the need for ambassadors among nations. This human dream of peace may one day be realized, but no prediction can be made whether such an achievement will render envoys and the practices associated with them from the beginnings of history superfluous.

---

[46] Somo Parpola, ed., *The Correspondence of Sargon II*, vol. 1, part 1, xiii-xiv.

BIBLIOGRAPHY

Bibliographical details have been kept to a minimum, especially the Greek. The initial letters of German and French adjectives and other terms have been capitalized here for the sake of uniformity with the English format.

NEAR EASTERN BIBLIOGRAPHY

The Amarna Letters
Knudtzon, J. A., *Die El-Amarna-Tafeln*, 2 vols. (Leipzig, 1915).
Mercer, S. A. B, *The Tell El Amarna Tablets*, 2 vols. (Toronto, 1939).
Moran, William L., ed., *The Amarna Letters*, (Johns Hopkins University Press, 1992).
Pritchard, James ed., 3rd ed., *Ancient Near Eastern Texts Relating to the Old Testament*.

Lexicon of Ancient Cultures
Brunner, Helmut et al., *Lexikon Alte Kulturen*, (Meyers Verlag, (Mannheim-Leipzig-Wien-Zürich, 1990-1993).

General Bibliography
Abdul Kader, M., "The Administration of Syro-Palestine during the New Kingdom," *Annales du Service des Antiquités de l'Egypte* 56 (1959) 105–1.
Albright, W. F., "A Case of Lèse Majesté in Pre Israelite Lachist, with Some Remarks on the Israelite Conquest," *BASOR* 87 (1942) 32–38.
----------, *From the Stone Age to Christianity*, 2nd ed. (Baltimore, 1946).
----------, *Archaeology and the Religion of Israel*, 3rd ed. (Baltimore, 1953).
----------, "The Amarna Letters from Palestine" in *CAH*, I. E. S. Edwards et al., eds, 3rd ed., vol. 2, pt. 2 (Cambridge University Press, 1975).
Altman, Amnon, "On the Legal Meaning of Some of the Assertions in the 'Historical Prologue' of the Kizzuwatna Treaty (*KBo* I, 5)," in Bar-Ilan, *Studies in Assyriology Dedicated to Pinhas Artzi*, (Bar-Ilan University Press, 1990) 177–205.

Anderson, Garry A., *A Time to Mourn, A Time to Dance: The Expression of Grief and Joy in Israelite Religion* (University Park, Pa., 1991).
Artzi, Pinhas," Mourning in International Relations," *Death in Mesopotamia: Mesopotamia* 8 (1980) 161–79.
----------, The Influence of Political Marriages on the International Relations of the Amarna Age," in *La Femme dans le Proche Orient Antique. Compte Rendu de la XXXIIIe Recontre Assyriologique Internationale* (Paris, 7–10 Juillet 1986) Jean-Marie Durand ed., 23–26 (Paris, Editions, *Recherche sur les Civilization*, 1987).
Averback, R. E. et al., eds., *Life and Culture in the Ancient Near East* (Bethesda, MD, 2003).
Avruch, Kevin, "Reciprocity, Equality, and Status-Anxiety in the Amarna Letters," in *Amarna Diplomacy*, R. Cohen and R. Westbrook, eds. (Johns Hopkins University Press, 1999) 154–63.
Balkan, Kemal, *Letter of King Anum-Hirbi of Mama to King Warshama of Kanish* (Ankara: 1957).
Barton, G. A., *The Royal Inscriptions of Sumer and Akkad* (New Haven, 1929).
Beckman, G., *Hittite Diplomatic Texts.* (Society of Biblical Literature Writings from the Ancient World) 7 (Atlanta, Scholars Press, 1996).
Bezold, C., *Oriental Diplomacy* (London, 1983).
Berridge, G. R., *Talking to the Enemy: How States without Diplomatic Relations Communicate* (London, 1994).
Bleiberg, E. L., *The Official Gift in Ancient Egypt* (University of Oklahoma Press, 1996).
Brinkman, J. A. in Paul Garelli, ed., *Le Palais et la Royauté* (Paris, 1974).
Bryce, T. R., "Some Reflections on the Historical Significance of the Talagalawas Letter," (*KUB* XIV 3) *Orientalia* 48 (1979) 91–96.
----------, "Ahhiyawans and Mycenaeans—An Anatolian Viewpoint," *Oxford Journal of Archaeology* 8 (1989) 297–310.
----------, *The Kingdom of the Hittites* (Oxford University Press, 1998).
----------, *The Trojans and Their Neighbors* (Routledge, 2006).
Carnevale, P. J. and D. G. Pruit, "Negotiations and Mediation," *Annual Review of Psychology* 43 (1992) 531–82.
Cassin, E., J. Bottero, and J. Vercoutter, eds., *Die Orientalischen Reiche II, Das Ende des 2. Jahrtausends*, in *Fischer Geschichte*, vols. 2–5 (Fischer Bücherei, 1966).
Charpin, D and J. M. Durand, "Le Traité entre Ibal-pi-El II d'Ešnunna et Zimrli-Lim de Mari" in *Marchands, Diplomats, Empereurs: Études sur la Civilisation Mésopotamienne Offértes à Paul Garelli*, D. Chapin and F. Joannès, eds. (Paris: Editions Recherche sur les Civilizations, 1991) 139–66.

Cohen, Raymond, *International Politics: the Rules of the Game* (London, 1981).
---------, "All in the Family: Ancient Near Eastern Diplomacy," in *International Negotiation* 1 (1996) 11–28.
--------, "On Diplomacy in the Ancient Near East: The Amarna Letters," in *Diplomacy and Statecraft*, 7 (1996) 245–70.
Collins, Billie Jean, ed., *A History of the Animal World in the Ancient Near East* (Leiden, 2002).
Cooper, J. and W. Hempel, "The Sumerian Sargon Legend," *JAOS* 103 (1983) 67–72.
Crown, A. D., "Tidings and Instructions: How News Travelled in the Ancient Near East," *JESHO* 17 (1974) 244–71.
Dalley, Stephanie et al, *The Legacy of Mesopotamia* (University of Oxford Press, 1998).
Drower, M., "The Amarna Age," in *CAH*, I. E. S. Edwards et al. eds., 483–93, 3rd edition, vol. 2. pt.2 (Cambridge University Press, 1975).
Edel, Elmar, ed., *Die Ägyptisch-Hethitische Korrespondenz aus Boghazköi in Babylonischer und Hethitischer Sprache. Vol 1. Umschriften und Übersetzungen.* Abhandlungen der Rheinisch-Westfälischen Akademie der Wissenshaften 77 (Opladen: Westdeutsche Verlag, 1994).
Edzard, D. O., "Die Beziehungen Babyloniens und Ägyptens in der Mittelbabylonischer Zeit und das Gold," *Journal of the Economic and Social History of the Orient* 3 (1960) 38–55.
Frandsen, P., "Egyptian Imperialism," in *Power and Propaganda: A Symposium on Ancient Empires*, M. Larsen, ed. (Akademisk Forlag, 1979) 167–81.
Fensham, Charles F., "Malediction and Benediction in Ancient Near Eastern Vassal-Treaties and the Old Testament." *ZAW* 74 (1962) 1–9.
Galán, J. M., "The Heritage of Thutmose III's Campaign in the Amarna Age," in *Essays in Egyptology in Honor of Hans Goedicke*, B. Bryan and D. Lorton, eds. (San Antonio, 1994) 91–102.
Gardiner, A., *The Kadesh Inscriptions of Ramesses II* (Oxford University Press, 1960).
Garelli, Paul, *Marchands, Diplomates et Empererus; Études sur la Civilisation Mesopotamienne Offérts à Paul Garelli*, D. Charpin et al. eds. (Paris, 1991).
Gelb, I. J., "The Word for Dragoman in the Ancient Near East," *Glossa* 2 (1968) 93–104.
---------, and B. Kienast, *Die Altakkadischen Königsinscriften des Dritten Jahrtausends v. Chr.* FAOS 7 (Freiburg-Beisgau, 1990).
Goetze, Albrecht, "The Kassites and Near Eastern Chronology," *JNS* 18 (1964) 97–101.
Grayson, Kirk, A., *Assyrian Royal Inscriptions*, 2 vols. (Wiesbaden, 1976).

----------, *Assyrian Rulers of the Third and Second Millennium to 1115 BC* 2 vols. (University of Toronto Press, 1987).

Hachmann, R., "Die Ägyptische Verwaltung in Syrien während der Amarnazeit," *Zeitschrift des Deutschen Palästina-Vereins* 98 (1982) 17–49.

Hallo, W. W., ed., *The Context of Scripture: Canonical Compositions from the Biblical World*, 2 vols. (Leiden, 1997–2000).

Harper, R. F., *ABL* (London and Chicago, 1982–1914).

Heimpel, Wolfgang, *Letters to the King of Mari* (Winona Lake, Ind., 2003).

Helck, W., *Zur Verwaltung des Mittleren und Neuen Reiches, Probleme der Ägyptologie* 3 (Brill, 1958).

----------, " Die Ägyptische Verwaltung in den Syrischen Besitzungen" *MDOG* 92 (1960) 1–13.

----------, "Die Beziehungen Ägyptens zu Vorderasien im 3. und 2. Jahrtausend v. Chr." *Ägyptologische Abhandlungen* 5 (Wiesbaden, 1971) 435–443.

----------, *Die Beziehungen Ägyptens und Vorderasiens zur Ägäis bis ins 7. Jh. v. Chr.* (Darmstadt, 1979).

Hoffner, Harry A., Jr., *The Laws of the Hittites: A Critical Edition* (Leiden, 1997).

Holmes, Y. L., "The Messengers of the Amarna Letters," *JAOS* 95 (1975) 376–81.

Houwink ten Cate, P. H. J. "Contact between the Aegean Region and Anatolia in the Second Millennium B.C." in A. Crossland and Ann Birchall, eds., *Bronze Age Migrations in the Aegean: Archaeological and Linguistic Problems in Greek Prehistory* (Park Ridge: 1974).

Kenyon, Kathleen, M., "Palestine in the Time of the Eighteenth Dynasty," *CAH*, 3rd ed., Pt. 1, pp. 575–81.

Korošec, Victor, "International Relations according to Cuneiform Reports from the Tell el-Amarna and Hittite State Archives" in *Zbornik Znanstvenih Razprav* 23 (1950) 390–97.

Kühne, Christian, *Die Chronologie der Internationalen Correspondenz von El Amarna* (Neukirchener Verlag, 1994).

Kühne, Hartmut, Hans-Jörg Nissen, Johannes Renger, eds., *Mesopotamien und Seine Nachbarn, Politische und Kulturelle Wechelbeziehungen im Alten Vorderasien vom 4.bis zum 1. Jahrtausend v.chr.*, 2 vols., in *Berliner Beiträge* (Dietrich Reimer Verlag, Berlin 1982).

Kuhrt, Amelie, *The Ancient Near East: c. 3000–330 BC*, 2 vols. (London, 1995).

Lambrou-Phillipson, C., "A Model for the Identification of Enclave Colonies," *Paper Delivered at the Sixth International Colloquium on Aegean Prehistory, 30 August -5 September 1987*.

Lanfranchi, Giovanni P., and Simo Parpola, eds., *The Correspondence of Sargon II, State Archives of Assyria (SAA)* 5 vols. (Helsinki University Press, 1990).
Larsen, Mogens Trolle, *BIN, Babylonian Inscriptions in the Collection of J. J. B. Nies*, 4: A T. Clay, *Letters and Transactions from Cappodocia*, (1927) 6.
---------, *The Old Assyrian City-State and Its Colonies, Copenhagen Studies in Assyriology*, vol. 4, (Copenhagen, 1976).
---------, ed., *Power and Propaganda: A Symposium on Ancient Empires* (Copenhagen, 1979).
Lassøe, J., *The Shemsharra Tablets*, (Copenhagen, 1959).
Leemans, W. F., *The Old Babylonian Merchant: His Business and Social Position* (Leiden, 1950).
Lewis, B., *The Sargon Legend: A Study of the Akkadiean Texts and the Tale of the Hero Who Was Exposed at Birth* (Cambridge Mass., 1988).
Liverani, Mario, "The Great Powers' Club," in R. Cohen and R. Westbrook, *Amarna Diplomacy*, (Johns Hopkins University Press, 1999) 15–27.
---------, *International Relations in the Ancient Near East, 1600–1100 BC* (Palgrave, New York, 2001).
Malamat, A., " 'Hazor' The Head of All Those Kingdoms," *JBL* 79 (1960) 12–20.
Meier, Samuel A., *The Messenger in the Ancient Semitic World* (Atlanta, Scholars Press, 1988).
---------, "Diplomacy in International Marriages," in R. Cohen and R. Westbrook, eds., in *Amarna Diplomacy* (Johns Hopkins University Press, 1999) 165–173.
Morrison, M. A. and D. I. Owen eds., *Studies in the Civilization and Culture of Nuzi and the Hurrians* (Winona Lake, Indiana, 1981).
McCarthy, Dennis J., S. J., *Treaty and Covenant* in *Analecta Biblica* (Rome, 1978).
Mercer, S. A. B., *The Tell El-Amarna Tablets*, 1 (Toronto, 1939).
Moran, W. L., "Some Reflection on Amarna Politics," in *Solving Riddles and Untying Knots: Biblical, Epigraphic, and Semitic Studies in Honor of Jonas C. Greenfield*, Ziony Zevit, Seymour Gitin, and M. Sokoloff, eds. (Winona Lake, Ind., 1995) 559–72.
Munn-Rankin, J. M., "Diplomacy in Western Asia in the Early Second Millennium B.C.E." *Iraq* 18 (1956) 68–110.
Murnane, W. J., *Texts from the Amarna Period in Egypt*, Society of Biblical Literature Writings from the Ancient World 5 (Atlanta, Scholars Press, 1995).
Nougayrol, I., *Le Palais Royal d' Ugarit IV—Textes Accadiens des Archives Sud Archives Internationles* (Paris, 1956).

Numelin, Ragnar, *The Beginnings of Diplomacy, A Sociological Study of Intertribal and International Relations* (New York, 1950).
Oded, B., *War, Peace and Empire: Justification for War in Assyrian Royal Inscriptions* (Wiesbaden, 1922).
Oppenheim, A. L., "A Note on the Scribes in Mesopotamia," *Studies in Honor of Benno Landsberger on the Occasion of His Seventy-fifth Birthday*. (University of Chicago Press, 1965).
Parpola, Simon, *The Correspondence of Sargon II, Part I, Letters from Assyria and the West (SAA)* (Helsinki, 1988).
Peoples, J. and G. Bailey, *Theory of Ethnicity: An Anthropologist's Perspective* (New York, 1983).
Perrot, J., "The Excavations at Tell Abut Matar, Near Beersheba," *IEJ* 5 (1955) 1–16.
Pfeiffer, R., *State Letters of Assyria (SLA)* in AOS 6 (1935) 21–34.
Pritchard, James, ed., *Ancient Near Eastern Texts Relating to the Old Testament*, 3rd ed., (Princeton Univ. Press, 1969).
Revilla, Claudio Ciofi, "Origins and Evolution of War and Politics," *ISQ* 40 (1996) 1–22.
Rheinhold-Kramer, R., "Arzawa: Untersuchungen zu Seiner Geschichte nach den Hethitischen Quellen," *Theth* 8 (1977) 2–4; 50–55.
Robins, G., *Women in Ancient Egypt* (London: British Museum Press, 1993).
Ryholt, K. S. B., *The Political Situation in Egypt during the Second Intermediate Period* (Museum Tusculatum Press, 1997).
Scalpinger, Anthony J., *War in Ancient Egypt* (Oxford, Blackwell, 2005).
Schaeffer, Claude, *Ugaritica* 7 (Paris, 1978).
Schulman, Alan R., "Some Remarks on the Military Background of the Amarna Period," *Journal of the American Research Center in Egypt* 3(1964) 51–69.
----------, "Diplomatic Marriages in the Egyptian New Kingdom," *JNES* 38 (1979) 177–83.
----------, "Aspects of Ramesside Diplomacy: The Treaty of Year 21," *JCSEA* 8 (1978) 112–130.
Sethe, K. and W. Helck, eds., *Urkunden des Ägyptischen Altertums IV: Urkunden der 18. Dynastie, 1–6* (Berlin, Akademie, 1955–58).
Several, Michael W. "Reconsidering the Egyptian Empire in Palestine during the Amarna Period," *PEQ* 104 (1972) 123–33.
Sigrist, Marcel, *Messenger Texts from the British Museum* (Maryland, 1990).
Soden, W. von, "Drei Mittelassyrische Briefe Aus Nippur," *AFO* 18 (1958) 368 ff.

Sollberger, E., *Corpus des Inscriptiones "Royales" Présargoniques de Lagaš* (Geneva, 1956).

----------, and J. R. Kupper, *Inscriptions Royales Sumériennnes et Akkadiennes. Paris Littératures Anciennes du Proche-Orient* (Lapo 3, 1971).

----------, "The So-Called Treaty between Ebla and Ashur," *Studi Eblaiti* 310 (1980) 129–55.

Théodoridès, Aristide, "Les Relations de l' Égypte Pharaonique avec ses Voisins," *RIDA* 22 (1975) 87–140.

Thompson, Stephen E., "The Anointing of Officials in Ancient Egypt," *JNES* 53 (1994) 15–25.

Veenhof, Klaas, R., *Aspects of Old Assyrian Trade and Its Terminology* (Leiden, 1972).

Watermann, Leroy, *Royal Correspondence of the Assyrian Empire*, 4 vols. (Ann Arbor, 1930–36).

Weidner, Ernst. F., *Politische Dokumente aus Kleinasie. Die Staatsverträge in Akkadischer Sprache aus dem Archiv von Boghazköi* (Leipsig, 1923).

----------, "Weisse Pferde in Alten Orient," *BiOr* 9 (1952) 157–59.

Weinfeld, M., "Covenant Terminology in the Ancient Near East and Its Influence on the West," *JAOS* 93 (1973) 190–99.

Wiseman, D. J., *The Alalakh Tablets* (London, British Institute of Archaeology at Ankara, 1953).

----------, " 'Is It Peace?'—Covenant and Diplomacy," *VT* 32 (1982) 317–22.

Westbrook, Raymond, "International Law in the Amarna Age" in *Amarna Diplomacy* (Johns Hopkins University Press, 1999) 33–34.

Yeivin, S., "Early Contacts between Canaan and Egypt," *IEJ* 10 (1960) 203.

Zaccagnini, Carlo, "The Merchant at Nuzi," *Iraq* 39 (1977) 171–89.

----------, "Patterns of Mobility Among Near Eastern Craftsmen," *JNES* 42 (1983) 245–64.

----------, "On Late Bronze Age Marriage," in *Studi in Onore di Edda Bresciani*, S. F. Bondi, ed., (Pisa, 1985) 593–605.

----------, "Aspects of Ceremonial Gift Exchange in the Near East during the Second Millennium BC in *Center and Periphery in the Ancient World*," M. Rowland, M. T. Larsen, and K. Kristiansen eds. (Cambridge University Press, 1987) 47–56.

----------, "The Forms of Alliance and Subjugation in the Near East of the Late Bronze Age," in *I Trattati nel Mondo Antico: Forma, Ideologia, Funzione*, L. Canfora et al. eds. (Rome, 1990) 37–79.

----------, "The Interdependence of the Great Powers," in *Amarna Diplomacy* (Johns Hopkins University Press, 1999) 141–153.

HOMERIC AND OTHER BIBLIOGRAPHY

Lexica

Chatraine, P., *Dictionaire Étymologique de la Langue Greque* (Paris, 1968–80).
Cunliffe, R. J., A Lexicon of the Homeric Dialect (University of Oklahoma Press, 1963).
Ebelin, C. et al., *Lexicon Homericum*, 2 vols, 1880–85.
Frisk, H., *Griechsches Etymologisches Wörterbuch* (Heidelberg, 1954–73).
Janin, Raymond, *Dictionnaire d' Histoire et de Geographie Ecclesiastique* 16 (Paris, 1969).
Snell, B. and H. Erbse, eds., *Lexicon des Frühgriechisschen Epos* (Göttingen, 1955–

Some Homeric Texts and Commentaries

General

Ameis, K. F., C. Hentze, and P. Cauer, *Homers, Ilias* (Leipzig, 1868–1932).
Dimock, G. F., trans. and ed., *The Odyssey*, 2 vols., in Loeb Classical Library, (Harvard University Press, 1995).
Dindorf, Chatraine, P., *Dictionnaire Étymologique de la Langue Grecque* (Paris, 1968-80).
Erbse, H., ed., *Scholia Graeca in Homeri Iliadem*, 7 vols. (Berlin, 1969–88).
Kirk, G. S., Gen. ed., *The Iliad: A Commentary* (Cambridge University Press, 1985–93)
Kontomiches, Pantazes, A superb metric rendition of the *Iliad* and the *Odyssey* in Modern Greek (Athens, 1976 and 1972).
Leaf, W., *The Iliad: XII^2* (London, 1900).
MaCleod, C. W. *Iliad Book XXIV* (Cambridge, 1982).
Pulleyn, Simon, *Homer Iliad I* (Oxford University Press, 2000).
Russo, Joseph, et al., *A Commentary on Homer's Odyssey*, 3 vols, (Oxford Univ. Press, 1989–92).
Standford, W. B., *The Odyssey of Homer*, 2nd ed., 2 vols. (St. Marin Press, 1958).
Wyatt, W. G. trans. and ed., *The Iliad*, 2 vols., in Loeb Classical Library, (Harvard University Press, 1999).

Anderson, M. S., *The Rise of Modern Diplomacy, 1450–1919* (Longman, 1993).
Anglo, S. *Spectacle, Pageantry, and Early Tudor Method* (Oxford University Press, 1997).

Aravantinos, Vassilis, "Old and New Evidence for the Palatial Society of Mycenaean Thebes: An Outline," *Proceedings of the Fifth International Conference in Politeia: Society and State in the Aegean Bronze Age*, (Aegaeum 12) University of Heidelberg, Archäologisches Institut, 10–13 April, 1994, Robert Laffineur and Wolf-Dietrich Niemeier, eds., (Liège, 1995) 613–621.
Arend, W., *Die Typischen Scenen bei Homer. Problemata: Forschungen zur Klassischen Philologie*, Heft 7 (Berlin, 1933).
Aro, Sanna and R. M. Whiting, eds., *The Heirs of Assyria, Melammu Symposia* 1 (Helsinki, 2000).
Astour, M., *Hellenosemitica: An Ethnic and Cultural Study in West Semitic Impact on Mycenaean Greece* (Leiden, 1967).
Åström. P. and K. Demakopoulou, "New Excavations in the Citadel of Midea 1983–84," *OpAth* 17 (1988) 19–25.
Åström P., K. Demakopoulou, and G. Walber, "Excavations in Midea 1985," *OpAth* 17 (1988) 7–11.
Austin, M. M., *Greece and Egypt in the Archaic Age*, PCPS suppl. 2 (Cambridge University Press, 1970).
Best, E., *The Maori* 2 (Wellington, 1924).
Bancroft, H. H., "The History of Mexico, in *Works of H. H. Bancroft*, vol. 9 (San Francisco, 1883).
-------, *The Native Races of the Pacific States of North America*, 4 (San Francisco, 1883–86).
Barber, R. L. N., *The Cyclades in the Bronze Age* (London, 1987).
Barth, F., "Ethnic Groups and Boundaries," *TAPS*, vol. 57, pt. 8 (Philadelphia, 1969).
Bernal, Martin, *Black Athena, The Afroasiatic Roots of Classical Civilization* (Rutgers University Press, 1987).
Boas, Fr., *General Anthropology* (New York, 1938).
Bon, Antoine, *Le Péloponnèse Byzantine jusqu'en 1205* (Paris, 1951).
Bouzek. Jan, *Greece, Anatolia and Europe: Cultural Interrelations During the Early Iron Age in Studies in Mediterranean Archaeology*, vol.122 (Paul Aström, 1997)
Bozeman, Adda, *Politics and Culture in International History* (Princeton, 1960).
Bowra, C. M., *Heroic Poetry*, (London, 1952).
Brenk, Frederick, E., S.J., *Dear Child*: "The Speech of Phoinix and the Tragedy of Achilles in the Ninth Book of the Iliad," *Eranos* 84 (1986) 77–86
Brown, G., *Melanesians and Polynesians* (London, 1910).

Burkert, Walter, *Die Orientalisierende Epoch der Griechischen Religion und Literatur, Sitzungsberichte der Bayerishen Akademie der Wissenschaften, Phil.- Hist. Klasse* (Stuttgart, 1984) abt. 1.

----------, *Greek Religion*, J. Raffan, trans. (Harvard University Press, 1985).

Burr, V., Νεῶν Κατάλογος, *Klio Beiheft* 49 (Leipzig 1944).

Buxton, R. G. A., ed., *From Myth to Reason? Studies in the Development of Greek Thought* (Oxford, University Press, 1999).

Cambridge Ancient History, 3rd ed., I. E. S. Edwards, C. J. Gadd, N. G. L. Hammond, and E. Sollberger (Cambridge University Press, 1973–).

Carpenter, Rhys, *Folk Tale, Fiction, and Saga in the Homeric Epics* (University of California Press, 1946).

Carter, Jane B. and Sarah P. Morris, eds., *The Ages of Homer* (Texas University Press, 1995).

Casalis, E., *My Life in Basuto Land* (London, 1889).

Chadwick, John, *The Mycenaean World* (Cambridge University Press, 1976).

Chrysos, Evangelos, "Byzantine Diplomacy A.D. 300–800: Means and Ends," in Jonathan Shepard and Simon Franklin, eds., *Byzantine Diplomacy, Papers from the Twenty-fourth Spring Symposium of Byzantine Studies, Cambridge, March 1990* (Variorum, 1992).

Clauss, D. B., "*Aidos* in the Language of Achilles," *TAPA* 105 (1975) 13–28.

Cline, Eric, H., "Amenhotep III and the Aegean: A Reassessment of Egypto-Aegean Relations in the 14th Century B.C." *Orientalia* 56 (1987) 1–36.

----------, *Sailing in the Wine Dark Sea: International Trade and the Late Bronze Age Aegean*, Bar International Series 591, (Oxford, Tempus Reparatum, 1994).

----------, "Egyptian and Near Eastern Imports at Late Bronze Age Mycenae," in *Egypt, Mycenae and the Levant*, W. Vivian Davies and Louise Schofield, (British Museum Press, 1995) 91–115.

----------, Tinker, Tailor, Soldier, Sailor: Minoans and Mycenaeans Abroad," in Laffineur Robert and W.-D. Niemeier, eds., *Politeia: Society and State in the Aegean Bronze Age* (Aegaeum 12) (University of Liège, 1995) 265–287.

----------, and Diane Harris-Cline, eds., "The Aegean and the Orient in the Second Millennium," *Proceedings of the 50th Anniversary Symposium, Cincinnati 18–20, April 1997* (Université de Liège 1998).

Coldstream, J. N., "Mixed Marriages at the Frontiers of the Early Greek World," *OJA* 12 (1993) 89–107.

Davis, J. L., "Review of Aegean Prehistory I: The Islands of the Aegean," *AJA* 96 (1992) 699–756.

Deger, Jalkotzy, Sigrid, "The Post Palatial Period of Greece: An Aegean Prelude to the 11th Century B.C. in Cyprus," in Vassos Karageorgis, *Proceedings of the International Symposium of the Archaeological Research Unit of the University of Cyprus and the Anastasios G. Leventis Foundation (30–31 October 1993): Cyprus in the 11th Century B.C. Nicosia 11–30.*

Delobson, A. A. D., *L' Empire du Mogho-Naba (Inst. De Droit Comp. Études*, xi) (Paris, 1933).

Demakopoulou, K., ed., *The Mycenaean World* (Athens, 1988).

---------, "Mycenaean Citadels: Recent Excavations on the Acropolis of Midea in the Argolid," *BICS* (1995) 151–61.

Demand, Nancy, "Models in Greek History and the Question of the Origins of the Polis" *AAB* 18 (2004) 61–86.

Dickinson, O. T. P. K., *The Origins of Mycenaean Civilization* (Göteborg: 1977). "Homer, the Poet of the Dark Age," *Greece and Rome* 33 (1986) 20–37.

----------, *The Aegean Bronze Age* (Cambridge University Press, 1994).

Donlan, Walter, "The Unequal Exchange between Glaucus and Diomedes in Light of the Homeric Gift-Economy," *Phoenix* 43 (1989) 15.

----------, "Duelling with Gifts in the *Iliad*: As the Audience Saw it," *Colby Quarterly* 20 (1993) 155–172.

----------, *The Aristocratic Ideal and Selected Papers* (Eauconda, 1999).

Drews, Robert, "PIE speakers and PA Speakers," *JIES* 25. (1997) 153–77.

Driessen, Jan, *An Early Dectruction in the Mycenaean Palace at Knossos: A New Interpretation of the Excavations Field-Notes of the South-East Area of the West Wing* (Acta Archaeological, Monograph 2, Louvain, 1990).

Drew, R., O. Dickinson, W. Ward, and M. S. Joulkowsky, eds. *The Crisis Years: The 12th Century B.C. from the Danube to the Trigris* (Dubuque, Iowa) 1992.

Eder, Brigitta, *Argolis, Lakonien, Messenien, von Ende der Mykenischen Palastzeit bis zur Einwanderung der Dorier* (Wien, 1998).

Edwards, Mark W., *Homer, Poet of the Iliad* (Johns Hopkins University Press, 1990).

Edwards, Ruth B., *Kadmos the Phoenician* (Amsterdam, 1979).

Ellis, W., *Narrative of Tour Through Hawaii, or Orewnybec* (London, 1862).

Eylmann, E., *Die Eingeborenen der Kolonie Südaustraliens* (Berlin, 1908).

Fenik, B. C., ed., *Homer: Tradition and Invention* (Leiden, 1978).

Finkelberg, Margalit, "Royal Succession in Heroic Greece, *CQ* 41 (1991) 303–16.

----------, "Anatolian Languages and Indo-European Migrations to Greece," *CW* 91 (1997) 3–20.
----------, "Time and Arete in Homer," *CQ* 48 (1998) 155–28.
----------, *Greeks and Pre-Greeks, Aegean Prehistory and Greek Heroic Tradition* (Cambridge University Press, 2005).
Finley, Moses I. "The Trojan War," *JHS* 84 (1964) 1–20.
----------, "Myth, Memory and History," in *History and Theory*, 4 (1965) 288.
----------, *The World of Odysseus*, 2nd ed. (Harmondsworth, 1979).
Foley, John M., *The Theory of Oral Composition, History and Methodology* (Indiana Univ. Press, 1988).
Frazer, J., *The Aborigines of New South Wales* (Sydney, 1892).
French, E. B. and K. A. Wardle, "Cultic Places at Mycenae," in R. Hägg and N. Marinatos, eds., in *Sanctuaries and Cults in the Aegean Bronze Age* (Stockholm, the Swedish Institute, 1981) 41–48.
French, E. B. and K. A. Wardle, eds., *Problems in Greek Prehistory* (Bristol, 1988).
Fridl, E ., *Vasilika* (New York, 1962) 60–64.
Forrer, Emilio, *Forschungen*, 2 vols. (Berlin, 1926–29).
Godart, L. and A. Sacconi, "Les Dieux Thébains dans les Archives Mycéniénnes" in *Académie des Inscriptions et Belles-Lettres. Comptes Rendus des Séances de l' Année, Jan.-Mar.* (Paris) 99–113.
Gordesiani, Rismag, "Zur Interpretation der Duale in 9. Buch der Ilias," *Philologus* 124 (1980) 163–74.
Graves, Robert, *The Greek Myths*, 2 vols. (Baltimore, 1961).163–74).
Greeenhalgh, P. A. L., *Early Warfare* (Cambridge University Press, 1973).
----------, "The Homeric *Therapon* and *Opaon* in their Historical Implications," *BICS* (1982) 81–90.
Gschnitzer, Fritz, "Die Stellung der Polis in der Politischen Enwicklung des Atltertums," *OA* 27 (1988) 287–302.
----------, "Phoinikisch-karthagisches Verfassungsdenken," in Kurt Raaflaub, ed., *Anfänge Politischen Denkens in der Antike* (Munich, 1993) 187–98.
Hägg, R. and Marinatos N., eds., *Sanctuaries and Cults in the Aegean Bronze Age* (Stockholm, 1981).
Hägg, Robin, "The Role of Libations in Mycenaean Ceremony and Cult" in *Celebrations of Death and Divinity in the Bronze Age Argolid," Proceedings of the Sixth International Symposium at the Swedish Institute at Athens, 11–13 June, 1988* (Stockholm, 1990) 177–211.
Hampe, Roland and Erika Simon, *The Birth of Greek Art: From the Mycenaean to the Archaic Period.* (Oxford University Press, 1981).

Haubold, Johannes, *Homer's Peoples, Epic Poetry and Social Formation* (Cambridge University Press, 2000).
Havelock, Eric A., "The Transcription of the Code of a Non-literate Culture," in *The Literate Revolution in Greece and Its Cultural Consequences* (Princeton University Press, 1972) 89-121.
Herskovits, J. J., *Dahomey, an Ancient West African Kingdom* 4 (New York, 1938).
Hooker, J., *Mycenaean Greece* (London, 1977).
Hope-Simpson, R., "The Seven Cities Offered to Achilles, *Iliad* ix 149 ff.; 221 ff.) *BSA* 61 (1966) 113–31.
----------, and O. T. P. K. Dickinson, *A Gazetteer of Aegean Civilization in the Bronze Age, vol. I: The Mainland and Islands* (SIMA 52, Göteborg, 1979).
----------, *Mycenaean Greece* (Park Ridge, N.J, 1981).
Houwink ten Cate, P. H. J., "Hittite Royal Prayers," *Numen* 16 (1969) 81–98.
----------, "The History of Warfare according to Hittite Sources: The Annals of Hattusilis I (Part II)," in *Anatolia* 11 (1984) 47–83.
Howitt, A. W., *The Native Tribes of South-Australia* (London, 1904).
Iakovides, S. "Das Werk Klaus Kilians," *AM* 108 (1993) 9–27.
Isager, S. and J. E. Skydsgaard, *Ancient Greek Agriculture. An Introduction* (London, 1992).
Jackson, A. and T. Rihll, "War and Society in the Greek World," in J. Rich and G. Shipley, eds., (London, 1993) 64–76; 77–107.
Jardé, Auguste., *The Formation of the Greek People* (London, 1926).
Jeffreys. E, M. Jeffreys, R. Scott et al., *The Chronicle of John Malalas, A Translation* (Melbourne, 1986).
Jeffrey, L, *Archaic Greece: The City States c. 700–500 B.C.* (London, 1976).
Jenkins, R. J. ed., *De Administrado Imperio: Commentary* (London, 1962).
Junod, H. A., *The Life of a South African Tribe*, vol. 2 (London, 1929).
Kakrides, John T., *Homeric Themes* (Thessalonike, 1981).
Karageorhis, Vassos, "Cultural Innovations in Cyprus Relating to the Sea Peoples," in Oren, E. D., ed., *The Sea Peoples and Their World: A Reassessment* (Philadelphia, 2000) 256–275.
Karavites, P., "Diplomatic Envoys in the Homeric World," *RIDA* 34 (1987) 41–100.
--------- *Promise-Giving and Treaty-Making, Homer and the Near East* (Leiden, 1992).
Kilen, J. T., "The Linear B Tablets and the Mycenaean Economy," in A. Morpurgo Davies and Y. Duhoux, eds., *Linear B: A 1984 Survey* (Bib-

liothèque des Cahiers de l' Institute de Linguistique de Louvain 26. Louvain 1985) 241–305.

----------, "Observations on the Thebes Sealings," in J. P. Olivier ed., Mykenaika: *Actes du IXe Colloque International sur les Textes Mycéniens et Égéens, Athènes, 2–6 October 1990*, BCH suppl.25 (Paris, 1992) 365–85.

Kilian, Klaus, "Zeügnisse Mykinische Kulturaübung in Tiryns," in R. Hägg and N. Marinatos, eds., *Sanctuaries and Cults in the Aegean Bronze Age* (Stockholm: Swedish Institute in Athens, 1981) 49-58.

----------, "The Emergence of Wanax Ideology in the Mycenaean Palaces," *OJA* 7 (1988) 291-302.

Kirk, G. S., *The Songs of Homer* (Cambridge University Press, 1962).

----------, *Language and Background of Homer* (Cambridge: Heffer, 1964).

----------, *Myth: Its Meaning and Function in Ancient and Other Cultures* (University of California Press, 1970).

Köhnken, Adolf, "Die Rolle der Phoinix und die Duale im I der Ilias," *Glotta* 53 (1975) 89–113.

Kougeas, Socrates, "Peri tôn Meliinkôn tou Taÿgetoy," in *Pragatiae Akademias Athênôn*, 15.3 (Athens, 1950) 1–34.

Koutelakis, Haralambos, Μεγαλιθικές Κατασκευές καί Κύκλωπες, *Corpus* 68 (Febr. 2005) 36–45.

Laffineur, R. and L. Basch, eds., *THLASSA. L' Égée Préhistorique et la Mer. Actes de la Treisième Recontre Égéenne Internationale de l' Université de Liège* (Aegaeum 7) (Liège, 1991).

Laffineur, R. and W.-D. Niemeier eds., *Politeia: Society and State in the Aegean Bronze Age* (Aegaeum 12), (Liège, 1995).

Lambert, W. G. and A. E. Millard, eds., *Atra-Hasis* (Oxford, 1949).

Lampsides, O., *Andreou Libadenou, Bios kai Erga* (Athens, 1975).

Lardinois, André, "The Wisdom and Wit of Many: The Orality of Greek Proverbial Expression," in *Speaking Volumes, Orality and Literacy in the Greek and Roman World, Mnemosyne* Suppl. 218 (Leiden, 2001) 95.

Latacz, Joachim, ed., *Homer's Iliad, Gesamtkommentar* (Saur-München, Leipzig, 2000). Prolegomena—Faszikel 2.

----------, *Troy and Homer, Towards a Solution of an Old Mystery*, K. Windle and R. Ireland trans. (Oxford University Press, 2002).

Lattimore, Richmond, *The Iliad of Homer* (University of Chicago Press, 1951).

----------, *Homer's Iliad. A Commentary on the Translation of Richmond Lattimore's Iliad* (Exeter University Press) by N. Postlethwaite, in *JHS* 122 (2000) 160–61.

Lesky, Albin, "Zum Hethithischen und Griechischen Mythos," *Eranos* 52 (1954) 8–17.
Levy, H. L., "Property Distribution by Lot in Present-Day Greece," *TAPA* 87 (1956) 42–46.
Long, A. A., "Morals and Values in Homer," *JHS* 90 (1970) 121–39 with a reply in *JHS* 91(1991) 1–15.
Lord, Albert Bates and Béla Bartók, *Serbo-Croatian Folk Songs* (Columbian University Press, 1951).
Lord, Albert Bates, *The Singer of Tales* (Harvard University Press, 1960).
---------, *Epic Singers and Oral Tradition* (Cornell University Press, 1991).
Louden, Bruce, *The Iliad. Structure, Myth, and Meaning* (The Johns Hopkins University Press, 2006).
Machteld, Mellink J., ed., *Troy and The Trojan War* (Bryn Mawr, Pa., 1986).
Martin, R. P., *The Language of Heroes* (Cornell University Press, 1989).
Mauss, Marcel, *Essai sur le Don*, trans. By Ian Cunnison, *The Gift, Forms and Functions of Exchange in Archaic Societies* (Norton Library, 1976).
Mavromatis, L., *La Fondation d' Empire Serve, Le Krailj Milutin* (Thessalonike, 1978).
Mellor, Ronald, "The Dedication on the Capitoline Hill," *Chiron* 8 (1978) 319–30.
Moravcsik, G. and R. J. Hemkins, eds., and trans. *Constantine VIII, De Administrado Imperio* (Washington D.C., 1967).
Mitchell, Lynnette G., *Greeks Bearing Gifts, The Public Use of Private Relationships* (Cambridge University Press, 1997).
Morganthau, Hans, *Politics Among Nations*, 3rd ed. (New York, 1966).
Morris, Ian, ed., *Classical Greece New Directions in Archaeology* (Cambridge University Press, 1999).
Morris, Sarah, "Homer and the Near East," in Morris and Powell, eds., *A New Companion to Homer* (Leiden, 1997) 599–623.
Mosley, Derek J., "The Size of Embassies in Ancient Greek Diplomacy," *TAPA* 96 (1965) 255–66.
----------, *Envoys and Diplomacy in Ancient Greece, Historia, Einzelschriften* 22 (Franz Steiner Verlag, 1973).
Muellner, Leonard, *The Anger of Achilles. Mênis in Greek Epic* (Cornell University Press, 2005).
Mylonas, G. E., "Priam's Troy and the Date of its Fall," *Hesperia* 33 (1964) 352–80.
----------, *The Cult Center of Mycenae, Proceedings of the British Academy* 67 (1981) 307–20.

Nagy, Gregory, *The Best of the Achaeans: Concepts of Hero in Archaic Greek Poetry* (Baltimore, 1979).

----------, *Homeric Questions* (Texas University Press, 1996).

Negbi, Ora, "The Libyan Landscape from Thera: A Review of Aegean Enterprizes in the Minoan IA Period, *JMA* 7 (1994) 73–112.

Niemeier, W.-D., "Greeks vs. Hittites: Why Troy is Troy and the Trojan War is Real," *Archaeology Odyssey*, vol. 5, issue 4 (2002) 24–35.

----------, "Miletus in the Bronze Age: Bridge Between the Aegean and Anatolia," *Bulletin of the Institute of Classical Studies*, 46 (2002–03) 225–27.

Nilsson, M. P., *The Mycenaean Origin of Greek Mythology* (Cambridge University Press, 1932).

--------- *Greek Folk Religion* (Harper Torch Books, 1961).

Oikonomides, N., "Byzantine Diplomacy, A.D. 1204–1453: Means and Ends," in J. Shepard and S. Franklin, eds., *Byzantine Diplomacy*, 73–88.

Olivier, Jean-Pierre, ed., *Mykenaika; Actes du IXe Colloque Internationale sur les Textes Mycénniens et Egéens, Athènes, 2–6 October 1990*, BCH, suppl. 25 (Paris, 1992).

Olshausen E and H. Biller, eds., *Antike Diplomatie*, in Wege der Forschung series (Darmstadt, 1979).

Page, D. L., *History and the Homeric Iliad* (University of California Press, 1959).

Parker, K. L., *The Euahlayi Tribe* (London, 1905).

Parry, Adam, "The Language of Achilles," *TAPA* 87 (1959) 1–7.

----------, ed., *The Making of Homeric Verse. The Collected Papers of Milman Parry* (Oxford, 1971).

Perlès, Catherine, *The Early Neolithic in Greece* (Cambridge University Press, 2001).

Phiillipson, C., *International Law and Custom of Ancient Greece and Rome* 2 (London, 1911).

Picard, Bertold, *Das Gesandschafstwesen* (Graz-Wien-Köln, 1967).

Polignac, F. de, *Cults, Territory, and the Origins of the Greek City-State* (Chicago, 1995).

Poulianos, Ares N., E *Proelefsê tôn Hellênôn, Ethnogenetikê Erevna. E Mathêmatikê Apodeixê gia tên Katagôgê tôn Hellênon*. Library of the Greek Anthropological Society, No. 9 (Athens, 2001).

Powell, B. B. and I. Morris, *A New Companion to Homer* (Leiden, 1997).

Price, Douglas ed., *Europe's First Farmers* (Cambridge Univ. Press, 2000).

Raaflaub, Kurt A. and Elisabeth Müller, eds., *Anfänge Politischen Denkens in der Antike: Die Nahöstlichen Kulturen und die Griechen* (München, 1993).

----------, "Politics and Interstate Relations in the World of Early Greek Poleis: Homer and Beyond," *Antichthon* 31 (1997).

----------, "A Historian's Headache, How to Read 'Homeric Society'" in *Archaic Greece: New Approaches and New Evidence* (Wales, 1998).

----------, "Homer, the Trojan War, and History," *The Classical World*, 9 (1998) 386–403.

----------, "Influence, Adaptation, and Interaction: Near Eastern and Early Greek Political Thought." In S. Aro and R. Whiting, *Melammu Symposia* (Helsinki, 2000) 51–64.

----------, "Archaic Greek Aristocrats as Carriers of Cultural Interaction," *Melammu* (2002) 1–26.

----------, "Die Beteutung der Dark Ages: Mykene, Troia und die Griechen," in C. Ulf, ed., *Der Neue Streit um Troia. Eine Bilanz* (Munich, 2003) 1–20.

Rattray, R. S., *Ashanti Law and Constitutions* (Oxford, 1929).

Rehak, P., ed., "The Role of Aegean Prehistory II: The Prepalatial Bronze Age of the Southern and Central Greek Mainland," *AJA* 97 (1993) 745–97.

Renfew, A. C., *The Emergence of Civilization* (London, 1972).

----------, *Before Civilization* (London, 1973).

----------, *Problems in European Prehistory* (Edinburgh University Press, 1978).

Renfew, Colin A. and E. A. W. Zubow, eds., *The Ancient Mind. Elements of Cognitive Archaeology* (Cambridge University Press, 1994).

Renfew, Colin. and K. L. Cooke, eds. *Transformation. Mathematical Approaches to Culture* (New York, 1979).

Rich, J. W., *Declaring War in the Roman Republic in the Period of the Transmarine Expansion* (Brussels, 1976).

Rivers, W. H. R., *Kinship and Social Organizations* (London, 1914).

Rousseau, Joseph, "The "Formula" in I. Morris and B. Powell, eds., *A New Companion to Homer* (1997).

Rowland, M., M. Larsen, and K. Kristiansen, *Center and Periphery in the Ancient World* (Cambridge University Press, 1987).

Rutter, J. B., "Review of Aegean Prehistory II: The Prepalatial Bronze Age of the Southern and Central Greek Mainland," *AJA* 97 (1993) 745–97.

Schachermeyr, Fritz, *Die Levante im Zeitalter der Wanderungen vom 13 bis zum 11 Jahrhundert v. Chr.* (Wien, Österreiche Akademie der Wissensaftler, 1982) ch. 1.

Schultz-Ewert, E. and L. Adam, *Eingeborenen Recht* (Stuttgart, 1929).

Scodel, Ruth, "The Autobiography of Phoenix: *Iliad* 9. 444–95," *AJPH* 103 (1982) 128–36.

----------, "The World of Achilles," *CPh* 84 (1989) 91–99.

Seaford, R., *Reciprocity and Ritual. Homer and Tragedy in the Developing City-State* (Oxford University Press, 1994).
Segal, Charles, "The Embassy of the Duals of Iliad 9.182–98," *GRBS* 9 (1968) 101–114.
----------, "Nestor and the Honor of Achilles," *Studi Mycenei ed Egeo-anatolici*, 13 (1971a) 90–105.
Shelmerdine, C. W., "Review of Aegean Prehistory VI: The Palatial Bronze Age of the Southern and Central Greek Mainland," *AJA* 101 (1997) 537–585.
Singer, Itamar, *Hittite Prayers*, H. A. Hoffner, ed. (Leiden, 2002).
Small, David B., "Surviving the Collapse: The Oikos and Structural Continuity between Late Bronze Age and Later Greece," in Gitin, S., A. Mazar, and E. Stern, eds., in *Mediterranean Peoples in Transition: Thirteenth to Early Tenth Centuries BCE. In Honor of Professor Trude Dothan*, (Jerusalem, 1998) 283–91.
Snodgrass, A. M., *The Dark Age of Greece* (Edinburgh University Press, 1971).
----------, "An Historical Homeric Society," *JHS* 94 (1974) 114–25.
----------, *Archaic Greece. An Age of Experiment* (London, 1980).
----------, *Archaeology and the Emergence of Greece* (Cornell University Press, 2006).
Sollas, W. J., *Ancient Hunters* (London, 1924).
Spencer, Sir Walter Baldwin, *Native Tribes of Central Australia* (London, 1914).
Stanley, K., *The Shield of Homer* (Princeton University Press, 1993).
Starr, C. G., *The Origins of Greek Civilization, 1100–650* (New York, 1962).
Symeonoglou, S., *The Topography of Thebes from the Bronze Age to Modern Times* (Princeton University Press, 1985) 26–63.
Theocharis, D. R., ed., *Neolithic Greece* (Athens, 1973).
Thomas, Carol, G., *Myth Becomes History* (Regina Books, 1993).
----------, *Decoding Ancient History* (Prentice Hall, 1994).
----------, "The Components of Political Identity in Mycenaean Greece," in Laffineur R. and W.-D. Niemeier, eds., *Politeia: Society and State in the Aegean Bronze Age* (Aegaeum 2) (University of Liège, 1995) 349–355.
----------, *Finding People in Early Greece* (University of Missouri Press, 2005).
Thomas, C. G. and C. Conant, *Citadel to City-State, The Transformation of Greece, 1200–700 B.C.E.* (Indiana Univ. Press, 1999).
Thomas, N. W., *Natives of Australia* (London, 1906).
Thomas, R., *Oral Tradition and Written Records in Classical Athens* (Cambridge, 1989).

--------- *Literacy and Orality in Ancient Greece* (Cambridge, 1992).
Thornton, A. "Once Again, The Duals in Book 9 of the Iliad," *Glotta* 56 (1978) 1–4.
Trevor, Bryce, *The Trojans and their Neighbors* (Routledge, 2006).
Tzedakis, Yannis and Holley Martlew eds., *Archaeology Meets Science, Minoans and Mycenaeans, Flavors of their Times*. (Athens, Ministry of Culture, 2001).
Vansina, J., *Oral Tradition and History* (London, 1985).
Vedder, H., *Die Bergdama S. W. Afrikas* (Hamburg University, 1923).
Ventris, Michael and John Chadwick, *Documents in Mycenaean Greek*, 2nd ed. (Cambridge University Press, 1973).
Visser, Edzard, *Homers Katalog der Schiffe* (Stuttgart and Leipzig, 1997).
----------, "Formale Typologien im Schiffskatalog der Ilias: Befunde und Konsequenzen," in H. H. C. Tristram ed., *New Methods in the Research of Epic* (Tübingen, 1998).
Waanders, F. M. J., *Studies in Local Case Relations in Mycenaean Greek* (Amsterdam, 1997).
Wainright, F. T., *Archaeology and Place-Names and History* (London, 1962).
Waitz, Th., *Anthropologie der Naturvölker* 6 (Leipzig, 1872).
Wardle, K. A., *Cities of Legend. The Mycenaean World* (London, 1997).
Warren, P. M., *The Aegean Civilizations*, 2nd ed. (Oxford, Phaidon: 1989).
Watson, Janet, ed., *Speaking Volumes: Orality and Literacy in the Greek and Roman World*, Mnemosyne Suppl. 218 (Leiden, 2001).
Wheeler, R. E. M., *Alms for Oblivion* (London, 1966).
Wees, Hans van, "Homeric Warfare," in Ian Morris and Barry Powell, eds., *A New Companion to Homer* (Brill, 1997) 599–623.
Wéry, Louise-Marie, "Le Fonctionnement de la Diplomatie à l' Époque Homérique," *RIDA*, 14 (1967) 169–206.
West, M. L., *The East Face of Helicon: West Asiatic Elements in Greek Poetry and Myth* (Oxford University Press, 1997). Review article in *JHS* 121 (2001) 172–73, "West on the East: Martin West's East Face of Helicon and Its Forerunners."
Westermarck, E., *The Origin and Development of the Moral Ideas*, 2 (London, 1908).
Whittaker, C. R. ed., *Pastoral Economies in Classical Antiquity* (Cambridge, 1988).
Williamson, R. W., *The Social and Political Systems of Central Polynesia* 3 (Cambridge, 1924).
Willcock, M. M., "Homer, the Individual Poet," *Liverpool Classical Monthly* 3 (1978) 11–18.

Worthington, Ian and John Miles Foley, eds., "Epea and Grammata, Oral and Written Communication in Ancient Greece," in *The Orality and Literature in Ancient Greece*, vol. 4, series, Mnemosyne, Suppl. 153, (Leiden, 2002).

Wyatt, William Jr., "Homeric *ATH*," *AJPh*. 103 (1982) 247–76.

INDEX

Ab, 43
Abi-Milku, 79
Abraham, 66, 177
Absalom, 73
Achaean(s), 4, 17, 68, 90, 91, 98, 100, 102, 104, 105, 106, 109, 110, 111, 112, 114, 115, 116, 118, 119, 120, 122, 123, 125, 126, 127, 129, 130, 131, 133, 139, 146, 147, 148, 150, 152, 153, 155, 159, 163, 175, 177, 180, 181, 182, 189
Acharnae, 12
Achilles, 99, 101, 102, 103, 105, 106, 108, 109, 110, 111, 112, 113, 114, 115, 116, 117, 118, 119, 120, 121, 122, 127, 129, 133, 138, 139, 146, 148, 149, 150, 151, 153, 154, 155, 157, 158, 160, 177, 179, 182, 192, 193, 195, 199
Adad-nirari, 65
aedos, 141
Aegean, ix, x, xi, 2, 3, 8, 9, 10, 11, 14, 20, 21, 72, 90, 91, 92, 93, 94, 95, 96, 97, 98, 110, 112, 116, 136, 142, 143, 145, 148, 154, 167, 169, 170, 171, 172, 183, 191, 197, 199, 201, 203, 206
Aeolus, 140, 141, 153
Aethe, 107
Aethon, 107
Agamemnon, 15, 17, 99, 102, 103, 104, 105, 106, 107, 108, 109, 110, 111, 112, 114, 115, 116, 119, 121, 122, 123, 124, 128, 129, 131, 139, 146, 148, 149, 150, 151, 153, 154, 155, 157, 158, 159, 162, 174, 177, 182, 190, 192, 193, 195, 199, 202

agorai, 141
Ahhiyawan(s), 90, 91, 97, 98
Ahimaaz, 59
Ai, 80
Aias (Aias Telamonius), 106, 113, 114, 116, 126, 130, 133, 139, 146, 148, 149, 150, 182, 193
Akhenaten, 15, 29, 48, 195, 202
Akkadian, 2, 15, 19, 177
Alašiya, 39, 57, 72, 83, 194
Alcinous, 121, 149
Alexander, 125
Amarna, ix, xi, xiv, 14, 15, 16, 19, 20, 21, 22, 23, 25, 26, 27, 29, 36, 39, 42, 44, 45, 46, 47, 49, 50, 53, 54, 56, 58, 61, 70, 71, 72, 77, 78, 79, 81, 83, 156, 157, 172, 173, 174, 176, 177, 179, 187, 188, 192, 196, 197, 198, 199, 200, 201, 202, 205, 207
Amenophis III, 15, 26, 29, 39, 45, 48, 50, 80, 177
Amenophis IV, 29, 55, 69, 195
Amman, 21
Amon, 68
Amphictyonic, 214
Anatolia, 3, 13, 91, 98, 100, 103, 125, 169, 191
anax, 136
Andromache, 106, 107
angelos, 100, 120, 125
Antenor, 67, 126, 127, 151, 161
Antheia, 162
Antilochus, 107
Antimachus, 161, 189, 190
Aphrodite, 124, 159

Apollo, 102, 103, 105, 109, 125, 129, 130, 133, 150, 166, 179
Apollo Smintheus, 103
Apollodorus, 7, 67
Apophis, 78
Aratta, xiv, 74
Arcadia, 9
Archaic, x, 93, 115, 154, 170, 203
Archilochus, 115
Ares, 13
Arete, 149
Argolid, 8, 9, 136, 137
Argos, 10
Aristotle, 157, 158, 180
Artatama, 42
Arzawa(n), 42, 43, 50, 80
Ashurbanipal, 76
Asia Minor, ix, 83, 98, 103
Asine, 137
Assur, 69, 72, 196
Aššur-uballit, 24, 30, 36, 38, 46
Assyria(n), ix, xiii, xiv, xv, 23, 24, 28, 30, 36, 38, 46, 55, 57, 60, 62, 65, 68, 72, 73, 76, 84, 177, 191, 195, 196, 199, 213, 218, 220
Atahna-Šamas, 57
athemiston, 141
Athena, 2, 13, 78, 109, 125, 129, 130, 134, 135, 137, 146, 152, 160, 162, 163
Athens, xii, xiii, 10, 95, 96, 107, 136, 157, 172, 175, 180, 182, 195
-ian, 157, 158
atimia, 105
Atreid(s), 102
Atreus, 100, 107, 159
Attarisya, 100
Attica, 10, 11, 94
Aziru, 34, 37
Babylon, 26, 40, 55, 71, 195
Babylonia(n), 16, 24, 28, 43, 193
Bacchae, 151
Bellerophon, 101, 152, 162
Beth-aven, 80

Bethel, 80
Bet-ili, 35
Boeotia(n), 10, 11
Boğazköy, 16, 22
Borus, 159
Briseis, 105, 109, 111
Bronze (Age), i, ix, x, 2, 4, 5, 7, 8, 9, 10, 11, 12, 16, 18, 20, 28, 71, 72, 89, 90, 91, 92, 93, 94, 96, 97, 98, 99, 100, 103, 109, 110, 112, 113, 117, 124, 126, 128, 136, 137, 139, 143, 146, 148, 159, 164, 167, 170, 171, 183, 192, 195, 197, 201, 203, 207, 209, 210, 211, 221
Burra-Buriyaš, 24, 26, 29, 35, 38, 40, 44, 45, 46, 47, 195
Busruna, 39
Byblos, 68
Byzantium
-ine, xiv, 12, 56, 67, 68, 70, 76, 172, 175, 200, 201, 223
Calchas, 102, 105, 151
Calypso, 134, 140, 153, 175
Canaan, 35, 37, 66, 78, 79
-ite, 20, 33, 78, 110
Cassandra, 159
Castor, 100, 105
Catholic, 12, 208
Chalandritsa, 10
Chavos, 10
Chloris, 159
Christian, 29, 94, 95, 166, 180
Chryseis, 104, 105, 109
Chryses, 101, 102, 104, 109, 111, 120, 150, 159, 179, 199
Cicero, 212
Cilicia, 50, 56, 80
Constantinople, 12, 67
Crete, 3, 83, 100, 203
-an, 166
Crisa, 11
Cyclopes, 140, 141, 152
Cyprus-Cypriot, 9, 10, 20, 83, 91, 154, 177, 194

Dark Ages, ix, x, 4, 5, 7, 8, 13, 18, 92, 93, 117
David, 17, 55, 56, 61, 62, 66, 73, 176, 191
Delphi, 11, 115, 166, 204
Delphinius, 166
Delta, 3
Demodocus, 149, 150
Derveni, 10
diactôr, 120
Diocles, 139, 153
Diomedes, 100, 107, 127, 152, 155, 157, 178
Dionysus, 13
Dorian(s), 9, 171
   pre-Dorian, 10
Dream, 128, 130, 162
Dreros, 166
Duke of Savoy, 208
Echecles, 159
Egypt, ix, xi, 2, 3, 5, 9, 14, 16, 17, 19, 20, 22, 23, 24, 26, 27, 28, 29, 30, 32, 33, 34, 35, 36, 38, 39, 40, 41, 42, 43, 44, 45, 46, 47, 48, 50, 53, 54, 56, 57, 63, 66, 68, 69, 71, 72, 73, 74, 76, 78, 79, 80, 82, 84, 94, 129, 169, 174, 182, 191, 192, 193, 195, 196, 199, 202, 206
   -ian, xiv, 13, 14, 15, 16, 17, 19, 20, 21, 23, 24, 26, 28, 29, 30, 31, 32, 33, 34, 35, 36, 37, 38, 39, 40, 41, 42, 43, 44, 45, 46, 47, 48, 50, 53, 54, 55, 58, 59, 60, 66, 69, 70, 72, 74, 78, 79, 80, 81, 84, 87, 98, 99, 107, 110, 142, 152, 154, 155, 156, 157, 165, 169, 173, 174, 177, 178, 182, 193, 195, 196
Ekallatum, 73
Elam
   -ite, 67, 76
Elis, 166
Elizabeth, 208
Enmerkar, xiv, 73

Epano Eglianos, 11
ephybrizôn, 103
Epigonoi, 7
epikertomeôn, 122
Erinyes, 132
Esau, 63
Euboea, 10, 95
Eumaeus, 97, 202
Euphrates, 3, 16, 169, 193
Euripides, 151
Eurybates, 97, 113, 146, 150
Eurycleia, 150
Eurymachus, 159
Eurystheus, 7
eusebeia, 105
Eziretai, 12
First Dynasty, 40, 53
Florence
   -tine, 210
France, 208, 211
Frank(s)
   -ish, 12
Franks(s), 12
Gaia, 124
geras, 103
Germonius, 1
Gilgamesh, 14, 109, 112
Gla, 11
Glaucus, 106, 155, 157, 178
Grotius, 1
Gubla, 34
Gutian
   -ium, 83
Haamašši, 31, 40, 55, 165
Haaramašši, 38
Hadoram, 56
Hamath, 56
Hammurabi, 58, 79, 83, 209
Hane, 34
Hani, 35
Hanum, 66
Hasor, 83
Hatti, 17, 28, 35, 55, 65, 69, 80, 176, 206

Hattusilis, 55, 65, 69, 70, 72, 77, 81, 83, 103, 110, 121, 129
Hattussa(s), 16, 80, 83
Haya, 46, 55
Hebrew, 13, 63, 70
Hector, 106, 107, 115, 116, 117, 118, 121, 123, 125, 126, 129, 130, 131, 133, 139, 148, 150, 160, 162, 163, 199
Hecuba, 106, 119, 120, 125, 150, 163
Helen, 67, 100, 101, 105, 123, 124, 125, 126, 127, 150, 153, 155, 161, 189, 192
Helenus, 125, 163
Helios, 124, 178
Hephaestus, 133, 159
Hera, 13, 118, 124, 128, 129, 130, 133, 162
Heracles, 7, 100
  idae, 7
Heri-Hor, 68
Hermes, 118, 120, 122, 134, 140, 151, 152
Herodotus, x, 7, 22
Hesiod, x, 2, 8, 101, 132
Hezekiah, 63, 65
Hippolochus, 106
Hittite, ix, xiii, 2, 13, 17, 19, 55, 56, 59, 60, 63, 65, 66, 69, 70, 76, 80, 83, 91, 98, 99, 103, 107, 109, 121, 125, 165, 176
Homer, i, ix, x, xi, 2, 5, 7, 11, 15, 18, 21, 55, 67, 87, 88, 89, 90, 91, 92, 96, 99, 100, 101, 104, 106, 108, 109, 111, 112, 113, 114, 119, 120, 121, 123, 125, 132, 135, 138, 140, 141, 143, 146, 149, 150, 152, 154, 155, 156, 159, 160, 162, 163, 164, 167, 173, 174, 175, 176, 178, 180, 182, 191, 193, 194, 202, 212
  -ic, x, xi, 2, 3, 4, 5, 7, 9, 13, 14, 15, 17, 18, 21, 87, 88, 89, 90, 91, 92, 97, 98, 99, 105, 106, 107, 108, 110, 111, 112, 117, 124, 127, 129, 132, 133, 135, 142, 143, 145, 146, 147, 150, 151, 152, 154, 155, 156, 158, 159, 163, 164, 166, 167, 169, 170, 171, 172, 173, 174, 175, 177, 178, 180, 181, 182, 183, 188, 189, 190, 192, 193, 194, 195, 197, 199, 203, 204, 205, 211
  pre-Homeric, x, 4, 5, 117, 123, 133
House G, 137
House of Columns, 10
Hurrian, 19, 177, 192
hybris, 115
Hyksos, 2, 3, 78
Hyllus, 7
Ida (Mt), 131
Idaeus, 55, 125, 126, 127, 147, 150, 151, 160, 163
Idomeneus, 159
Ilion, 91
Ilus, 191
Ionia(n), 10
Iris, 117, 118, 119, 125, 127, 129, 130, 131, 132, 133, 147, 150, 160, 163, 178
Iron (Age), ix, 88, 90, 91, 99, 128
Iršappa, 42
Ishi-Adad, 71
Ishtar, 129, 177
Išme-Dagan, 71
isotês, 157
Israel, xiv, 63, 73, 91, 138
Ithaca, 134, 135, 137, 139, 140, 153, 155, 182
Jâ-besh-gil-e-ăd, 63
Jacob, 63
Jašmah-Adad, 60, 74
Jericho, 80
Joab, 62, 63
Joram, 56
Joshua, 80
Kadašman-Enlil, 23, 26, 28, 29, 33, 38, 39, 43, 44, 45, 71, 83, 173

Kadašman-Turgu, 66
Kadesh, 59, 193
Kahat, 165
Kalbaya, 43
Kamose, 78
Karaduniyaš, 24
Kasi, 29
Kassite(s), 16
kelefse, 131
Keliya, 31, 32, 38, 39, 40, 48, 55, 79, 165, 193, 201, 202
ke-se-nu-wi-ja/xenwia, 154
Kizzuwatna, 55, 59, 76
Knossos, 154, 203
Korakou, 10
Kumidu, 34
Kummea(n), 58
Kuretes, 101
Kurinnu, 165
Kush, 53, 78
  -ite, 63
Laban, 66, 177
Laertes, 97, 160
Lampus, 107
Laodice, 125
Larsa, 83
lawagetas, 97
Lefkandi, 95, 96
Leto, 122
Levant, 2, 9, 14, 16, 20, 21, 72, 79, 80, 138, 145
  -ine, 2, 21, 42, 78
Linear (Writing) B, 5, 8, 9, 13, 88, 145, 154, 165, 203
Lotus-eater, 140, 141
Lycia(n), 152, 162
Lyon, 210
Madduwatta, 100
Mane, 31, 32, 34, 36, 38, 40, 41, 46, 55, 79, 165, 178, 193, 201
Maori, 167
Mari, xiii, 17, 39, 58, 68, 73, 77, 79, 83, 99, 172, 176
Mattiwaza, 165

Mediterranean, xiv, xv, 1, 2, 5, 16, 21, 54, 70, 74, 79, 82, 91, 95, 97, 100, 167, 169, 172, 191
Meleager, 101
Melingoi, 12
Menelaus, 105, 107, 120, 121, 122, 123, 124, 125, 126, 129, 137, 138, 139, 148, 150, 151, 155, 156, 159, 160, 161, 175, 182, 189, 192, 199
Menidi, 12
Mesopotamia(n), ix, xi, 2, 3, 5, 14, 19, 23, 39, 42, 44, 51, 58, 60, 65, 68, 70, 72, 73, 74, 77, 81, 94, 99, 109, 124, 169, 176, 177, 191, 213
Messene, 135, 139, 153, 164, 195
Messen-ian, 165
Metapioi, 166
Methana, 137
Midea, 10
Milan, 208
Miletus, 91, 98
Millawanda, 98
Mimmuwareya, 23
Minoan, ix, x, 3, 165, 168
Minos, 11, 203
Mitanni, 3, 16, 31, 32, 34, 36, 40, 41, 46, 48, 64, 80, 139, 165, 193
Morea, 12
Mursilis, 17, 28
Muwatallis, 59
Mycenae, 9, 10, 11, 15, 20, 72, 89, 96, 136, 177, 181, 203
  -an, ix, 1, 4, 5, 6, 8, 9, 10, 11, 13, 18, 20, 21, 88, 89, 90, 91, 92, 93, 96, 97, 98, 99, 101, 112, 116, 136, 137, 139, 152, 153, 154, 165, 167, 168, 170, 171, 175, 182, 192, 194, 203, 213, 233
  post-Mycenaean, 182
Myrmidon, 120, 122, 151
Nausicaa, 159
Neleus, 100, 159
Neo-Assyrian, 55, 73, 213

Nestor, 7, 55, 99, 100, 107, 110, 112, 113, 114, 121, 128, 135, 136, 137, 139, 146, 148, 153, 155, 156, 182
New Kingdom, ix, 3, 13, 20, 40, 50, 53, 71, 79, 129
Nichoria, 10
Nile, 73, 93, 169
Nimmureya, 32, 34, 42
Nineveh, 177
Niobe, 121
Nippur, 23, 55
Niqmepa, 28
Nubia, 169
Odius, 113
Odysseus, 14, 30, 55, 90, 92, 97, 104, 106, 111, 113, 114, 115, 116, 121, 129, 134, 135, 137, 139, 140, 141, 146, 148, 149, 150, 151, 153, 154, 155, 159, 160, 161, 162, 164, 175, 182, 189, 191, 192, 193, 195, 199, 201, 202
Oedipus, 151
Old Babylonian, 23, 65, 67, 76
Old Kingdom, 53
Old Testament, xiii, 13, 165, 177
Olympia(n), 118, 166, 204
Olympus(Mt), 12, 118, 128, 130, 132, 134
Ops, 97
orator et ambaxiator, 208
Orestes, 134, 152
Orthodoxy, 12
Ortilochus, 139, 153
Othryoneus, 159
Ouranus, 124
Paddatissu, 56
Palestine, xv, 19, 21, 34, 94, 178
Panachaean, 160
Pandarus, 161
Panhellenic, 166
Paris, xiii, 12, 22, 57, 105, 123, 124, 126, 127, 129, 130, 132, 161, 162, 175, 180, 189, 223
Patras, 94

Patroclus, 106, 107, 109, 114, 117, 129, 133
Pausanias, 7
Peisistratus, 137, 139, 148, 150, 153, 182
Peleus, 106, 114, 122, 159
Peloponnese, 7, 8, 10, 11, 12
-sian, 12, 111, 195
Penelope, 134, 159, 202
Pentheus, 151
Pericles, 157, 195
Perieres, 159
Perseid(s), 7
Persian(n), 56, 68, 73, 151, 157, 172, 214
Phaeacia(n), 149, 150, 175
Pharaoh, 23, 24, 25, 26, 27, 28, 30, 33, 35, 36, 37, 38, 40, 41, 43, 44, 45, 46, 47, 50, 53, 57, 59, 66, 69, 71, 72, 76, 79, 80, 81, 83, 84, 129, 174, 178, 195
Pherae, 139
Philistine, 110
philotimon, 107
Phoenician, 91
Phoenix, 112, 114, 115, 153, 155, 156, 182
Podargus, 107
Polites, 130
Polyctor, 120
Polydeuces, 100, 105
Polydora, 159
Polymele, 159
Poseidon, 13, 130, 131, 132, 134, 136, 147, 163
Priam, 11, 101, 105, 117, 118, 119, 120, 121, 122, 127, 130, 139, 148, 150, 151, 152, 159, 161, 163, 178, 199
Proteus, 152, 162
proxenos, 208
Pudehepa, 76
Pylian, 99, 111

Pylos, 9, 10, 15, 96, 134, 135, 136, 138, 139, 148, 153, 154, 182, 203
Qatanum, 177
Questorium, 67
Rahat, 80
Ramses II, 59, 66, 69, 76, 81
Res Publica Christiana, 207
Rhodes, 98
Rib-Addi, 34, 47
Rib-Hadda, 33, 37, 79
Sabat-Enlil, 72
Samuel, 42, 88
Sargon II, King, 62, 76
Sargon of Agade, 62
Saul, 17
Sea People(s), 9, 91, 170, 206
Second Intermediate, 3, 78
Semitic, 56, 65
Shamash, 124, 165, 178
Shamshi-Adad, 59, 60, 72, 177
Shaushka, 177
Shemsharra, 59
Shulgi, 58, 65, 73
Sidon, 79
Sinuhe, 14
Sixth Dynasty, 53
Slav(s), 11
 -ic, 11
Smenkhare, 15
Solomon, 138, 157
Sophocles, 106, 151
Sparta, 124, 134, 137, 139, 153, 171, 182, 189
Styx, 124
Subrian, 58
Sudan, 78, 158
Sumer, 142
Sumerian, 2, 62, 65, 68, 129
Sunaššura, 65
Suppiluliumas, 17, 60, 165
Susa, 83
Sutahapshap, 69
Sybaris, 166
Syria, 3, 19, 169

Syria-Lebanon, 3
Syro-Palestine, 3
Tadu-Heba, 32
Tagi, 37, 45
Talthybius, 102, 126, 146, 150
Tammuz, 43
Tanis, 68
Tarhundaradu, 80
Telemachus, 120, 121, 122, 134, 135, 136, 137, 138, 139, 146, 148, 150, 152, 153, 155, 156, 175, 182, 192
Tešub, 110, 165
Teye, 31, 40, 45
Theano, 125, 163
Thebaid, 101, 132
Thebes, 7, 12, 15, 68, 96, 100, 101, 130, 203
 -an, 101
themistes, 168
Thera, 3
therapon, 151, 182
Therapon, 151, 152
Thessaly, 10
Thetis, 118, 121, 122, 127, 128, 160
Thracian, 110
Thucydides, x, 7, 10, 11, 93, 157, 180
Tigris, 169
timê, 70, 124, 128
Tiryns, 8, 10, 11, 136
Tou, 56, 95, 96
Toumba, 95, 96
Troad, 68, 103
Trojan, ix, 5, 7, 11, 14, 55, 67, 89, 90, 91, 92, 93, 97, 98, 99, 100, 102, 103, 106, 107, 116, 120, 123, 125, 126, 127, 129, 130, 146, 147, 160, 161, 163, 189, 192, 199, 204
 Pre-Trojan, 99
Troy, 4, 11, 15, 17, 67, 89, 90, 96, 102, 106, 111, 114, 115, 121, 125, 127, 130, 132, 151, 153, 155, 160, 161, 189, 199
Tudhaliyas, 65, 125
Tulubri, 39, 165

Tuni-ibri, 48
Tunip, 35
Turkish, 96
Tušratta, 31, 32, 34, 38, 40, 41, 44, 46, 47, 48, 50, 76, 174, 177, 178, 191, 193
Tydeus, 100, 101
Tyre, 79
Ugarit, 2, 21, 22, 28, 176, 191
Un series, 136
Uriah, 55, 62, 63
Urzaba, 62
Venice, 201, 208
vox populi, 109
wanax, 97, 136
Wen-Amon, 68
Wilusa, 91
WuNoddles, 203
Xanthus, 107, 138
xenia, 158
Xenia, 156
xenos, 154
Xeropolis, 10
Xerxes, 129, 151
Yamhad, 73
Yanhamu, 37
Zephyr, 141
Zeus, 13, 108, 113, 117, 118, 119, 120, 122, 124, 125, 127, 128, 129, 130, 131, 132, 133, 140, 150, 155, 160, 162
Zimreddi, 79
Zimri-Lim, 58, 79
Zubi, 74
Zuzu, 76
Zygouries, 11